D1499192

The Crowd
Funding Services
Handbook

The Wiley Finance series contains books written specifically for finance and investment professionals as well as sophisticated individual investors and their financial advisors. Book topics range from portfolio management to e-commerce, risk management, financial engineering, valuation and financial instrument analysis, as well as much more. For a list of available titles, visit our website at www.WileyFinance.com.

Founded in 1807, John Wiley & Sons is the oldest independent publishing company in the United States. With offices in North America, Europe, Australia and Asia, Wiley is globally committed to developing and marketing print and electronic products and services for our customers' professional and personal knowledge and understanding.

The Crowd Funding Services Handbook

*Raising the Money You
Need to Fund Your Business,
Project, or Invention*

JASON R. RICH

WILEY

Published by John Wiley & Sons, Inc., Hoboken, New Jersey.
Published simultaneously in Canada.

For general information on our other products and services or for technical support, please contact our Customer Care Department within the United States at (800) 762-2974, outside the United States at (317) 572-3993, or fax (317) 572-4002.

Wiley publishes in a variety of print and electronic formats and by print-on-demand. Some material included with standard print versions of this book may not be included in e-books or in print-on-demand. If this book refers to media such as a CD or DVD that is not included in the version you purchased, you may download this material at http://booksupport.wiley.com. For more information about Wiley products, visit www.wiley.com.

Library of Congress Cataloging-in-Publication Data:

Rich, Jason.
    The crowdsource funding services handbook : raising the money you need to fund your business, project, or invention / Jason R. Rich.
       pages   cm. — (Wiley finance)
      Includes index.
      ISBN 978-1-118-85300-9 (cloth); ISBN 978-1-118-94907-8 (ebk);
      ISBN 978-1-118-94908-5 (ebk)
      1. Crowd funding. 2. Venture capital. 3. New business enterprises—Finance.
  I. Title.
  HG4751.R49 2014
  658.15'224—dc23

                                                          2014013800

Printed in the United States of America.
10 9 8 7 6 5 4 3 2 1

This book is dedicated to all of the visionaries, entrepreneurs, investors, small business operators, and creative people who have already used crowd funding to make their dreams a reality.

I'd also like to give a shout-out to some of the talented YouTubers, including Tyler Oakley, Jack and Finn Harries, and Markus Butler (and the members of the YouTube Boyband), who have discovered how to utilize crowd funding in order to rally their massive audiences and raise hundreds of thousands of dollars for some very worthwhile charities and causes.

Contents

Acknowledgments

Thanks to Tiffany Charbonier and Meg Freeborn for their ongoing assistance as I was writing the manuscript for this book and for their hard work when it came to having the book published. Thanks also to everyone at John Wiley & sons who contributed their talents to the publication of this book.

I'd also like to thank the crowd funding experts who are featured in this book as well as my literary agent, Jeff Herman. My gratitude also goes out to my close friends and family for their ongoing love and support.

About the Author

Jason R. Rich (www.JasonRich.com) is the best-selling author of more than 55 books, as well as a frequent contributor to numerous national magazines, major daily newspapers, and popular websites. He's also an accomplished photographer and blogger. Some of his recently published books include *Your iPad at Work, 4th Edition; iPad and iPhone Tips and Tricks, 3rd Edition; iPad and iPhone Digital Photography Tips and Tricks*; and *The Ultimate Guide to YouTube for Business*. Please follow Jason Rich on Twitter (@JasonRich7).

Introduction

So you think you have an amazing idea for a project, business, event, or product that you want to create, and you believe that your best option for funding it is to use a reward- or presale-based crowd funding approach? Congratulations! You've overcome the first hurdle involved with creating and managing a successful crowd funding campaign. You have an idea. But what you're about to discover is that there are many additional hurdles to overcome. Crowd funding is not a get-rich-quick scheme!

To create and manage a successful crowd funding campaign that ultimately reaches its funding goal will take time, some money, careful preplanning, extensive research, and a lot of hard work on your part. Sorry, there are no shortcuts. If you want to fund your project idea, you'll need to manage a wide range of tasks simultaneously, make a series of intelligent decisions, and put forth the necessary time and effort. If, and only if, you're willing to do this will your crowd funding efforts be successful.

As you're about to discover, thousands of project creators, just like you, have managed to get a vast array of different types of projects fully funded using one of the popular crowd funding platforms like Kickstarter, Indiegogo, FundAnything, or RocketHub, for example. However, more than half of the projects that are published on these services fail to meet their funding goals. There are a wide range of reasons why some projects are successful but others are not when it comes to reward-based crowd funding.

The Crowd Funding Services Handbook was written to be an easy-to-understand, comprehensive guide for helping just about anyone create and manage a successful reward- or presale-based crowd funding campaign that will allow them to raise the money needed to complete their project idea and make it a reality. Not only will this book help you prepare for the challenges that lie ahead and assist you in overcoming the most common pitfalls that cause crowd funding campaigns to fail, it will also help you fully develop your project idea and then choose the best crowd funding platform to work with, based on your overall objectives. It's your job to come up with a brilliant project idea and then make sure there's a demand for that idea. Then, by following the strategies offered in this book, as well as using the expert advice that's shared by the handful of crowd funding experts whose interviews are featured in the final three chapters of this book, you'll be at a huge advantage when it comes to planning, creating, and managing your reward- or presale-based crowd funding campaign, regardless of which crowd funding platform you choose to work with.

Whether you're looking to invent and launch a product, establish a business, generate revenue from artwork you've created, write a book, record an album, produce a movie, develop a fashion line, create a smartphone/tablet app or accessory, create a computer or video game, or produce some type of event or performance, crowd funding can be the answer you need to get that project idea funded, so you can make it a reality.

Never before has there been a solution for everyday people seeking funding for projects that does not involve giving up equity or ownership in their company or idea, taking on a tremendous amount of risk, or potentially having to go into substantial debt. The concept of reward-based crowd funding is relatively new, evolving quickly, and becoming increasingly more popular and viable with each passing month.

From *The Crowd Funding Services Handbook*, you'll learn the secrets for success when it comes to getting your unique project idea funded, assuming you're willing to put in the long hours of hard work that are required to plan, create, and manage a successful crowd funding campaign and then have the wherewithal and drive to transform your project idea into something that's real and viable once it's funded.

This book will help you develop realistic goals and clear up common misconceptions about what reward- or presale-based crowd funding is all about, then walk you through the process of using a service like Kickstarter or Indiegogo, for example, to create and manage your crowd funding campaign. You'll learn how to attract highly targeted backers and supporters using social media, online advertising, public relations, and other means, and then cater to the wants and needs of that audience, which will play a pivotal role in the funding of your project idea.

While every project idea is different, and there are no preset formulas to follow that guarantee success, *The Crowd Funding Services Handbook* will help you learn all about what's involved with running a successful reward- or presale-based crowd funding campaign that's customized to your project idea and the target audience you're trying to reach.

Using easy-to-understand language and concepts, *The Crowd Funding Services Handbook* will help you learn all about crowd funding and save you time, money, and potential aggravation or disappointment when it comes to creating and managing your own crowd funding campaign for your project. No previous experience is necessary, but being able to tap the power of social media and the Internet in order to find, reach out to, and attract financial backers who are interested in your project will be important. Having previous business, marketing, advertising, public relations, finance, and/or social media experience, as well as creativity, will all be beneficial, as will any other business-related skills and experience you bring to the table.

Keep in mind that as a project creator looking to get your project idea funded, you are expected to be an expert when it comes to the scope of your project. The other core knowledge that's needed for crowd funding can be acquired from this book and from the resources that are recommended throughout it.

As you're about to discover, instead of pursuing traditional investors, taking out loans, or leveraging your personal credit, crowd funding can help you raise the money you need to fully fund your business, project, or invention by allowing you to reach out to everyday people and get them excited enough about your project idea that they become willing to financially support it.

The first step in pursuing a successful crowd funding campaign is to understand what crowd funding is and is it not. Introducing you to how the popular crowd funding platforms work is the focus of Chapter 1, "How Crowd Funding Works: The Basics." So, let's get started!

The Crowd
Funding Services
Handbook

How Crowd Funding Works: The Basics

In recent years, crowd funding has become an extremely popular and viable way for entrepreneurs, inventors, artisans, small business operators, fundraisers, musicians, charities, and people from all sorts of backgrounds and from all walks of life, to quickly, legally, and systematically raise the money needed to launch a new business, invent and sell a new product, fund some type of for-profit or nonprofit project, or somehow transform a business-related dream into reality.

Thanks to services like Kickstarter, Indiegogo, FundAnything, RocketHub, and Selfstarter, creating and launching a reward-based or presale-based crowd funding campaign has never been easier. However, it's important to understand that these days, the term crowd funding is being used very broadly.

In reality, there are big differences between reward-based crowd funding and equity-based crowd funding (which we'll explore later). What you need to know now is that the majority of this book focuses on reward-based or presale-based crowd funding, which is what platforms like Kickstarter, Indiegogo, and many others offer. That being said, the popularity of crowd funding is expected to grow a whopping 92 percent in 2014.

What creating and managing a successful crowd funding campaign involves is continuously and quickly evolving due to changes in technology, the growing popularity of crowd funding, and laws being passed on the state and federal level.

While you've probably heard many stories about inventors, small business operators, creative people, or entrepreneurs who had an amazing idea, launched a crowd funding campaign, and in less than a month, raised $5 or $10 million, when initially all they were seeking was a few hundred thousand dollars, it's essential that you understand that not all crowd funding campaigns become successful. In fact, many fail.

For every crowd funding success story, there are many failures. From this book, not only will you learn about the types of crowd funding projects that tend to be successful, plus learn proven strategies that can make your campaign a success, you'll also learn why so many campaigns stumble. Understanding why some crowd funding campaigns fail puts you at a tremendous advantage, because you'll know early on what mistakes and pitfalls to avoid and what strategies to pursue to achieve success.

WHAT CROWD FUNDING IS . . . AND ISN'T

Reward- or presale-based crowd funding allows you to reach out to your friends, relatives, professional acquaintances, like-minded people with similar special interests, and/or a niche target audience of people—in other words, your network—in order to get them to help you fund your business idea, invention, or project. You also typically need to reach out to the general public (the crowd) to expand your network of supports and backers.

In its simplest form, crowd funding is a viable alternative to more traditional ways of raising capital through investors, bank loans, or by utilizing credit. (Before crowd funding, individuals often found it necessary to use credit cards to fund start-ups, for example.) Reward-based crowd funding is open to everyone; it can be done without having to hire a team of lawyers, accountants, and financial experts, and it's very inexpensive to pursue.

What makes reward-based crowd funding work is the Internet and your ability to utilize online social networking to reach a targeted audience. Running a crowd funding campaign requires you to reach out to a target audience—using online social networking, email, online advertising, public relations, and other methods that we'll be exploring—sell them on your project idea, and get potential backers to support your project financially.

A crowd funding campaign is typically hosted on a specialized online service, like Kickstarter or Indiegogo, which are two of the most popular reward-based crowd funding platforms. On the crowd funding platform you choose to work with, your project idea is given its own web page and URL (website address), from which you manage your crowd funding campaign.

However, while a platform like Kickstarter or Indiegogo hosts and helps you manage your campaign, it is your responsibility to populate that web page with all of the information someone will need in order to get excited about your project. This typically includes creating an attention-getting promotional video and populating the campaign's web page with compelling text, photos, and other content you deem appropriate in order to communicate your message. Then it's your responsibility to drive an abundance of targeted traffic to your campaign's website. Your goal is to transform visitors to your crowd funding campaign's web page into backers who opt to support your project financially.

If you begin your crowd funding campaign with a great idea that's viable, you're able to quickly and succinctly communicate your idea online, and then generate a strong interest in it, you can be successful. But, along the way, a lot can go wrong. And what you need to understand right from the start is that managing a reward-based crowd funding campaign requires a significant time commitment on your part. There are no shortcuts.

Thanks to services like Kickstarter and Indiegogo, as well as countless others that you'll soon become familiar with, what crowd funding offers is an opportunity that's never before been so readily available. Reward-based crowd funding provides the ability for just about anyone to share with the public their viable idea for a business, invention, or project and attract people (the crowd) who become passionate about that idea and help to financially support it and make it a reality. What crowd funding is not, however, is a get-rich-quick scheme.

Crowd funding can take on many different forms, each of which uses its own method for raising money and funding businesses, inventions, individuals, or projects. All, however, rely on your ability to reach out to the online world and self-market your campaign using online social networking (Facebook and Twitter, for example), email, online advertising, public relations, and the other tools available to you.

Before you even think of launching a crowd funding campaign, a lot of research and preplanning need to be done. Again, there are no shortcuts if you want to be successful. You'll also need to invest a significant amount of time toward marketing, promoting, advertising, and managing your reward-based crowd funding campaign as well as in proactively communicating with your potential backers and actual backers (those who have supported your campaign financially).

LET'S TALK CROWD FUNDING LINGO

In its current online form, crowd funding is a relatively new practice, and like the Internet itself, it's changing and evolving quickly and continuously. As a result, a lot of new terminology has been created that relates to crowd funding. So, before you delve too deeply into pursuing your own crowd funding campaign, let's take a few minutes to identify some key terms you'll soon be using as part of your everyday crowd funding–related vocabulary.

We'll start with the concept of *reward-based crowd funding* and *presale-based crowd funding*. In the past, if you had a business or project idea and needed funding for it, one way to raise that capital was to seek out investors. In exchange for providing financial capital, investors received equity or partial ownership in the company or project that was being funded. In financial terms, they were making an investment.

Reward-based crowd funding does not involve traditional investors, nor does the person or organization that's running the crowd funding campaign wind up giving up any equity or ownership of their company or project. Instead, a reward-based crowd funding campaign involves seeking out *backers* (everyday people) who financially contribute to the funding of a business, product, or project in exchange for something of value, such as a reward, perk, experience, and/or the product they're helping to fund.

In other words, backers are not making a traditional investment, nor are they making a donation. When individuals decide to back a project, in some cases they're simply pre-purchasing a product based on the idea for that product, knowing that it could take several months, or even years, for the product to actually be designed, manufactured, and made available to them and the public.

Beyond just giving inventors with little or no start-up capital the opportunity to raise money to make their invention or product ideas a reality, reward-based crowd funding is also currently being used by all sorts of creative people to fund a wide range of project types.

For example, musicians are using reward-based crowd funding to pay for the recording of albums, fund tours, or purchase equipment. Movie producers are using crowd funding to raise money to film, edit, duplicate, and distribute their movies. Entrepreneurs and start-ups are using reward-based crowd funding to launch or expand their businesses.

Some writers are using reward-based crowd funding to self-publish their books, while other creative people are using this funding method to produce shows, performances, conferences, or works of art.

Likewise, computer and video game developers, software engineers, and mobile device app developers are all successfully using reward-based crowd funding to raise the money needed to create a new game, software program, or app.

Inventors are using crowd funding very effectively to raise the money needed to design, manufacture, and launch their product ideas. As a result, thousands of new high-tech gadgets and cool products have already been introduced to the world, not by huge corporations, but by individuals (like yourself), business start-ups, or established small businesses that without the existence of crowd funding would not have had the financial resources to achieve their goals (since traditional funding methods typically aren't available to them).

Whatever it is that someone is using reward-based crowd funding to raise money for is referred to as a *project*. When people begin using a crowd funding service like Kickstarter or Indiegogo to do their crowd funding, this is referred to as running a crowd funding *campaign*.

The people or organizations that launch a reward-based crowd funding campaign to fund their projects are the projects' *creators*, and the people they're seeking out to help fund their projects (and also help promote them) are the *backers* or *supporters*. Remember, there is an important distinction between a backer or supporter and an investor or donor.

Again, when people become backers or supporters of a reward-based crowd funding campaign, they receive something of value (a reward or perk) in exchange for their financial support. They are not, however, making an investment that could theoretically become more valuable. Likewise, they are not making a donation out of the goodness of their hearts, because they are receiving something of value in return for their support.

The online-based service used to host and help manage a crowd funding campaign is referred to as a *crowd funding platform*. Kickstarter and Indiegogo are popular examples of reward-based crowd funding platforms. However, at the time this book was being written, instead of using an independent crowd funding platform to host a crowd funding campaign, some project creators were opting to host and manage their own campaigns on their own websites or blogs. This can be done using tools offered by services like Selfstarter.

What you'll learn from Chapter 3, "Introduction to Crowd Funding Platforms and Services," is that each crowd funding platform offers its own unique set of tools for creating and managing a crowd funding campaign. Some platforms, like FundAnything, are open to all project creators. Others, like Kickstarter, are open only to "creative projects," while some platforms are open only to certain types of projects, such as the development and creation of consumer-oriented, high-tech projects or to nonprofit fund-raising campaigns.

In addition to each platform offering something unique that tends to work best for certain types of campaigns, each charges fees based on how much money is raised and has different policies for collecting and distributing the funds raised. So, depending on what you're trying to accomplish with your crowd funding campaign, you'll want to be sure to choose a crowd funding platform or self-hosted option that offers the tools, functionality, and flexibility you need.

When a product is being created as a result of reward-based crowd funding, in some cases the campaign's creator focuses exclusively on presales as opposed to offering backers rewards and perks. In this case, the campaign promotes a product idea. The goal is to fund the design and manufacturing of that product. The backers simply pre-purchase the product, often at a discount, while it's still in the idea phase, because it's a product they want to own and use, and it's something they're excited about and want to help make a reality. In this case, the reward or perk the backer receives is the product itself as soon as it becomes available. There are numerous crowd funding platforms that cater specifically to this type of presale campaign approach.

For other types of reward-based crowd funding, in addition to or instead of just preselling the product, rewards or perks are offered. This is the approach used by the Kickstarter and Indiegogo platforms, for example. In exchange for supporting a project financially, the project creator comes up with a menu of unique rewards to offer, at different price points, that a backer can acquire. These rewards or perks tend to be exclusive, limited, and only available to campaign backers.

One of the key components to a successful reward-based crowd funding campaign is offering rewards and perks that will be of interest to your backers and entice them to help fund your project with higher levels of financial support. A lot of creativity typically goes into creating the rewards associated with a campaign. Chapter 4, "Preplanning Your Crowd Funding Campaign," focuses in part on helping you develop rewards and perks to offer to your backers, if this is the type of crowd funding campaign you choose to pursue.

In addition to reward-based or pre-purchase crowd funding campaigns, several other forms of crowd funding are quickly evolving. *Equity-based crowd funding* is still in its infancy and involves using crowd funding techniques to raise money for a business or project, but in this case, the investors who support a project do receive equity in the business or project. These are more traditional investment opportunities, and they can legally be promoted to the public; thanks to the Jumpstart Our Business Startups (JOBS) Act, they are open to almost everyone, not just designated credited investors.

Equity-based crowd funding is being used by start-up businesses and established businesses of all sizes and in many industries. It's also starting to become popular in the real estate industry. This type of crowd funding is also taking several distinct forms, which the JOBS Act has been designed to regulate.

Taking advantage of equity-based crowd funding requires the use of lawyers and other experts to implement. This form of crowd funding is touched upon in this book, but is not the primary focus of it, in part because at the time this book was being written, major components of the JOBS Act had not been fully enacted by the U.S. Congress.

However, millions of entrepreneurs, inventors, and creative people of all types have discovered that using reward-based crowd funding is an extremely viable way to raise the funds needed to make their ideas and dreams a reality.

NINE COMPONENTS TO A SUCCESSFUL CROWD FUNDING CAMPAIGN

The first important lesson you need to learn, right now, is that to successfully use reward-based crowd funding, you need a great, well-thought-out, and viable idea. It can be an idea for a product, invention, business, service, or just about anything else. Your project needs to be something about which you are personally knowledgeable and truly passionate.

Ideally, the idea for your business, invention, or project should be unique and innovative, but at the very least, it must be legal and offer an obvious benefit or a solution to a problem or an exciting new twist on something that's already in the market.

Second, it's absolutely essential that you properly identify the target audience for your project. You need to be able to find and reach many people who will share your passion and excitement for your idea. At the same time, you need to ensure that your project is something that your target audience will want. When it comes to reward-based crowd funding, having a great idea for a project is useless if there's no demand for it.

Third, you need to do research. After developing your idea and proving its viability, the next step is to figure out—logistically and financially—exactly what it will take to make it a reality. Then, determine if crowd funding can be a useful tool to help you achieve your goals. If you determine crowd funding is a viable option, the next task is to research the best crowd funding approach to take and which crowd funding platform to use.

There are many crowd funding platforms out there, and no two are alike. It's essential that you find a crowd funding platform that's ideally suited to your particular project. In this book, you'll learn about several popular crowd funding platforms and self-hosting services, but more importantly, you'll learn what you need to understand when choosing which service to work with.

Fourth, your promotional video is an extremely important tool. While it's not required by all crowd funding platforms, without a doubt your most important tool for soliciting backers and communicating details about your project and crowd funding campaign will be the promotional video you produce. In three minutes or less, your promotional video needs to tell your story, demonstrate your product, and convince potential backers to financially support your project.

The focus of Chapter 7, "Producing Your Promotional Video," is on scripting, shooting, editing, and producing a promotional video that will capture the attention of your target audience. The production quality of your promotional video must meet or exceed the expectations of your target audience, while expertly and creatively communicating a lot of information in a very concise and visually appealing way.

Fifth, you need to create and expand your network. This includes friends, family, people in your target audience, and others you can easily reach and promote your campaign to. Your network should be large and composed of people who will become backers and support your project financially. As you market your crowd funding campaign, you'll also want to encourage your backers to share details about your campaign with their own networks (via Facebook, Twitter, LinkedIn, email, etc.). This virtual word-of-mouth promotion is essential and will help you quickly expand your network and identify additional backers.

Crowd funding is all about reaching out to the crowd to help get your project funded. Without an established network and the ability to use the Internet to effectively communicate with people in your network, running a successful crowd funding campaign will be much more challenging.

Sixth, you need to expertly communicate your project idea and details about your crowd funding campaign with others using a wide range of online-based resources. At the same time, you need to understand that when you reach out to potential backers, you'll only have a few brief seconds to capture their attention. As a result, your marketing message needs to be clear, succinct, well thought out, and be able to generate the desired response from the people it reaches.

Seventh, it's vital that you understand exactly what it will take to be successful. One of the biggest mistakes people make is not doing enough research as they're getting started, so they're not properly prepared once their crowd funding campaigns kick off.

Another all-too-common mistake is miscalculating your budget. If you able launch a successful campaign and raise the money you thought you needed, what happens when those funds aren't enough to make your idea a reality? Or, what happens when you have promised your backers results within 30 days only to discover that you'll need six months to turn your idea into a reality? These are situations you'll learn how to address later in this book.

Eighth, having realistic expectations is also essential. Reward-based crowd funding is not a get-rich-quick scheme or an easy way to raise thousands or millions of dollars in a few days or weeks. Throughout this book, you'll be introduced to many successful crowd funding experts, as well as entrepreneurs, small business operators, inventors, artists, and other creative individuals, like yourself, who have successfully used crowd funding to transform their ideas into reality. What you'll discover as you learn about the experiences these people had, or when you go out and speak with others on your own about crowd funding, is that you will need to invest weeks or maybe months preparing to launch a successful crowd funding campaign.

Then, once the campaign has launched, you'll need to invest hundreds, maybe thousands, of man hours to successfully manage and promote the campaign. If you're successful, an even greater investment of time, effort, expertise, and resources will be needed to use the funds raised to actually launch your business, bring your invention to market, or make your project idea a reality.

Each step along the way, as you prepare and manage your crowd funding campaign, will require a diverse set of skills. You'll need to juggle many different responsibilities, develop new areas of expertise, seek out help from proven experts in various fields, and remain focused while avoiding the common problems and pitfalls so many people experience when trying to use crowd funding to raise money.

Simply using many of the crowd funding platforms is easy and straightforward. If you know how to use any web browser and you're proficient surfing the Internet, you have the skills needed to use a crowd funding platform. Many of the crowd funding platforms have made using their service as easy as creating a listing on eBay to sell an item.

However, creating and managing a successful crowd funding campaign is not so easy. The more you know about business, finance, sales, marketing, advertising, promotions, public relations, storytelling, online social networking, video production and editing, and effective interpersonal communication, the better off you'll be. These are just some of the core skills you'll need to operate a successful crowd funding campaign.

So, if you already have the necessary skills and experience, terrific! However, if you're honest with yourself and know that you're a great inventor, for example, but that you lack the ability to communicate well with other people, you'll either need to fine-tune your skill set or seek help from experts who already possess the skills and experience you need for success.

Finally, the ninth component in a successful crowd funding campaign is to understand right from the start, that no two reward-based crowd funding campaigns are identical. What worked in the past for one business, invention, or project may not work for another. Even after you do all of your research and planning, be willing and able to adapt and fine-tune your strategies as you go. Flexibility and the ability to react quickly to the response from actual and potential backers is important.

Unfortunately, running a successful crowd funding campaign is not an exact science. Every campaign you see on Kickstarter, Indiegogo, or any other crowd funding platform, has its own story, its own challenges, a unique target audience, and its own potential group of backers. Your own creativity, dedication, and persistence as well as your ability to adapt will play a huge role in your success.

COMMON MISCONCEPTIONS ABOUT CROWD FUNDING

The concept of crowd funding is still relatively new. As a result, most every-day people have no clue what it is, how it works, or what's involved in becoming a backer for a project they're interested in supporting. With each passing month, however, reward-based crowd funding is becoming more popular and more widely used.

However, as you launch your crowd funding campaign, you may discover that your target audience is not technologically savvy and not familiar with the crowd funding concept. Educating potential backers about how this process works is one additional hurdle you'll need to overcome to be successful.

Don't launch a crowd funding campaign with the misconception that your potential backers and target audience are as knowledgeable about crowd funding and how it works as you are. There are still many people out there who are not comfortable making online purchases from reputable companies, much less willing to financially support crowd funding campaigns.

If these people are part of your target audience, you will face a challenge trying to convince them to fund your project, which in essence means asking them to pre-purchase something that doesn't yet exist from an unknown and often unproven company, and then wait a long time to receive the product or perk.

Make sure you understand who your target audience is and that you launch your crowd funding campaign with an established network that's composed of people who understand your project and are likely to support it financially.

As you'll discover from reading the in-depth interviews with crowd funding experts that are featured in Chapters 13, 14, and 15, the biggest misconception people have about crowd funding is the "if you build it, they will come" mentality. As a project creator, simply publishing and launching a reward-based crowd funding campaign on a platform like Kickstarter or Indiegogo is not a guaranteed formula for success.

In reality, people are not going to magically stumble upon your campaign's web page and become a backer of your project. The crowd funding platform and the various Internet search engines are not going to drive qualified and interested backers to your campaign. That simply is not going to happen.

After coming up with an awesome project idea and creating a well-thought-out reward-based crowd funding campaign for it, and then publishing that campaign on an appropriate platform, your work is only beginning. It's now your responsibility to actively and continuously drive traffic to your campaign and solicit backers. The focus of Chapter 8, "Promoting Your Campaign," is on how to successfully market, advertise, and promote a reward-based crowd funding campaign.

This is going to require the use of social networking (Facebook, Twitter, etc.), email, and potentially online advertising, in addition to a well-orchestrated public relations effort. Creators of successful crowd funding campaigns, regardless of which platform they use, implement a multifaceted marketing, promotional, and advertising strategy that begins before the launch of the campaign and continues until the campaign ends. During the actual campaign, a significant time (and sometimes financial) commitment is needed to implement these strategies, without which your campaign will not attract backers.

IT IS ESSENTIAL TO CREATE AN ACCURATE TIME FRAME AND BUDGET

Another common misconception about reward-based crowd funding is that the project creator can randomly come up with an outrageously high and unsupportable funding goal, such as $1 million, when all that's really needed is $10,000, and that backers are going to provide them with all of the money they ask for with no strings attached. This, too, is false.

As you'll discover in Chapter 5, "Crunching the Numbers," it's essential that prior to launching your crowd funding campaign, you set a funding goal that is achievable, realistic, and viable.

In terms of achievable, you need to know that you'll be able to reach an ample number of backers, who will allow you to generate enough funds to reach your goal. If you know your existing network comprises 5,000 potential backers, and each will give an average of $25.00, you will probably have a difficult time raising more than $125,000 from your campaign unless you do an incredible job with your marketing, promotional, public relations, and advertising efforts and are able to attract an abundance of total strangers to your campaign.

In terms of being realistic, don't assume your crowd funding campaign will go viral and that you'll raise $10 million or more with little or no effort. The campaigns that do manage to go viral and achieve these incredible results are almost always backed by extensive advertising, marketing, promotional efforts, and public relations campaigns that were created and implemented by skilled and experienced professionals. And a lot of money and resources were put behind those campaigns.

Only a miniscule number of reward-based crowd funding campaigns actually go viral on their own, without tremendous financial and marketing support. However, to achieve success, your campaign does not need to go viral. It simply needs to reach enough people in your target audience so you can fund your project.

This might mean attracting several hundred or a few thousand backers, not hundreds of thousands of backers. Especially for smaller-scale crowd funding projects, when you only need to raise thousands of dollars, focusing on making a campaign go viral is counterproductive and a waste of time and resources.

After reading this book, you should be able to calculate a realistic funding goal for your campaign, based on your idea, target audience, available resources, and other key factors. Finally, make sure your funding goal is viable. Once you figure out how much money you want to raise, make sure it's enough to actually fund your project, taking into account unexpected expenses and problems, the fees you'll need to pay to the crowd funding platform, and the fees charged by the third-party credit card payment processor that handles the campaign's financial transactions.

Another important consideration is your time frame. Realistically, you'll need to create three separate time frames for your project and make sure that each is achievable. First, you'll need to set aside ample time to do research and preplan your campaign. This could take days, weeks, or months depending on your knowledge, experience, and resources.

Next, you need to come up with a realistic time frame for your crowd funding campaign's duration. Depending on the platform, a campaign can last anywhere from a few days to 90 days (or longer), although the average campaign length is 30 days. The campaign duration you select is basically how much time you'll have to drive traffic to your campaign's page, convert visitors into backers, and reach your funding goal.

You will also need to prepare in advance for what happens after your crowd funding campaign ends. If you've successfully reached your funding goal, you now have to make your project a reality. During the campaign, you'll need to provide your backers with a projected time frame for the project's completion, so they know that if they prepurchase your product or help fund your project they will receive the product or perk within 60 days, 90 days, six months, or one year after the campaign ends.

Once you promise your backers results, it's important to deliver what you have promised on time and on budget. Unfortunately, due to poor planning and other factors, delays are commonplace when it comes to turning a funded project into a reality. Efficiently and properly dealing with pitfalls, delays, challenges or budget miscalculations is essential if you want to maintain the support of your backers. Thus, as you'll learn in Chapter 13, "Interviews with Crowd Funding Experts," maintaining an open and honest line of communication with your backers, right from the start, is extremely important.

AGAIN, THERE ARE NO SHORTCUTS

Creating and managing a successful reward-based crowd funding campaign will rely on your ability to efficiently and effectively handle each component of the campaign, either on your own or by hiring consultants or third-party agencies that have specific skills and experience to support you and your efforts.

Thanks to services like Kickstarter, Indiegogo, and many others, it's currently possible to get almost any type of project funded, as long as it is legal and not offensive. However, to achieve your funding goals, you'll need to start with a great idea; develop realistic expectations for what's possible using reward-based crowd funding; know and understand your target audience; and be ready to implement the promotional, marketing, advertising, and public relations efforts related to your campaign in a cost-effective and efficient way.

Each chapter of *The Crowd Funding Services Handbook* focuses on one or more aspects of the reward-based crowd funding process. Beyond the knowledge you'll obtain from this book, your own creativity, passion, and dedication to your project will be key components to its success. If done correctly, just about anyone can use crowd funding to raise money to make an idea a reality.

As you'll discover, crowd funding offers some other key advantages when it comes to determining the viability of a project idea without investing and risking a fortune. Many established companies are using crowd funding as a marketing and market research tool in addition to a means to raise capital.

CROWD FUNDING CAN BE USED TO RAISE MONEY FOR PEOPLE AND CHARITIES, TOO

Crowd funding can be used to raise money for individuals and charities, as well. In Chapter 13 you'll learn about a crowd funding platform called Upstart that uses established crowd funding techniques to help individuals raise money for themselves in order to pursue their entrepreneurial goals or seek out higher levels of education.

You'll also discover how the CrowdRise, Prizeo, and Start A Cure crowd funding platforms, for example, are changing the way fund-raising is being done by charities and how businesses are able to handle their charitable donations, while at the same time boosting their brand awareness and enhancing their overall image. These crowd funding platforms are also making it easy for everyday people to raise money for charities they're passionate about helping and to extend the reach of their efforts on a national or international scale.

Using the knowledge and insight you acquire from this book, chances are you, too, will discover how you can best take advantage of reward-based crowd funding to raise the capital needed to fund your project idea, or, at the very least, determine that using one of the newly evolving equity-based crowd funding options is better suited to help you achieve your business objectives.

THE FUTURE LOOKS VERY BRIGHT FOR CROWD FUNDING

For the right type of project, reward-based crowd funding offers a relatively quick and low-risk way to raise capital without having to give up equity in or partial ownership of the project idea. Never before has this type of capital been available to everyday people. In the relatively short time that reward-based crowd funding has been in existence, thousands upon thousands of products, businesses, and projects have been funded.

According to the Fundable crowd funding platform, which offers crowd funding tools specifically for small businesses (which you'll learn more about in Chapter 3, "Introduction to Crowd Funding Platforms and Services"), by the end of 2014, reward-based crowd funding will help to create at least 270,000 new jobs and inject more than $65 billion into the global economy.

By 2020, crowd funding could be responsible for generating $3.2 trillion in economic value per year, and help create 2 million new jobs. These figures could potentially go even higher as outstanding elements of the JOBS Act are enacted by the U.S. Congress and everyday people over the age of 18 are allowed to participate in equity-based crowd funding projects as investment opportunities.

There's no better time than right now to look into the feasibility and opportunity that reward-based crowd funding (or potentially equity-based crowd funding) can offer to your project idea. So let's get started!

CHAPTER 2

What Types of Businesses, Projects, and Inventions Can Get Funded

In This Chapter

- Define your project idea and determine if it could benefit from crowd funding.
- Discussion of projects that used crowd funding and why their campaigns worked.
- Determine whether a popular crowd funding platform like Kickstarter will meet your needs or if you should consider a smaller, more specialized platform for your project.

You already know that just about any type of project idea can get funded using reward-based crowd funding, assuming the right combination of factors comes into play. Keep in mind, not all project ideas and campaigns are suitable for all crowd funding platforms. Choosing the right platform for your project idea is essential.

Also, just because you think you've come up with a brilliant project idea, that doesn't mean there will be a demand for it. Even if you have come up with a great idea and there is a demand for it, a crowd funding campaign can still fail to get funded if you don't convey the right details about your project in the right way, or if some aspect of your marketing message or campaign is off target.

On any given day, there are thousands of crowd funding campaigns running simultaneously on each of the popular crowd funding platforms, and the scope of each project is as different as the individuals who have created them.

PROFILES OF PROJECT TYPES THAT CAN BE
SUCCESSFUL USING REWARD-BASED CROWD FUNDING

As you'll discover, projects need to have a beginning and an end. That said, the scope of a project can involve inventing and manufacturing a product, recording music, creating art, running an event, starting a business, opening a restaurant, funding the production of a movie, expanding a business, designing and launching a clothing line, creating a mobile app, publishing software, producing a play or musical, designing a smartphone or tablet accessory, or fund-raising for a charity.

The possibilities are governed only by your imagination, your ability to find a crowd-funding platform that your project is compatible with, and your ability to get the project funded. Let's take a look at just a small sampling of the types of projects that reward-based crowd funding can work with.

If you visit the Kickstarter (www.kickstarter.com) crowd funding platform, for example, and scroll to the bottom of the home page, under the Discover heading you'll see an option labeled Most Funded.

Click on this option to see project listings for the all-time most successful projects funded on this platform. Reviewing this section and taking time to familiarize yourself with the projects it includes will allow you to discover the types of projects that work well on Kickstarter. Be sure to watch the promotional videos that accompany each project and study what the project creators did to make their campaigns stand out and become successful.

As of early 2014, Kickstarter's biggest success story was the Pebble smart watch (www.getpebble.com), which was funded back in May 2012. The company's goal was to raise $100,000, but the campaign attracted more than 85,000 backers, and ultimately raised more than $10.2 million. The Pebble smart watch has since gone on to sell hundreds of thousands of units and is currently sold through the company's website as well as at major consumer electronics retailers.

As a result of the Pebble smart watch's success, hundreds of other innovative accessory products for smartphones and tablets have wound up being funded using Kickstarter and other platforms. In many cases, these are products that were invented by everyday people, who, without crowd funding, would never have been able to bring their product ideas to market.

Thus, products related to smartphones and tablets, including accessories and apps, have become a wildly popular category on Kickstarter and other reward-based crowd funding platforms. In fact, in Chapter 15, you'll learn about two successfully funded smartphone accessory products—the Tile and the Hammerhead—by reading in-depth interviews with their inventors.

The Ouya video game console (www.ouya.tv) is another of Kickstarter's biggest success stories. This gaming system uses the popular Android operating system and was funded back in August 2012. The funding goal for this project was $950,000, but after attracting more than 63,000 backers, the campaign raised more than $8.5 million. Today, the $99 video game console is supported by a library of more than 500 games, and it's available from the company's website.

Another well-funded project hosted on Kickstarter was for a motion picture production based on the successful *Veronica Mars* television series. This project was funded in April 2013, and it immediately became the fastest project on Kickstarter to raise $2 million. The project was also the all-time highest funded project within Kickstarter's film category, and, with more than 91,500 backers, was supported by the most backers of any project in Kickstarter's history. The Veronica Mars Movie Project had a funding goal of $2 million but wound up raising more than $5.7 million.

Granted, The Veronica Mars Movie Project had an advantage in that the campaign was immediately supported by fans of the *Veronica Mars* television series, but by studying this Kickstarter campaign (www.kickstarter.com/projects/559914737/the-veronica-mars-movie-project), you can see how the product's creators (the movie's producers) used unique rewards and limited edition memorabilia to incentivize potential backers, while at the same time allowing fans to preorder copies of the DVD and Blu-ray editions of the movie, which was released on March 14, 2014 (www.theveronicamarsmovie.com).

As of early 2014, the fourth most successful project ever funded on Kickstarter was for the *Torment: Tides of Numenera* role-playing computer game. This campaign ended in April 2013. Its funding goal was $900,000, but after attracting more than 74,400 backers, it wound up raising just under $4.2 million.

By studying this campaign (www.kickstarter.com/projects/inxile/torment-tides-of-numenera), you can see, again, how rewards at different price points were used as incentives, which ultimately helped to attract nine backers who pledged $10,000 each, although most pledges were in the $39 to $130 range. You'll also see that unlike most promotional videos used in conjunction with Kickstarter campaigns, the video for this project was almost seven minutes long and included a preview of the gameplay, as well as interviews with the game's creators.

Produced by InXile entertainment, *Torment: Tides of Numernera* was not the first project for which the company used Kickstarter to successfully fund. However, using its experience creating and managing previous crowd funding campaigns for other computer game projects, the company was able to fully utilize its existing network to expand its game lineup with *Torment: Rides of Numerenera* (www.torment.inxile-entertainment.com).

The majority of Kickstarter's other all-time most funded projects were also computer or video games produced by independent game developers, although consumer electronics products and gadgets also dominated the top 20 most funded campaign spots as of early 2014.

It's important to realize that while the Most Funded listing on Kickstarter is populated by projects that raised in excess of $1 million, thousands upon thousands of other projects have been successfully funded for nowhere near $1 million. By returning to the main Kickstarter web page and clicking on the Popular option that's found under the Discover heading (or by visiting www.kickstarter.com/discover/popular), you can peruse through more than 129,000 project campaigns that are currently underway and performing well.

This listing of Kickstarter projects comprises projects that fit into all of Kickstarter's various categories, which (as you'll discover in Chapter 12: "Get Started Using Kickstarter.com") include Art, Comics, Dance, Design, Fashion, Film & Video, Food, Games, Music, Photography, Publishing, Technology and Theater.

On any given day, you're apt to find innovative and interesting projects with campaigns underway. For example, the Silic shirt was a project whose campaign ended on January 26, 2014. This unique shirt would be made from a self-cleaning, soft and breathable fabric with hydrophobic nanotechnology, allowing it to be resistant to stains from sweat, liquids, and other sources.

The Silic shirt's funding goal was $20,000, but after attracting approximately 4,000 backers, the majority of whom pledged between $40 and $88, the campaign actually raised approximately $284,000. In the three-minute promotional video for this campaign (which can be seen by visiting www.kickstarter.com/projects/741186545/a-shirt-that-cleans-itself), a prototype of the shirt was used to demonstrate just how stain-resistant the Silic shirt is, while its inventors explained the technology behind the shirt, its manufacturing process, and told viewers that the fabric is safe, inexpensive, and comfortable to wear.

Like so many of the best promotional videos used on Kickstarter and other reward-based crowd funding platforms, the video for the Silic shirt ends with a call to action, which includes the inventor saying, "We hope that with your support, we can turn our dream into a reality. We can't do it without you." In addition to the powerful and well-produced video, the Kickstarter page for the Silic shirt included a detailed text-based description of the product, additional videos and illustrations that explained how it works, plus video clips of national publicity the product had already received.

By exploring other projects that Kickstarter classified as Popular, it's easy to see that some of the product-related projects are not targeted to a mass-market audience and are very narrow in their appeal. For example, there's the Onewheel: Self-Balancing Electric Skateboard. The campaign for this project also came to a close in late January 2014, after dramatically exceeding its funding goal with only 832 backers.

The funding goal for the Onewheel (www.kickstarter.com/projects/ 4422853/onewheel-the-self-balancing-electric-skateboard) was $100,000, but as the campaign ended, it had raised almost $500,000. One interesting thing to look at related to this campaign was its use of *stretch goals*.

Kickstarter, and some other crowd funding platforms, allow campaign creators to introduce stretch goals partway through a campaign. These are secondary funding goals that are typically much higher than the original funding goal. A stretch goal is typically introduced to help continue to build excitement for a project that's close to being fully funded, so that the campaign can raise extra money.

Each stretch goal that's introduced by the project's creator is a promise to introduce something new to the project if that stretch goal is met. Using the Onewheel campaign as an example, as it came close to reaching its $100,000 funding goal, the first stretch goal was introduced. This goal was for $300,000. If this goal was met during the campaign, the project's creators would incorporate integrated LED lighting into the Onewheel skateboard.

As this goal was close to being reached during the campaign, a second stretch goal was introduced. If a new funding goal of $400,000 was reached, the developers of the Onewheel would create and introduce an iPhone and iPad app to be used in conjunction with the skateboard. Not only did the introduction of these stretch goals help the campaign raise a lot more money than was originally planned, they also allowed the campaign to maintain a high level of excitement among its backers, encouraging them to both pledge more money and help promote the campaign to their networks so that the stretch goals would be met and the Onewheel product would ultimately be more useful and fun to use.

Just like rewards used in most reward-based crowd funding campaigns, stretch goals are extremely useful tools to help successful campaigns become even more successful by leveraging the excitement that's already been created around the project and building on it so the project can be made even better with the additional help of its backers.

In addition to its use of stretch goals, the Onewheel project was supported by a well-produced video (just over three minutes long), as well as a successful public relations campaign that resulted in an onslaught of international media attention for this cutting-edge, albeit expensive ($1,300), skateboard.

Another example of a project that required only a few backers to be fully funded was one for Coin Rings (https://www.kickstarter.com/ projects/103571640/coin-rings), a project created by a recent college graduate who earned a bachelor's degree in product design. These handcrafted pieces of jewelry are created from actual coins. Unlike most projects on Kickstarter, this one featured no promotional video. It simply relied on a handful of digital photos to showcase product samples and the creation process of the rings.

The Coin Rings project's funding goal was just $400, but it wound up raising approximately $12,000, thanks to 298 backers who got excited about the project. As a result of the campaign's initial success, two stretch goals were introduced. A handful of interesting rewards, priced between $20 and $80, were also used to entice backers to support this project.

While the Coin Rings project is an example of a smaller-scale project that didn't need to raise a fortune to be successful, and the Pebble smart watch is an example of a multimillion-dollar project, each category within Kickstarter (and similar platforms) contains many projects from everyday people that require more funding than individuals might be willing or able to invest on their own but that is easily achievable using reward-based crowd funding.

Let's take JordyCakes, for example (www.kickstarter.com/projects/124 1134086/jordycakes-custom-cake-and-cupcake-boutique). At the age of 16, Jordy became a creative cake artist and was selling her creations to a small group of local clients, including friends and family. By the age of 20, her business had grown to the point where she needed a professional kitchen and storefront. So she turned to reward-based crowd funding and launched a campaign with a funding goal of $10,000.

Her goal was to expand her business (www.jordycakessweets.com) with a retail location in the Chicago area and be able to create cakes and cupcakes for birthdays, weddings, baby showers, and other events where people wanted to celebrate something with a custom cake that she describes in her promotional video as "high-quality, high-class works of art that taste as good as they look."

Thanks to 245 backers, she ultimately raised approximately $14,000. Her Kickstarter campaign featured a just over one-minute video, a handful of photos, and some basic information about her goals.

Meanwhile, recording artists and musicians have also discovered a way to leverage their existing fan bases and expand their audience in order to raise money to independently produce albums, fund tours, acquire new instruments or equipment, pay to have new merchandise created, or, as you'll discover in Chapter 15, "Experienced Crowd Funders Share Their Secrets," acquire a new tour bus.

In fact, the digital era we're now in has changed the music industry as a whole in many different ways and has resulted in the old business model no longer working. Today, instead of being signed to a major record label, independent recording artists and musicians can experience tremendous ongoing success, in part, because they now have access to enough capital to independently fund their music projects.

By visiting Kickstarter, for example, and browsing through the Most Funded music projects, you'll discover thousands of successful campaigns that have raised anywhere from a few thousand dollars to over one million dollars for the project creator's music-related endeavors.

As of early January 2014, the most funded music project of all time on Kickstarter was created by Amanda Palmer and the Grand Theft Orchestra (www.kickstarter.com/projects/amandapalmer/amanda-palmer-the-new-record-art-book-and-tour). The project involved recording new music, creating an art book, and touring. This campaign's funding goal was $100,000, but thanks to 24,883 fans and backers, it ultimately raised almost $1.2 million.

One reasons for this campaign's overwhelming success was the promotional video that accompanied it. During the three-minute video, recording artist Amanda Palmer stood in front of the camera, but instead of talking, she held up handwritten signs with messages to her fans and potential backers. Not a word was spoken. Instead, a sampling of the group's music was played in the background. The campaign also focused on Amanda Palmer's artwork, and did an excellent job rallying her existing fans, while providing enough information to help recruit new fans and backers.

In addition, this campaign offered a unique collection of rewards, ranging in price from $1 to $10,000, although the vast majority of backers pledged between $25 and $50.

As this campaign makes clear, having an established network in place prior to a campaign's launch is a huge benefit, as is a unique and attention-getting promotional video and interesting and exclusive rewards that potential backers will want.

As with any other category on Kickstarter, the Music category is also populated by thousands of projects from both up-and-coming and established musicians and recording artists who have created campaigns to raise lesser amounts of money (typically under $10,000), by reaching out to their existing fan bases (networks).

On Kickstarter, most of the all-time most funded projects are computer and technology-related products, but restaurants, specialty food products, retail stores, skate parks, book publishers, movie theaters, yoga centers, and winemakers are among the many other types of projects that have successfully been funded.

Like Kickstarter, Indiegogo also supports the creative community and has project categories for Art, Comic, Dance, Design, Fashion, Film, Gaming, Music, Photography, Theater, Transmedia, Video/Web, and Writing, as well as cause-related categories for Animals, Community, Education, Environment,

Health, Politics, Religion and Verified Nonprofits and entrepreneurial categories for Food, Small Business, Sports, and Technology.

By studying existing projects on Kickstarter and other platforms, it's easy to see that certain types of projects have the ability to raise more funds than others. While some technology-related projects, for example, are able to raise hundreds of thousands or even millions of dollars, the all-time most funded projects within Kickstarter's Dance category, for example, have all raised under $50,000, and, with the exception of one project in the Fashion category, as of early 2014, the all-time most funded projects in the Fashion category all raised less than $450,000, while in the Theater category, the all-time most funded project had raised just over $175,000.

It's important to develop realistic funding goals for your project, based on what's possible on the various crowd funding platforms, by looking at the successes that past projects have been able to achieve. So, if your dance-related project needs in excess of $250,000, chances are that a single reward-based crowd funding campaign on Kickstarter, for example, will not allow you to achieve this funding goal, at least based on the past pledging behavior of backers for other dance projects.

Thus, if your financial needs exceed what appears to be possible on a particular platform, you have a multitude of options. First, you can attempt to ignore the precedent on a platform and launch your campaign anyway, in the hope you can make it go viral or reach a broad enough group of backers to fund your project. This will pose a huge challenge, especially if your funding goal appears too high and winds up raising a red flag in the minds of potential backers who come to believe your funding goal is unattainable or unrealistic.

Second, you can narrow the focus of your project and set a lower funding goal. This option tends to work well if you have a dedicated network and you're able to run several consecutive crowd funding campaigns, each with a related but slightly different goal, where one builds on the success of the previous one in order to achieve your ultimate funding goal.

Third, you can pursue more traditional methods for raising capital. Fourth, you can investigate other crowd funding platforms that might work better for your project. For example, for small businesses and start-ups, Fundable offers both a reward-based and equity-based crowd funding platform in one. The process used for designing, launching, and managing a campaign varies greatly, based on which crowd funding approach you take on this platform. This platform has already helped small and start-up businesses raise more than $70 million.

Like most crowd funding platforms, Fundable welcomes a wide range of project ideas but prohibits projects involving things like alcohol, contests, credit services, drugs, gambling, tobacco products, weapons, and other controversial products or business practices.

On the Fundable platform, some of the biggest success stories (as of early 2014) include the iPen2 (a technology-related product that raised $260,000), Ube (an automated home lighting system that raised $760,650), *Yosemite Big Walls: The Complete Guide* (a comprehensive guidebook to big wall climbing in Yosemite, which raised $24,730), Garagelo (a smartphone control for existing garage door openers, which raised $30,448), Voilà Chocolat (a line of handcrafted, artisanal chocolates, which raised $600,000), the LulzBot TAZ 3D Printer (a desktop 3D printer by Aleph Objects, Inc., which raised $294,548), and Sprizzi Drink Company (an in-home soda-making machine, which raised $622,000). You can take a look at what made these and other campaigns successful by visiting www.fundable .com/browse/funded.

REWARD-BASED CROWD FUNDING IS ALSO A POWERFUL FUND-RAISING TOOL

Just as there are specialty crowd funding platforms for small businesses, technology-based products, and other types of specialized or vertical market-oriented ventures, there are also a growing number of specialty platforms designed for fund-raising.

The CrowdRise funding platform is being used by individuals who want to raise money for a favorite charity, as well as by businesses of all sizes that want to expand their corporate giving through the use of crowd funded campaigns that have the secondary advantage of helping to enhance a business's brand awareness and reputation while raising funds for a good cause.

For example, if you're planning to run a marathon or participate in a walkathon for a particular cause, the CrowdRise campaign can help you solicit and manage pledges using the same types of tools that are used by profit-oriented companies that utilize crowd funding.

The Prizeo platform has also reinvented how everyday people, as well as businesses and organizations, can raise money for worthwhile causes using reward-based crowd funding. One incredible example of this is the Prizeo campaign completed in late 2013 by twin brothers Jack and Finn Harries, who run a wildly successful YouTube channel called JacksGap (www.youtube.com/jacksgap). At the time their Prizeo campaign launched, JacksGap had over 3 million subscribers.

Visit the campaign's page on Prizeo (www.prizeo.com/prizes/jacksgap/a-london-rickshaw-run-experience) and you'll see that after gathering a group of friends, Jack and Finn Harries (who are in their early 20s) traveled across the world, from their home in the U.K. to India, in order to participate in the three-week-long Rickshaw Run. During this 3,500-kilometer trek across the width of India, Jack and Finn's team drove small tuk-tuk vehicles to raise money for the Teenage Cancer Trust.

Thanks to their highly dedicated network of young fans from YouTube and other social media services, the campaign wound up raising in excess of $177,496 for the Teenage Cancer Trust and allowed Jack and Finn to produce a series of videos for their YouTube channel that chronicled their adventure. These inspirational, entertaining, and educational videos wound up attracting a worldwide audience in the millions. The success of this campaign is an excellent example of a project creator leveraging an existing network (on YouTube, Facebook, Twitter, etc.) to raise funds for a charity, using creative promotional videos and exclusive rewards to attract backers.

Meanwhile, a Los Angeles–based YouTuber in his mid-twenties, named Tyler Oakley, recently leveraged his online popularity and his more than 4.3 million YouTube subscribers in order to raise upwards of $526,000 for The Trevor Project using Prizeo. This campaign exceeded its funding goal of $150,000 in three days.

More details about this wildly successful fund-raising campaign can be found at www.prizeo.com/prizes/tyler-oakley/an-LA-date. Meanwhile, to learn more about the talented Tyler Oakley, you can visit his YouTube Channel at www.youtube.com/user/tyleroakley.

Another approach to fund-raising using crowd funding is used by a platform called Start A Cure. If you're passionate about raising money for cancer research, Start A Cure (which you'll learn more about in the next chapter) is a crowd funding platform that takes a unique approach. It allows individuals to fund specific researchers working at top-rated institutions, like Johns Hopkins, UCLA, and Harvard, who are focusing their research on specific types of cancer.

Whatever idea you have related to a business, product, project, or charitable cause that needs to be funded, chances are that with a bit of research, you'll be able to pinpoint a crowd funding platform that can be used to raise the money you're seeking. But remember, coming up with that great idea and then selecting an appropriate crowd funding platform is only the beginning, and accomplishing these two important steps will not necessarily guarantee your success.

BECOME AN EXPERIENCED PROJECT BACKER BEFORE BECOMING A PROJECT CREATOR

If you're already kicking around a project in your head, one of the first things you should do is invest some time exploring the various crowd funding platforms. During this exploration, you want to accomplish several important things, including:

- Get to know how the popular reward or presale-based crowd funding platforms function. Discover what features are offered on each, how projects are showcased, and what tools are available that will allow you to profile your project.
- Look for project campaigns that are similar to yours and gauge the level of success they're having on the various platforms.
- Watch many promotional videos for all types of projects. Learn as much as you can about the various approaches these videos take, and start thinking about how you'll produce your own video.
- Become a backer of projects on several of the platforms you're thinking about using. You don't have to spend a fortune, but you should participate on some level in at least a dozen different projects prior to launching your own crowd funding campaign. This will allow you to experience how project creators communicate with backers, witness each campaign's process from start to finish, and allow you to experience crowd funding from a backer's perspective. Doing this will help you understand how to better attract and interact with backers when it comes time to creating and managing your own campaign.
- Look for campaigns that are targeting the same audience that your project will appeal to, even if the project itself is vastly different. Examine the primary message these campaigns convey, the content and quality of the promotional video, and which elements of those existing campaigns are appealing to the target audience and why. Pay attention to aspects of the campaign such as its duration, funding goal, the number of backers the campaigns have attracted, and the rewards that are being offered that the backers seem to really like. Ask yourself, what is it about the campaigns that got the audience really excited about the project?
- As you study campaigns that are working, and that have surpassed their funding goals, try to figure out some of the reasons why this happened. Look for elements of the campaign that were done well and see what approaches those project creators took with their campaigns. At the same time, look at project campaigns that are currently underway but that are not performing so well. Eventually, you should be able to look at a project's page on whatever platform it's being featured on, and determine for yourself why it's failing. Once you can do this confidently and consistently, chances are you've developed a good understanding of how reward-based crowd funding works, and you're ready to pursue your own campaign for your own project.
- As you explore the various crowd funding platforms, determine for yourself if hosting your project's campaign on that specific platform will be beneficial to what you're trying to accomplish. For example, will the campaign page you can create on that platform appeal to your target

audience and allow you to properly showcase your project in a way that will excite potential backers?

■ Figure out what it takes for a project to get featured on a platform, not just listed on it. As you later create your own project and the campaign for it, what will you do so it stands out? How will you utilize the resources offered by the platform to help make your campaign a success?

■ Determine whether your project's campaign would benefit from stretch goals and how these stretch goals could be used in the later phases of your already successful campaign to enhance your project idea and raise more money. Based on examples of stretch goals you notice being used by other campaigns, start brainstorming creative stretch goals for your own campaign that will further increase excitement for your project among backers and potential supporters.

You can read everything there is to read about each of the crowd funding platforms, but this will not replace the need for you to experience using the various platforms firsthand as you become acquainted with how reward-based crowd funding actually works.

While exploring the various crowd funding platforms, you'll discover that each offers online tutorials designed to help project creators become acquainted with the platform. One you narrow down which crowd funding platforms you may be interested in using, peruse these online resources so you develop an understanding of what sets each platform apart from its competition. As you do this, pay particular attention to the fees associated with using the platform and the rules related to receiving the funds you raise based on whether your reach your funding goal.

By the time you're done exploring the various reward-based crowd funding platforms, not only will you be proficient in understanding how they work, you'll also know whether your project could do well on a specific platform and whether the platform offers the features and functions you'll need to achieve your funding goal.

Since you already know that one key component to a crowd funding campaign's success is selecting the right platform for your project, this research will help you make the right decision. With this in mind, remember once again that there are no shortcuts. You'll need to invest whatever time is necessary to explore the various platforms and become a backer of a handful of projects.

When it comes to choosing a crowd funding platform, one common mistake is skipping the research and opting to go with a platform like Kickstarter or Indiegogo that is extremely popular and well-established. In some cases, you may wind up going with one of these platforms, but this should not be a default decision until you've researched other suitable crowd funding platforms for your project.

If you'll be raising capital to launch a small business that doesn't involve creating, manufacturing, and selling some type of project or a creative endeavor, a platform like Kickstarter may work, but you might discover another platform, like Fundable, which caters to small business start-ups, is more appropriate for your project. Or, if you think a straight presale approach will work better for your campaign, as opposed to offering rewards to backers, a self-hosted service like Selfstarter might be more suitable for your project. Without exploring the various platform options firsthand after determining what you're trying to accomplish using crowd funding, your ability to make an intelligent platform choice will be hampered and based on incomplete information.

HOW TO FIND SPECIALTY CROWD FUNDING PLATFORMS

Sometimes special interest projects require a specialty crowd funding platform to achieve success. The focus of Chapter 3, "Introduction to Crowd Funding Platforms and Services," is on helping you find alternative crowd funding platforms beyond Kickstarter and Indiegogo. In this chapter, you'll learn about just a few of the specialty crowd funding platforms that cater to specific types of projects that you might want to consider if your project doesn't fit the guidelines required by Kickstarter, for example.

Thanks to the fast-growing popularity of crowd funding, new platforms are launched almost weekly. Some of these platforms are open to all types of projects, while others cater to specific types of projects. Beyond the popular platforms profiled in Chapter 3, you can also use any search engine (such as Google, Yahoo!, or Bing) to help you find and learn about additional crowd funding platforms that might be suitable for your project.

Within the search field of your favorite search engine, enter the search phrase "crowd funding" or "reward-based crowd funding." To find more specialized crowd-funding platforms, use a search phrase like "crowd funding for small business," "crowd funding for inventors," "crowd funding for fund-raisers," "crowd funding for artists," and so on.

CHAPTER 3

Introduction to Crowd Funding Platforms and Services

In This Chapter

- Learn about several popular reward-based crowd funding platforms.
- Discover crowd funding platforms that cater to specific types of projects.
- Get the scoop on self-hosted crowd funding options.

Anyone who knows anything about reward-based crowd funding has heard about Kickstarter and most likely Indiegogo, as well. However, as you'll discover from this chapter, there are a growing number of additional reward-based crowd funding platforms, some of which are designed to handle very specific types of projects, while others take a very different approach to crowd funding than Kickstarter and/or Indiegogo that you may find appealing.

Each platform has its own features, options, and fees associated with it and often takes a unique approach when it comes to collecting funds from backers and dispersing those funds to project creators. What's nice about using a reward-based crowd funding platform to host your campaign is that all of the tools needed to create and manage your campaign are online, and each project is given its own unique web page and website address (URL) that's hosted by the platform.

Thus, the project creator can create, launch, and manage a reward-based crowd funding campaign with any computer or device that has Internet access and a web browser. No specialized software or programming is required. The majority of these platforms offers tools that are as easy to use as a word processor but allow a campaign page to be populated with customized content, including text-based descriptions and bios, digital photos, company and/or product logos, and of course, one or more promotional videos.

This chapter offers profiles of popular crowd funding platforms, as well as a self-hosted option. Each platform profile includes pricing information, as well as details about the features and functions that set it apart from its competition.

The platforms featured in this chapter are just a sampling of the many reward-based crowd funding platforms that are available, and new platforms and self-hosted options are constantly being introduced. It's important to understand that these services are continually evolving and growing in popularity. For that reason, the descriptions of the various crowd funding platforms given here may not reflect a platform's most recent updates or evolution.

GENERAL REWARD-BASED CROWD FUNDING PLATFORMS

This section profiles a handful of popular reward-based crowd funding platforms that have the broadest appeal in terms of the types of campaigns that can be managed from them. Because Kickstarter is a pioneer in the reward-based crowd funding arena, and it continues to be the most popular platform of its kind in existence (with literally tens of thousands of success stories), the entire focus of Chapter 12, "Get Started Using Kickstarter.com," is on using this platform.

FundAnything

Website	www.fundanything.com
Key Features	This platform is open to any type of project, except for projects that are deemed offensive or that use objectionable content.
Fees	FundAnything charges a 9 percent commission on all contributions that are collected. However, if a project reaches its published funding goal, 4 percent is given back to the project creator, so FundAnything's fee is a flat 5 percent. The independent payment processing company used by FundAnything charges a separate fee of approximately 3 percent. There are no start-up fees.

Pros/Cons	Unlike Kickstarter, for example, FundAnything accepts any type of project. There is no project preapproval process. Also, once a backer pledges money to a project, those funds (minus the fees charged by FundAnything and the payment processing company) are transferred to the project creator within 24 hours.
	One potential drawback is that FundAnything is less well-known than Kickstarter and Indiegogo, which could impact the success of a public relations effort for a campaign, if journalists are not already familiar with the platform.

In addition to creating a platform that allows for virtually any individual, company, or organization to quickly create and publish a reward-based crowd funding campaign, FundAnything offers a handful of online tools to guide project creators through the project creation, publishing, and promotions process.

Available from the platform's website (http://fundanything.com/en/how#handbook) is the free FundAnything Handbook, which breaks down the process of creating, publishing, and promoting a campaign into 10 easy-to-follow steps.

Like all reward-based crowd funding platforms, FundAnything requires a project's creator to set a goal amount for the campaign. This is the total amount that the project needs to raise and should be based on a careful calculation of the anticipated budget related to the entire project (including costs associated with running and promoting the crowd funding campaign itself).

Using the online tools offered by FundAnything, a project's creator also needs to create an attention-getting title for the campaign, which should be informative as well as keyword friendly. Like most platforms, FundAnything allows a logo to be added to the campaign's page.

FundAnything encourages the use of a promotional video as part of a campaign but doesn't require it. It is up to the project's creator to select the appropriate category and subcategory within the FundAnything platform that the project best fits into.

The main categories include: Creative Arts, Causes, Personal, and Business Ideas. Under each main category are a selection of more narrowly focused subcategories to choose from. Under Creative Arts, subcategories include: Art, Design, Fashion, Film & Video, Gaming, Music, Photography, Theater & Dance, Web Projects, and Writing. Under the Causes category, subcategories include: Animals, Community, Nonprofit, Politics, Religion, Schools, Sports, and Volunteering.

The Personal category allows individuals to use reward-based crowd funding to raise money for almost any specific personal use. Subcategories include: Celebrations, Competitions, Education, Family Needs, Funerals & Memorials, Hopes & Dreams, Medical, Pets, and Weddings.

Finally, the Business Ideas category caters to start-ups, small businesses, entrepreneurs, and even larger businesses that want to expand, for example. This category has just two subcategories: Business and Technology.

An important part of any campaign is its detailed description. Using text, this is where project creators should clearly and concisely describe their project, include their bio, explain to potential backers how much money is needed, how the money will be used, and why the project is relevant or important. The FundAnything platform walks project creators through the process of creating a detailed description as a campaign is being set up, but it's up to the project creator to compose the text and add whatever additional content is deemed appropriate.

Another key component of all FundAnything campaigns are the rewards. On this platform, rewards can be just about anything, but it's important to create rewards that potential backers will find appealing.

Once a FundAnything campaign is set up and published, the platform helps project creators link their existing social media accounts directly to the campaign's page, making it easier to promote the campaign using services like Facebook and Twitter, as well as direct email.

After a campaign gets underway, FundAnything provides the additional tools needed to continuously update the campaign, stay in contact with backers, and send out the promised rewards to the appropriate backers.

As with any crowd funding campaign, it's a smart strategy to peruse the platform's successful campaigns, as well as campaigns that are currently underway in the category you believe your project will ultimately fit into.

To determine what FundAnything deems to be the best campaigns currently running on the platform, take a look at the platform's Featured Campaigns section (http://fundanything.com/en/search/category?cat_id=27).

In terms of funding, one feature many project creators appreciate is that money received from backers is transferred directly to the project creator within 24 hours, and whether or not the project gets fully funded, the monies received are kept by the project creator (minus fees). The potential drawback to this occurs if a project does not reach its funding goal, but backers still expect to receive the reward(s) that were promised.

To learn more about the FundAnything platform, be sure to read the interview with Brad Wyman, the platform's chief crowd funding officer, which is featured in Chapter 13, "Interviews with Crowd Funding Experts."

FundRazr

Website	www.fundrazr.com
Key Features	FundRazr accepts virtually any type of project and offers a handful of easy-to-use features when it comes to creating, managing, and promoting a campaign, as well as interacting with backers.
Fees	There are no start-up costs associated with using FundRazr. Project creators pay a 5 percent commission on all funds received, as well as a payment processing fee of 2.9 percent, and a $0.30 per transaction fee. All money raised, minus the fees, is paid directly to the project creator.
Pros/Cons	FundRazr does not financially penalize project creators if their funding goal is not met. All money raised (minus the fees) are transferred directly to the project creator's account, and can be accessed almost immediately. The service accepts 10 different currencies, and allows for project backers to come from 20 countries, including the United States, UK, Canada, Europe, and Australia. Backers can also financially support a project via PayPal. One potential drawback is that FundRazr is lesser known than Kickstarter and Indiegogo, which could impact the success of a public relations effort for a campaign.

Since its launch in 2008, FundRazr has hosted more than 40,000 reward-based crowd funding campaigns and has allowed for more than $40 million to be raised by project creators from more than 20 different countries. As with most reward-based crowd funding platforms, getting started with FundRazr is free. As a project creator, you only pay when funds are actually raised and collected from backers. Since projects do not need to be approved in advance by FundRazr, once a campaign is created, it can go live and start collecting funds from backers within minutes.

Using the platform's built-in promotional tools, existing social media accounts (including Facebook, Twitter, Google+, LinkedIn, and Pinterest) can be linked to a campaign, plus direct mail can be used to drive traffic to a campaign's page. All funds collected are transferred directly to the project creator's PayPal or WePay account almost immediately (minus fees), so project creators have access to raised funds while a campaign is still underway.

FundRazr is open to projects created by individuals, communities, groups, organizations, nonprofits, businesses, political groups, and entrepreneurs. Unlike some platforms, FundRazr allows for projects of a personal nature (such as the funding of a college education, the payment of medical bills, or covering the cost of a wedding, for example). However, the same reward-based crowd funding tools can also be used to fund business projects; manage a fundraising campaign for a nonprofit or political group; or to fund the creation of products, artistic projects, or just about anything else that's legal.

Indiegogo

Website	www.indiegogo.com
Key Features	Next to Kickstarter, Indiegogo is the second most popular reward-based crowd funding platform in the world. Unlike Kickstarter, however, there is no approval process for projects.
Fees	Indiegogo charges no set-up fees. A flat commission of 9 percent is taken on all funds raised. However, if a campaign reaches or exceeds its funding goal, 5 percent of the fees taken are given back to the project creator, so the actual commission paid is only 4 percent. An additional 3 percent fee is charged by the third-party payment processing company.
Pros/Cons	There is no waiting to get a new project approved, so once you create and publish your project with Indiegogo, you can begin promoting it and collecting funds from backers. Indiegogo is open to all types of projects, including for-profit creative ventures, business ventures, and personal projects.
	One nice feature of Indiegogo is that project creators can choose whether they want to keep all the money raised, whether or not a project reaches its funding goal, or only keep the money if the funding goal is met or exceeded.

At any given time, there are thousands of active reward-based crowd funding campaigns utilizing the Indiegogo platform. Many project creators like this platform because of its flexibility and customizability. The platform launched in 2008 as a way for independent filmmakers to fund their projects, but in 2009, the platform opened itself up to accept all types of projects. According to the company's website, "Our belief is that anyone, anywhere who is passionate and works hard should be able to raise money."

In addition to offering an entire section of its website that's dedicated to teaching people how to effectively use reward-based crowd funding to raise money for their projects, Indiegogo offers project creators the opportunity to email its Help Center and receive personalized responses to questions.

When it comes to doing your research, Indiegogo allows you to browse through and view campaigns. To do this, click on the Browse option that's displayed at the top of the main web page, and then select the Popular Now, Final Countdown, New This Week, Most Funded, or Hot Perks option. You also have the option to browse projects based on their category.

Main project categories include Creative, Cause, or Entrepreneurial, and each category has a selection of subcategories. For example, under the Creative category, subcategories include: Art, Comic, Dance, Design, Fashion, Film, Gaming, Music, Photography, Theater, Transmedia, Video/Web, and Writing.

By clicking on the Most Funded option, you can take a look at the campaign pages for the most successful campaigns hosted by Indiegogo and pinpoint what elements of each campaign worked well, ascertain why they were successful, and then apply similar strategies when creating and managing your own campaign.

What's nice about the Indiegogo platform is that it's designed for non-tech-savvy project creators and backers, so using the various online tools to create and/or contribute to a campaign is an easy and straightforward process. You can be confident that your potential backers will easily be able to navigate and use the platform to help fund and promote your project using one-click social media integration.

Because the Indiegogo platform is well-known, getting media attention for your campaign through an optional public relations effort may be a bit easier. Most journalists and bloggers are already familiar with Indiegogo and consider it to be a reputable crowd funding platform. As a result, they often seek out story ideas about campaigns currently underway on Indiegogo and other well-known platforms.

Kickstarter

Website	www.kickstarter.com
Key Features	This is the best known and most widely used reward-based crowd funding platform in the world. Projects must conform to Kickstarter's creative criteria and be approved before appearing on this platform. Kickstarter defines an acceptable project as "Something with a clear end, like making an album, a film, or a new game. A project will eventually be completed, and something will be produced as a result."

Fees	When a project reaches or exceeds its funding goal and is funded, Kickstarter charges a 5 percent commission on the funds collected. In the United States, payment processing is done by Amazon Payments, which charges between 3 percent and 5 percent for this required service. For projects based outside of the United States, a different third-party payment processing service is used, which also charges between 3 and 5 percent.
Pros/Cons	Kickstarter uses an all-or-nothing approach to project funding. If a project reaches or exceeds its published funding goal, the funds collected are transferred to the project creator at the conclusion of the campaign (minus fees). However, if the campaign does not meet its funding goal, those who chose to support the project are never charged, the project creator receives nothing, and no fees are paid.

Kickstarter launched in 2009 as a reward-based crowd funding platform. As of January 2014, more than 55,000 projects have been successfully funded using this platform, and more than $960 million had been raised for them. As with so many of today's reward-based crowd funding platforms, project creators who use Kickstarter retain all ownership over their project and are fully responsible for it. Anyone (age 18 or older in the United States, United Kingdom, Canada, Australia, or New Zealand) is allowed to publish a project on the platform as long as the project adheres to Kickstarter's guidelines.

One differentiator between Kickstarter and some competing platforms is its all-or-nothing approach for projects trying to get funded. The benefit to this is that if a project fails to reach its funding goal, the project creator is not obligated to fulfill orders, provide rewards to backers, or try to complete the project with insufficient funds. Project creators can retain their credibility and fine-tune and relaunch their campaigns, if they choose to.

On other platforms, if a project fails to reach its funding goal, but the project creator received some funds from participating backers, those backers are still entitled to whatever rewards were promised, which often requires that the project creator attempt to complete the underfunded project or run the risk of disappointing backers and losing credibility.

As of January 2014, almost 131,000 individual projects had been published on the Kickstarter platform, and thanks to the hard work of the project creators, 43.62 percent of those projects were successfully funded. Of those successfully funded projects, 35,269 of them raised between $1,000 and $9,999, while 56 raised in excess of $1 million.

All projects published on Kickstarter must clearly fit within one of the platform's established categories, which include: Art, Comics, Dance, Design,

Fashion, Film & Video, Food, Games, Music, Photography, Publishing, Technology, and Theater.

All projects must be creative in nature and have a clearly defined goal with a clear end. Thus, someone with an idea to launch a business that involves the invention or manufacturing of a technology product, for example, would most likely be welcome on Kickstarter, but many other types of more traditional business ventures are not suited to this platform.

One key differentiator between Kickstarter and some other reward-based crowd funding platforms is that Kickstarter cannot be used to raise money for causes, whether a well-known charity, a scholarship program, or what Kickstarter refers to as a "fund my life" project. Kickstarter is exclusively for funding "creative projects," which are more clearly defined on the platform's website (www.kickstarter.com/help/guidelines).

One perk project creators receive as a result of hosting and managing their projects' campaigns on Kickstarter, is that they can leverage the popularity of the Kickstarter platform, which has attracted more than 5.5 million project backers, and is well known and respected by the media. Kickstarter also boasts a large pool of active repeat backers. These are people who actively explore the Kickstarter platform looking for multiple projects to support. While you, as the project creator, can't rely on these backers to completely fund your project, this group can be used to supplement your own network of backers that you drive to your Kickstarter campaign page.

Be sure to read Chapter 12, "Get Started Using Kickstarter.com," for a more in-depth overview of the Kickstarter platform, how it works, and what sets it apart from other platforms. It's important to understand these differentiators and whether they can be used to your advantage prior to launching your campaign.

RocketHub

Website	www.rockethub.com
Key Features	This reward-based crowd funding platform has teamed up with the A&E television network to provide certain project campaigns and related success stories with a vast television audience. RocketHub also allows project creators to keep all funds raised (minus fees), regardless of whether a campaign reaches its funding goal. For first-time project creators, RocketHub offers an online Success School (www.rockethub.com/education), which provides a comprehensive and easy-to-follow tutorial for using the RocketHub platform to create, launch, manage, and promote a reward-based crowd funding campaign.

Fees	For projects that reach or exceed their funding goals, RocketHub charges a 4 percent commission on funds collected. There is also a 4 percent fee charged by the payment processing service. For projects that do not reach their funding goals, RocketHub charges an 8 percent commission on all funds raised, plus the payment processing service charges a 4 percent fee.
Pros/Cons	For projects that are truly unique and show promise on the RocketHub platform, the opportunity to receive national television coverage on the A&E network is a huge perk. Plus, for newcomers to the reward-based crowd funding arena, the platform's Success School is a very useful information-packed resource.

RocketHub is open to all types of projects, as long as they're legal and in good taste. The platform's partnership with the A&E television network allows selected projects to be introduced to a national television audience and potentially receive funding directly from the A&E network. According to RocketHub, "A&E looks for exceptional stories, passionate project leaders and crowd validation (i.e., funding momentum). They are also looking for a general fit with the interests of their audience."

Even if a project is not specifically selected to receive support from A&E, the RocketHub platform offers a robust collection of tools and services that make creating, launching, managing, and promoting a campaign a straightforward process (although a considerable time commitment is still required to manage and promote a campaign, just as it is on all platforms).

You can learn more about RocketHub directly from Brian Meece, the platform's CEO, by reading the in-depth interview with him that's featured in Chapter 13.

SPECIALTY REWARD-BASED CROWD FUNDING PLATFORMS

Unlike the reward-based crowd funding platforms profiled in the previous section, the platforms profiled within this section cater to specific types of projects and typically offer a more specialized set of tools for designing and managing a campaign. Here, you'll also learn about crowd funding platforms that can be used for fundraising as well as platforms that take a very unique approach to crowd funding.

CrowdRise

Website	www.crowdrise.com
Key Features	CrowdRise uses reward-based crowd funding, but opens these tools up to individuals, businesses, and organizations that want to raise money for a charity or worthwhile cause. This includes companies that want to manage branded fund-raising campaigns for a charity in order to rally their customers or clients, while enhancing their public image. CrowdRise currently supports more than 1.6 million recognized charities worldwide.
Fees	The CrowdRise platform earns money by taking a commission on the donations raised. This commission is between 3 and 5 percent, plus a potential monthly fee, a third-party credit card processing fee of 2.9 percent, and a $0.30 per transaction fee. Three different pricing plans are offered and it's up to the individual charities (not the people raising the money) to choose which pricing plan will be applied.
Specialty	The goal of CrowdRise is to make fund-raising fun, both for the individuals, organizations, or companies trying to raise donations and for the people making the donations. The platform offers a wide range of interesting, fun, and highly engaging ways an individual, business, or organization can go about raising money for a worthwhile cause of their choosing. CrowdRise is a platform designed exclusively for fund-raising.

Chapter 13 features an interview with Robert Wolfe, the founder of CrowdRise. In it, he discusses why he created and launched the CrowdRise platform and how he's gone to great lengths to make fund-raising more interactive, fun, and successful.

As you'll discover, CrowdRise offers tremendous flexibility for people running crowd funding campaigns to raise money for their favorite charities. For example, a child (with the help of a parent) can launch a campaign in conjunction with his or her birthday party. Instead of accepting traditional gifts for themselves, children can solicit donations for favorite charities, such as the animal shelter in their hometown.

Meanwhile, an individual who is planning to participate in a walk-athon or marathon, for example, can use CrowdRise in conjunction with social media to solicit and manage donations, if they are raising money for a cause. Companies of any size can also create highly engaging, fully branded, and widely publicized fund-raising campaigns for charities they support.

CrowdRise offers project creators an array of online tools to help them create unique campaign pages. These pages can include, text, photos, video, and other content to convey relevant details about the campaign to potential donors. It is then the project creator's responsibility to promote the campaign using social media, email, and/or other resources.

Using CrowdRise, just about anyone can create a fund-raising page on the platform for their favorite charity or a cause they're passionate about. Then, social media is used to promote the campaign and drive traffic to the page. CrowdRise collects the donated funds and forwards them directly to the charity (minus fees and commissions). For the person, organization, or business that publishes and manages the campaign on the CrowdRise platform, there are no fees to pay whatsoever, and all donations made to U.S.-based 501(c)(3) charitable organizations are tax deductible. Donors automatically receive an email after making a donation that meets the donation documentation requirements of the IRS.

Dragon Innovation

Website	www.dragoninnovation.com
Key Features	This crowd funding platform is designed exclusively to support inventors of technological products and gadgets that are being designed, manufactured, and marketed from scratch. Dragon Innovation provides a team of experts who specialize in manufacturing and online marketing, for example, who help all approved projects succeed on this platform. The focus is on providing project creators with the extensive up-front preparation that is needed to design, manufacture, distribute, and market a technology-based product, as well as the support needed once a project is funded.
Fees	Every project concept goes through a thorough prescreening (vetting) process by Dragon Innovation's team of design, manufacturing, and marketing experts. For this initial consultation, there's a fee of $5,000. Once a project is fully funded, Dragon Innovation charges a 5 percent commission on the funds raised, and a third party charges for payment processing. After a project is funded, the project creator can continue working with Dragon Innovation's experts on a retainer basis.

Specialty	Dragon Innovation is primarily a consulting firm that works with inventors developing cutting-edge technologies and hardware. The company launched its own crowd funding platform to help its clients' projects get funded. Only projects that are approved by Dragon Innovation's team are accepted onto its proprietary reward-based crowd funding platform, and, as a result, the platform's overall success rate in getting projects funded is exceptionally high.
	The focus of this platform is on working with entrepreneurs looking to build consumer scale products, not on supporting ideas from what the company calls hobbyists or hackers.

For people with ideas for technology-based products that they want to design, manufacture, market, distribute, and sell, Dragon Innovation offers a perfect solution. As you'll discover from reading the interview with Scott Miller, CEO of Dragon Innovation, in Chapter 13, several things set Dragon Innovation's platform apart from its competition.

First, a project must be approved by a team of design, marketing, and manufacturing experts before a crowd funding campaign is launched for it on this platform. What Dragon Innovation brings to the table are teams of recognized experts, each with decades of experience in their fields, who work closely with each inventor to fully develop a project and its campaign before it launches. This includes developing a thorough and detailed budget and accurate funding goal, based on all of the unique challenges an inventor faces when trying to design and manufacture a new product either domestically or overseas.

Second, once a project is approved for the Dragon Innovation platform, the company's team of crowd funding and marketing experts helps the project creator design and launch an appropriate campaign and ensure that the project creator has the resources to properly manage that campaign.

Due to the individualized attention that each project receives, a project creator has a significantly better chance of reaching or exceeding his funding goal. Then, project creators can continue working with Dragon Innovation's team to bring their funded project ideas to fruition. As of early 2014, the Dragon Innovation platform was only open to U.S.-based projects, although the tooling and manufacturing process for the invention can be (and often is) handled overseas.

Like Kickstarter, Dragon Innovation's crowd funding platform has adopted an all-or-nothing approach to funding. If a project meets or exceeds its funding goal, the funds are collected from backers and forwarded to the project creator (minus the fees). However, if a project fails to reach its funding goal, no money is collected, and the project creator receives no money. The up-front fee of $5,000 is nonrefundable.

Another way that Dragon Innovation's platform differentiates itself, aside from focusing exclusively on technology (hardware) related projects, is that it works almost exclusively with project creators (inventors) seeking to raise between $200,000 and $1 million (or more) to design, create, manufacture, and sell a product and launch a company around that the product.

To learn more about the types of projects that have been successfully funded using Dragon Innovation's platform and that are currently being hosted by the platform, visit www.dragoninnovation.com/projects. To ensure that each project gets the most individualized attention possible, as of early 2014, only about 40 new projects are published on this platform each month.

Fundable

Website	www.fundable.com
Key Features	Designed exclusively for small business operators and entrepreneurs, Fundable can be used as either a reward- or equity-based crowd funding platform. Which option you choose as a project creator will determine how a project is handled by the platform. The reward-based crowd funding component of the platform is typically used by companies looking to raise less than $50,000 and retain all ownership of and equity in their business and project. Equity-based crowd funding can be used by companies looking to raise between $50,000 and $10 million. Backers of these projects must be accredited investors, and the project creator must offer an equity stake in the company (or project).
Fees	Fundable charges a flat monthly fee of $179 for the duration that a campaign is active on the platform. There are no percentage fees charged by Fundable, but a separate fee from the third-party payment processing company will apply.
Specialty	For reward-based crowd funding, Fundable offers many of the tools, services, and features you'd otherwise find on platforms like Kickstarter or Indiegogo, but the projects on this platform are all small-business or entrepreneurial in nature. The equity-based crowd funding component of this platform is based on what's now permissible through the Jumpstart Our Business Startups (JOBS) Act.

For small businesses and entrepreneurs looking to raise capital for their for-profit business ventures, Fundable offers both reward and equity-based crowd funding options, as well as a different (and more competitive) fee structure than most competing platforms charge. It's entirely the responsibility of the project creators to market and promote their campaigns, drive web traffic to their campaign pages, and then use the content on those pages to convert people into backers who make financial commitments to the projects.

The Fundable platform allows project creators to offer rewards to their backers and recommends offering between three and eight tiers of rewards during a campaign. Just as on other platforms, these rewards can involve preorders for a product, services, or recognition (which might include offering exclusive or limited-edition swag).

As you'd expect from a platform that caters to small business and entrepreneurs, the projects hosted on this platform often include new inventions and products. You can preview a sampling of successful campaigns that have been hosted by Fundable by visiting www.fundable.com/browse, and then clicking on the Successful button.

Prior to a project being published, it must be submitted and approved by Fundable.

Prizeo

Website	www.prizeo.com
Key Features	Prizeo is a reward-based crowd funding platform designed specifically for fund-raising by charities and not-for-profit projects. This platform continues to be used by high-profile companies, celebrities, athletes and YouTube personalities, for example, to raise money and boost awareness for charities these people or organizations are passionate about or spearhead. In exchange for financial donations, donors can win once-in-a-lifetime experiences with celebrities, as well as receive exclusive merchandise (rewards).
Fees	Prizeo keeps 10 percent of the revenue raised by a project and forwards the remaining 90 percent of the proceeds directly to the applicable charity.
Specialty	Prizeo uses a contest-based model as well as rewards to attract donors (backers) to fund-raising projects hosted on this platform. To help project creators with their campaigns, Prizeo offers scalable technology, graphic design, video and production services, payment processing, and it handles all legal accounting aspects of a campaign. Prizeo also helps with public relations, marketing, promotions, and prize fulfillment.

To fully understand how Prizeo works—and how it dramatically differs from other reward-based crowd funding platforms that focus on fund-raising—it's useful to visit www.prizeo.com/prizes and take a look at both the successful campaigns that have been hosted by this platform and those that are currently running on it.

Among the campaigns hosted by Prizeo, a number have been connected to celebrities such as Will Ferrell, Snoop Dogg, Michael Phelps, Mariah Carey, Donald Faison, Eva Longoria, the cast of *High School Musical*, Justin Bieber, YouTubers Jack and Finn Harries, Avril Lavigne, Muhammad Ali, Khloe Kardashian, members of One Direction, Alicia Keys, Kobe Bryant, and Samuel L. Jackson.

The charities that benefited financially (through donations) from these campaigns are diverse and include The Snoop Youth Football League, Michael Phelps Foundation, St. Jude Children's Research Hospital, The Eva Longoria Foundation, GimmeMo', FCancer, Typhoon Haiyan Relief, Teenage Cancer Trust, World Wildlife Fund, Alzheimer's Association, and many others.

When a new campaign launches on Prizeo, it's typically supported by one or more high-profile companies as well as a celebrity or an athlete. Most offer one or more grand prizes that include some type of one-of-a-kind interaction with the featured celebrity. Everyone who donates to a campaign becomes eligible to win the grand prize drawing, which is held at the conclusion of the fund-raising campaign. However, based on the amount of a donation, donors also automatically receive rewards, which often include limited-edition and/or autographed items.

The campaigns are all hosted online by Prizeo and have their own unique web page on the Prizeo platform. All campaigns are promoted using social media, email, public relations, and other marketing and promotional efforts.

Prizeo offers companies the opportunity to sponsor specific campaigns and benefit from the promotion and publicity they receive by being active in them. For celebrities, athletes, YouTube personalities, and other high-profile people, Prizeo offers a chance to build and enhance their brand while helping to raise money for a good cause. Donors receive exclusive or limited-edition prizes for their financial participation in a campaign plus the chance to win an opportunity to interact in some way with their favorite celebrities or athletes. Companies interested in participating in a future Prizeo campaign or donating prizes to a campaign should email corporate@prizeo.com. Representatives of celebrities, athletes, or individuals interested in participating in a future campaign should email celebrity@prizeo.com.

Start A Cure

Website	www.startacure.com
Key Features	Start A Cure is a nonprofit fund-raising platform that works with well-respected doctors, researchers, educational institutions, research facilities, and laboratories focused on finding a cure for various types of cancer.
Fees	If a project reaches or exceeds its funding goal, Start A Cure retains a 5 percent commission to maintain the platform, and an additional percentage (around 3 percent) is paid to the third-party payment processing company.
Specialty	Start A Cure works only with accredited experts, doctors, and organizations. All projects must be related to finding a cure for cancer and preapproved by Start A Cure's volunteer panel before they can be published on the platform.

Start A Cure was launched in March 2013 and has adopted a unique approach to crowd funding for cancer research. This platform allows backers to support specific researchers or research projects that are focusing on finding a cure for a specific type of cancer. Thus, backers are able to target their donations to areas of cancer research they are most passionate about.

In exchange for their donations, backers get a firsthand look at cutting-edge research that's being done, and in some cases, unprecedented access to world-renowned researchers and doctors. Individual doctors, laboratories, research facilities, and universities, for example, use Start A Cure to fund specific research projects.

Start A Cure has three main goals. First, it seeks to help fund the cure for cancer. Second, it serves to reveal the often hidden faces of those conducting cutting-edge cancer research, and third, it aims to build hope for the men, women, and children diagnosed with cancer.

All projects submitted to Start A Cure are reviewed by a volunteer review board. Once a project is approved, the same types of crowd funding tools offered by more mainstream platforms are used to raise money and boost awareness for specific cancer-related research projects. Doctors, hospitals, patients, and everyday people can all participate in the fund-raising efforts.

Start A Cure has adopted an all-or-nothing approach to funding projects. Only projects that meet or exceed their funding goal receive the donations from their backers. When a funding goal is not met, the credit or debit cards from the supporting backers are not charged. To see what types of cancer research projects are currently being assisted by Start A Cure, visit http://startacure.com/start-a-cure. The Start A Cure platform is managed by Malecare Cancer Support (www.malecare.org).

Upstart

Website	www.upstart.com
Key Features	Upstart is unique in that it allows individuals to use crowd funding to raise money for their own personal career or entrepreneurial goals. In other words, backers invest in someone's potential and future income. This is a hybrid form of crowd funding that is somewhat related to equity-based crowd funding in that backers must be accredited investors. Upstart is used by individuals (mostly recent graduates) to pursue entrepreneurial goals and fund further education. In exchange for backers' financial support, participants pay back a fixed percentage of their income for a predetermined number of years.
Fees	Upstart charges a 3 percent commission on the funds collected, and it charges an account maintenance fee to its accredited investors.
Specialty	Upstart is all about funding individuals with entrepreneurial aspirations who want to launch a business, for example, but don't have the capital that's required and don't necessarily meet the requirements of most traditional lending institutions.

Upstart does not nicely fit into the reward or equity-based crowd funding model used by other platforms. It has pioneered a new and innovative way for recent graduates, among others, to fund their entrepreneurial goals or pursue higher levels of education without taking on huge amounts of debt or exposing themselves to high levels of financial risk. To learn more about this unique crowd funding platform, read the interview with Upstart founder Dave Girouard in Chapter 13.

Even if you are not someone who qualifies to participate in the Upstart platform, learning more about it offers an interesting insight into how these platforms are quickly evolving in order to cater to the highly specialized funding needs of individuals, small businesses, and entrepreneurs.

GoFundMe

Website	www.crowdfunding.com
Key Features	GoFundMe is a service that allows individuals to raise money for any personal purposes, such as paying off debts, starting a business, funding a vacation, paying for a wedding, covering college tuition, funding a funeral or memorial, or pursuing a hobby or creative endeavor. Like other crowd funding platforms, GoFundMe users employ social media to solicit donations. It can be used to fund just about anything.
Fees	The GoFundMe platform charges a 5 percent commission based on the funds raised. The payment processing company also charges a commission of between 2.9 and 4.25 percent, depending on the focus of the project.
Specialty	GoFundMe allows individuals to raise money for just about anything. Rewards do not need to be offered by project creators, and there are no presales of products.

GoFundMe works a bit differently from all of the other reward-based crowd funding platforms featured in this book. While project creators must set a funding goal, there is no time limit to achieve that goal. A campaign can remain online for any duration of time. Plus, people who use GoFundMe to raise money for their project are simply soliciting outright donations; there are no products to presell or rewards for various size donations. Project creators receive all the money given to them by their donors (minus fees), whether or not their funding goal is actually met.

As with any type of crowd funding campaign, someone's ability to achieve success using GoFundMe depends on the size and dedication of their network and the project creator's ability to use social media to solicit donations from family, friends, and other members of their online network. While GoFundMe is not a reward-based or equity-based crowd funding platform, the same types of online tools and resources are used to create and manage a campaign, and social media is used to promote campaigns.

A SELF-HOSTED REWARD-BASED CROWD FUNDING OPTION

In addition to the many online platforms that will host your campaign, there are a growing number of self-hosted crowd funding options that allow individuals, businesses, and organizations to create and manage their own reward- or presale-based crowd funding campaigns, and host them on their own websites or blogs.

Currently, the most popular tool set for self-hosted, reward-based crowd funding is called Selfstarter. What's great about this option is that it's open source, which means there are no fees to use it, and it's highly customizable. However, you will need to host your campaign's website yourself or work with a web hosting service, and you must have at least a basic understanding of website design, publishing, and hosting.

Selfstarter

Website	http://selfstarter.us
Key Features	If you have the wherewithal to host your own crowd funding campaign and website that is based on presales of a product or service, Selfstarter offers the software-based tools needed to create and host this type of campaign on your own website or blog.
Fees	Free
Pros/Cons	When you self-host a crowd funding campaign, you are responsible for all aspects of it, not just its creation, management, and promotion.

Selfstarter is an open-source collection of software-based tools that allows you to design and build your own presale-based crowd funding solution and collect funds from your backers through Amazon Payments or the payment processing service of your choice. The platform was originally created by a company called Lockitron (www.lockitron.com), after its project idea (for a smartphone-controlled deadbolt door lock) was rejected by Kickstarter.

Ultimately, Lockitron used its own crowd funding platform to raise more than $2.2 million from 14,704 backers. The company then turned around and made its source code available to the general public for free.

Using the Selfstarter tools, it's possible to design and launch a fully customizable presale-based crowd funding website for any type of product. As the project creator, it is your responsibility to populate the website with content (text, photos, video, etc.), and then to promote the campaign and drive traffic to your site. In addition to all of the skills needed to create and run this type of crowd funding campaign, you will need some familiarity with website programming and design, and you'll need to provide your own hosting service for the site.

For product-driven crowd funding campaigns, Selfstarter is a viable option because there are no platform-imposed rules to adhere to or website templates that your campaign's content must fit into. The Selfstarter software can be downloaded from https://github.com/lockitron/selfstarter.

To help you decide whether Selfstarter is a potential option for your project, take a look at Lockitron's campaign website (www.lockitron.com), to see what this self-hosted crowd funding platform is capable of. The Tile is another example of a smartphone-compatible product that was funded thanks to a highly successful presale-based crowd funding campaign that used Selfstarter.

To learn more about Tile and its campaign, check out the interview with Nick Evans, the founder of Reveal Labs, in Chapter 15.

Preplanning Your Crowd Funding Campaign

Before you publish your crowd funding campaign on a platform and start trying to promote it to potential backers, there's a lot of preparation that you must do to help ensure a successful campaign. How much prep work will be necessary, and how long these tasks will take, will depend on a variety of factors, including the skills and resources at your disposal, the scope of your project idea, your target audience, and your ultimate goals for the campaign.

For most project creators, the key steps involved in the preparation of a successful, reward-based crowd funding campaign include:

- Defining and fine-tuning your project idea
- Pinpointing your target audience
- Performing research in regard to your project's viability and the opportunities for funding the project offered by various crowd funding platforms
- Choosing an appropriate crowd funding platform
- Creating your campaign's rewards (if applicable)
- Developing a time line and schedule for the campaign, and a separate time line for the project itself
- Building or expanding your network

- Creating an overall marketing message
- Preparing the content for your crowd funding campaign, including the production of a promotional video
- Preplanning the promotional efforts for your campaign, including how social media, email, paid online advertising, public relations efforts, and more traditional marketing activities will be utilized
- Gathering the support from experts you'll need to create and manage the crowd funding campaign, and putting into place the experts you'll need to bring your project to fruition after it's funded
- Calculating a detailed budget for the crowd funding campaign and the overall project

Only after these tasks have been completed should you actually consider logging onto a reward-based crowd funding platform in order to create and ultimately launch a campaign for your project. Keep in mind, in most cases, once a campaign launches, you'll have a predetermined and finite amount of time to promote your project and get it funded. Based on extensive research conducted by virtually all of the reward-based crowd funding platforms, as well as crowd funding experts and the firsthand experiences of campaign creators, running a 30-day campaign tends to work best for most projects. However, most platforms allow you to preset the duration of your campaign and choose a duration between one week and 90 days.

Knowing once your campaign launches that you have 30 days, for example, to achieve success, you'll want to have laid the foundation for a successful campaign in advance and not waste valuable time having to gather the information you need during the actual campaign. It's essential that during those first few hours or days of your campaign, you're able to rally your core network and begin to generate enough hype and excitement for your project so it translates immediately into an influx of financial support, which you'll then continue to build upon.

Some of the most important tasks related to preplanning and creating a reward-based crowd funding campaign have been given their own chapters within this book. In this chapter, however, we'll take a closer look at the list of crowd funding campaign tasks that are an integral part of the preplanning process. As you're about to discover, it all starts with a great project idea.

DEFINE AND FINE-TUNE YOUR PROJECT IDEA

Everything related to crowd funding starts with a project idea. To develop and fine-tune that idea as much as possible, before revealing it to the general public, you will need to ask yourself a lot of questions and then come up with honest and well-thought-out answers to these questions.

For example, what is the scope of your project idea, and what would you like to get funded? Do you have an idea for an invention? Are you looking to start a business? Do you have a hobby that you want to somehow transform into a revenue-generating venture? Are you a musician who wants to record an album or go on tour or a filmmaker with an idea for your next movie project?

Perhaps you're a chef who wants to publish your own cookbook, open a restaurant, or manufacture and distribute a food item. Maybe you're a painter, jewelry maker, sculptor, or photographer who wants to somehow showcase and/or sell your work.

Whatever you have for an idea, write it down. Now, determine what your short-term and long-term goals are for the project. In other words, what would you like to accomplish within the next six months for your short-term goals, and how would you like to see your project idea develop beyond one year?

Are you truly passionate about your project idea? Is this something you want to dedicate a lot of your time, energy, and resources to for the next few months or potentially the next several years? Is this project idea something that you'll enjoy talking about with your friends and family as well as sharing with total strangers? Will you be able to motivate others to get excited about your project idea? Are you willing to put your personal and professional reputation on the line to make your project idea a reality?

Specifically, why are you passionate about this idea? What makes it special or unique? How will making your project idea a reality benefit you and the people who financially support it? What impact will it have on the people who are somehow exposed to your project? What positive impact will your project have on your community or on society as a whole? Why will people care about your project?

These are just some of the questions you'll need to answer for yourself before starting to pursue the project. If you can't answer any of these questions, either you haven't done enough research, or the idea may not be something that's viable or worth pursuing.

Let's assume you've come up with a very special project idea that you are passionate about. Next, ask yourself what makes it unique or special? How is it different or better than similar ideas that already exist?

If you think you've come up with a brilliant idea that you're excited about, what other types of people will be interested in it? How big is that pool of potentially interested people? In other words, will there be a demand for your project idea, and will other people be interested in helping you make it a reality by providing their financial support?

Consider the scope of your project idea. Is this something that you have the education, skills, experience, and drive to make a reality, provided you were given the funds to do so? Is this project idea viable, and it is realistically something that you could successfully pursue? If not, what additional skills, knowledge, or resources would you require?

As you fine-tune your project idea into something that could potentially be funded through a reward-based crowd funding platform, think about everything you'll need to accomplish in order to go from the idea stage to fully realizing your project idea and making it a reality. Do you have the wherewithal, dedication, available time, and enough energy to pursue this?

Once you've developed the core idea for your project, sit down and write out an informal business plan for it. This business plan should describe everything you'll need to accomplish in order to make your idea a reality, and include information about what challenges you'll potentially need to overcome. Flush out your project idea as much as possible, and then start thinking about how you'll be able to market the idea for your project to potential backers in a way that's easy to understand. Determine how you will quickly be able to demonstrate to potential backers that your idea is a good one, viable, and something you can make a reality.

In one sentence, how will you describe your project idea and its benefits? Using one additional sentence, can you explain why you're the best person to make your project idea a reality or spearhead the project?

PINPOINTING YOUR TARGET AUDIENCE

After coming up with your brilliant project idea, you need to determine two important things. First, who will help fund the project, and second, who will want to purchase or experience it once it's a reality?

This first group of people will be your primary target audience that you want to reach during your crowd funding campaign. This should include people you are already in contact with or can easily reach via email or social media. The second group should be composed of people you can reach out to during your campaign and who you believe will become very interested in and excited about your project once they learn about it.

As you invest the time to pinpoint your target audience, learn as much as you can about them. Knowing their average age, income, spending/shopping habits, education level, social media habits, career/job details, marital status, hobbies, how technologically savvy they are, special interests, and other pertinent details about them will help you focus your marketing message so it appeals directly to them.

As you are preparing your marketing message and developing the content to populate your crowd funding campaign's web page, you'll want to put yourself into the shoes of your target audience, think like them, and adjust your campaign to appeal to them by looking at things from their perspective.

DO YOUR RESEARCH

There are several types of research you'll want to do before launching your campaign. This research will include getting to know everything possible about your project, its target audience, its potential competition, and how you'll overcome whatever challenges you might face in bringing the project to fruition.

You'll also need to determine if there's a market for your project idea, the size and scope of the potential market, and how you'll best reach potential backers. Another aspect of your research should focus on the crowd funding campaign you plan to launch.

As you figure out the scope of your crowd-funding campaign, determine what assistance you'll need, and then find the right experts to help you prior to the campaign's launch. Your research can take many forms. Some can be done online. Some will require you to seek out experts and tap their knowledge. You might also benefit from reading industry-specific trade journals or consumer-oriented publications that relate to your project or its target audience.

Regardless of what your project idea entails, plan on spending time exploring the various crowd funding platforms firsthand and reviewing as many project campaigns as possible. Focus specifically on campaigns that are relevant to your own project idea or its target audience. Use this research to help determine what will be necessary to make your campaign a success.

CHOOSE AN APPROPRIATE CROWD FUNDING PLATFORM TO HOST YOUR CAMPAIGN

The previous chapters focused a bit on some of the popular crowd funding platforms and their unique and sometimes proprietary approaches to reward-based crowd funding. By researching each platform for yourself, you should be able to choose one that's a really good fit for your project idea.

When choosing which platform to utilize, consider the following:

- The reputation of the reward-based crowd funding platform
- The features and functions that platform offers for creating, managing, and promoting a reward-based crowd funding campaign
- The integration the platform allows you to establish with the popular social media services (Facebook, Twitter, etc.)
- From a design or visual standpoint, the level of personalization or customization that's possible when creating your campaign's web page
- The tools available to help you manage the campaign, keep track of and communicate with backers, and monitor traffic to the web page

- The fees associated with using the platform, including the payment processing fees charged by a third party
- How, when, and under what conditions you'll receive the funds from your backers
- What specialized or personalized support or services the platform offers to its project creators

Ultimately, you want to choose a platform that offers everything you want or need as the project creator but that will also be easy to navigate and appealing to your target audience. After all, if your potential backers are not comfortable using the platform, they won't feel comfortable financially supporting your project.

CREATE YOUR CAMPAIGN'S REWARDS

You already know that not all crowd funding campaigns use rewards. Some focus simply on presales of a product. However, if your project will include rewards for your backers, it's absolutely essential that you come up with a selection of rewards that are unique, exclusive, and appealing to your target audience.

Ultimately, it will most likely be the rewards you offer, in addition to the project idea itself, that a potential backer will use to determine how much financial support they want to give to your project. All of your project's rewards should somehow include a "thank-you" for each backer and, when possible, some type of recognition for their support. The rewards should also give them behind-the-scenes or exclusive access to follow the progress of your project as it's being developed. This can be done using a blog, web page, or email.

Backers should also be among the first to experience your project once it's finished. For example, if you've created a product, your backers should get their hands on the product before the general public. If your project involves producing a show, movie, or event, your backers should be the first admitted to see it.

Then, in exchange for higher levels of financial support, come up with personalized, limited edition, and exclusive rewards that have value to your backers and that cannot be acquired elsewhere. For example, if your project involves producing a show or concert, a top-tier reward might include the best possible tickets to the show, an invitation backstage, the opportunity to attend a dress rehearsal or sound check, a private meet and greet, plus autographed memorabilia.

If your project involves producing a movie, some top-level rewards might include:

- A walk-on role in the movie
- A day-long set visit during the movie's production
- Having a character in the movie named after the backer
- A script autographed by the entire cast
- A movie poster autographed by the entire cast
- A prop that was used in the movie and that is autographed by the actor who used it
- An invitation to the movie's premier and/or cast party
- An acknowledgment in the movie's closing credits

Invest whatever time is needed to research the rewards offered by other project campaigns that are similar to yours, and then brainstorm unique reward ideas that will have tremendous appeal to your target audience. Keep in mind, wealthy people who will be able to provide the most financial support for your project will appreciate rewards that can't typically be purchased, such as exclusive experiences that are tied directly to the project. This can also include providing direct access to or personalized experiences with the project's creators.

PLAN YOUR SCHEDULE

Once again, depending on the scope of your project, it might take you several weeks or months to do all of the preplanning that goes into launching a successful reward-based crowd funding campaign, so make sure you allocate the time that's needed to accomplish each of the necessary tasks without cutting corners.

Next, plan a detailed time line for your crowd funding campaign. If your campaign is slated to last for 30 days, what tasks will you need to accomplish on each day? When will you publish updates? Based on what-if scenarios you create, what actions will you take to generate more excitement for your campaign if it experiences a lull? Determine when and if stretch goals will be introduced, and what they will entail.

You also need to develop a tentative schedule in advance related to what will happen once your project gets fully funded. You'll need to share this information with potential backers. How long do you anticipate it will take to bring your project to fruition? When making this initial projection, be sure to include a cushion in case things go wrong. You're always better off giving yourself a longer time line and then launching the project earlier than projected, rather than having to explain delays to your project backers.

When creating your schedules, make sure they're realistic, based on the scope of your project and your available resources. For example, if you plan to rely on a public relations effort to generate media and blog attention for your project idea and crowd funding campaign, you'll need to launch this aspect of your campaign and reach out to journalists, producers, and bloggers several weeks (and in some cases several months) prior to a campaign's launch in order to adhere to the lead times these media outlets work under.

Likewise, if you plan to use paid advertising to promote your campaign in traditional printed publications, this, too, needs to be done well in advance of your campaign's actual launch. Keep in mind, the lead time for running paid ads within a printed publication is much longer than the lead time to launch a Facebook or Google AdWords online advertising campaign. It is important to preplan all of these prior to the launch of your campaign so that the ads appear at exactly the right time to have the most impact possible.

BUILDING OR EXPANDING YOUR NETWORK

The term *crowd funding* was created for a reason. It means something. To successfully raise funds for your project, you'll need to reach out to people and solicit the financial support needed for your project from the public (the crowd), as opposed to traditional investors. Initially, it will likely be your core network that supports your project, because these people know you and will want to support you.

Your core network (i.e. your inner circle of contacts) will include friends, family, online acquaintances, and perhaps people you've worked with in the past (customers, clients, coworkers, schoolmates, etc.). Before launching your crowd funding campaign, make sure you build up this network so it's as large as possible. Be sure to gather each person's name and email address and connect with them on the various social media platforms.

If you represent an established business, music group, or band, or you interact with a large group of customers, clients, fans, or followers, these people also need to be included within your broader network and approached as soon as your campaign gets underway. These are people who already know you and your reputation and who will likely be more willing to support your project than will total strangers.

It's essential that you build up your network to be as large as possible prior to the launch of your campaign. If you don't already have a network that includes an inner circle of at least several hundred people plus several thousand other people who could become potential backers, invest whatever time and resources are needed to expand your network prior to launching your crowd funding campaign.

In other words, long before you launch your campaign, you'll want to become active on the various social media services (Facebook, Twitter, Google+, LinkedIn, Instagram, etc.) and organically grow your network. Again, based on the scope of your project, this might entail creating personal social media accounts or setting up accounts specifically for your business, organization, or project, and then rallying online support from people on the various networks. Building up a presence on social media costs nothing, but it can be a time-consuming process.

Next, think beyond your existing network and figure out how to reach people in the general public who you don't yet know but who will most likely be interested in your project idea when they learn about it. This group is your target audience. You'll need to work hard to find and reach these people. This can often be done by acquiring email lists, targeting them on social media services, using online advertising, reaching out to special-interest groups, or by launching a public relations campaign.

Keep in mind, only a small percentage of the people in your overall network will actually help to fund your project. Hopefully a high percentage of people from your inner circle will become backers, but as you go beyond your inner circle, the percentage of people you reach out to who will ultimately become backers will drop off considerably. Thus, the larger your network, the better.

It is a good strategy to begin reaching out to your network prior to your crowd funding campaign's launch. Try to start sharing information about your project idea and generating as much hype about it as possible without using a hard-sell message. Keep in mind, as you reach out to every person in your network, you always have two main goals.

First, you want them to become backers and to help fund your project. Second, whether or not they financially support your project, you want each person to share details about your project with their own online networks. This includes posting messages on Facebook and Twitter on your behalf.

The promotional support you receive from people in your network will be extremely valuable and will help you quickly and effectively grow your own network and get the word out about your project. Not only do you want to encourage people in your network to share details about your project with others, you want to make it extremely easy for them to do this, and then offer them some type of thank-you for their assistance, making them feel like they are an important part of your project's success.

The focus of Chapter 6, "Targeting Your Backers and Supporters," is on building and expanding your network, and then in Chapter 9, "Interacting with Your Backers Using a Blog," you'll discover ways to maintain communication with your backers throughout your crowd funding campaign and beyond.

CREATE YOUR OVERALL MARKETING MESSAGE

After you've come up with your brilliant project idea and have pinpointed your target audience, one key factor in your success will be your ability to communicate details about your project idea to that audience in order to obtain their support. This happens through your marketing, advertising, and promotional efforts.

Using the range of tools and resources at your disposal, you'll need to reach out to and contact the individuals in your network as well as total strangers within your target audience, get them to visit your campaign's web page, and then rely on the content you've published on that page to transform them from potential supporters into actual financial backers.

The marketing message you develop for your project idea needs to be consistent, easy to understand, concise, relevant, and targeted specifically to your audience. Understand right from the start that you realistically only have about five seconds to capture someone's attention. Then, if you manage to get their attention, you need to keep it long enough to get them to financially support your project and/or help promote it. This can be a huge challenge, and it should be something you're prepared for.

Your crowd funding campaign's overall marketing message starts with the headline for the campaign. This should be short, descriptive, relevant, and catchy. It should include keywords that people might use to find your project when using the search function built into the platform you're using to host your campaign as well as when using an Internet search engine such as Google, Yahoo!, or Bing.

As you create your crowd funding campaign, you'll typically be required to compose a more detailed text-based description of your project, provide a biography of the project creator(s), and include additional information about the scope of the project.

Beyond using just text, you'll also have the opportunity to use a logo, photographs, and perhaps multimedia content (including animations). Plus, most crowd funding campaigns feature a short promotional video.

Using the text-based content and photos, you'll have about five seconds to convince visitors to your web page to click on the play button and watch your promotional video. Then, you'll have an additional 5 to 10 seconds to capture their attention with that video. The attention span of people using the Internet is very short, so make every second that you have someone's attention count.

Each element of your marketing message should be consistent and relevant. At the same time, you want to share different pieces of information about your project using different media. For example, the text-based description of your project might include details about why you've chosen to pursue the project, while the promotional video goes into detail describing the specific project, who it will appeal to, and why it's relevant to the potential backer.

Use compelling content and avoid redundancy or anything that's irrelevant. Try to ensure that everything related to your campaign is synergistic. For example, any email, advertising, or social media engagement you have with potential backers should contain consistent imaging and messaging and include the URL for your campaign's web page as well as your primary web page or blog, if applicable.

The color scheme you select, the logo you use, the photos you showcase, everything in your video, and the wording of your messaging should also come across as coherent and relevant, so it's obvious that it all originates from a single, well-thought-out campaign that focuses specially on your project idea and caters to your target audience.

The vocabulary and graphical elements included within your overall marketing message should be appropriate for your target audience's level of education. How you present your content is as important as what you actually say. For example, if you're targeting middle-aged, college-educated men who have an annual income over $50,000, the color scheme, background music, images, and vocabulary you use to communicate your message to these people will be very different from what you would use to appeal to teenagers and young adults who play video games, listen to rap music, and enjoy skateboarding.

This synergistic approach to the content used to market and promote your project idea applies to everything published on your campaign's web page as well as all content you create that is shared through social media, email, online advertising, and through your public relations efforts. In order to be successful with this, it is essential that you truly understand your project idea and why people will want to support it. In addition, you must have a good grasp of who your target audience is and what will appeal to them, especially in regard to your project.

PREPARE THE CONTENT FOR YOUR CROWD FUNDING CAMPAIGN

As you begin to fine-tune your project idea, research the various platforms, and analyze other campaigns that have been successful, you'll discover that the majority of successful crowd funding campaigns have several things in common—one of which is a well-produced, clever, informative, entertaining, visually engaging, concise, and attention-getting promotional video.

In three minutes or less, your video needs to introduce your project idea to potential backers and get those people excited enough about your project that they want to help fund it. Unfortunately, there is no video production formula to follow that results in a successful promotional video. Every video is as unique as the project idea itself, yet many have similar components that help the video achieve its goals. You'll learn more about producing a successful promotional video in Chapter 7, "Producing Your Promotional Video."

Keep in mind, in most cases, your promotional video does not need to be a slick Hollywood-style production or have the production quality of a professionally produced television commercial. It does, however, need to be good enough to appeal to your target audience, meet their expectations, convey the right information, and do an excellent job of helping you build a potential backer's confidence in you and your ability to achieve your goals.

If you forego basic video production quality standards, this could easily tarnish your credibility, and cause potential backers to question your ability to bring your project idea into fruition if it gets funded. Even if you have no video production budget, and opt to use a low-end video camera (such as the camera built into your smartphone) to shoot your video, it's essential that every shot be in focus, and that you figure out how to incorporate crystal clear audio into the production.

A promotional video that doesn't convey the right information or that fails to appeal to your target audience will almost definitely result in your overall crowd funding campaign failing, even if you start off with an incredible project idea and there is a demand for that idea.

PREPLAN THE PROMOTIONAL EFFORTS FOR YOUR CAMPAIGN

Starting a reward-based crowd funding campaign with a great idea is essential. However, once your campaign launches, on whichever platform you choose, your success in getting your project idea funded will depend in large part on the effectiveness of your promotional efforts. Thus, the focus of Chapter 8, "Promoting Your Campaign," is on helping you create a multi-faceted, achievable, and far-reaching promotional campaign that will take full advantage of the tools you have at your disposal.

While most reward-based crowd-funding campaigns rely heavily on social media and direct email in order to pinpoint and reach out to potential backers, your campaign will most likely also benefit from paid online advertising, a public relations effort (which targets the media as well as bloggers), and more traditional promotional efforts that take place both online and in the real world.

The promotional efforts you pursue for your campaign will depend a lot on the scope of your project, its target audience, your available budget, and the amount of time you're willing to dedicate to this important element of your crowd funding efforts. The more preplanning you do in regard to the promotional efforts you intend to use once your campaign kicks off, the more time you'll have to actually implement those plans and focus on your potential backers when the campaign is underway.

GATHERING THE SUPPORT SERVICES AND EXPERTS YOU'LL NEED

Running a successful crowd funding campaign and then making your fully funded project a reality is most likely something you will not be able to do single-handedly. Thus, you'll need to put together a team of people, each with specific skills and experience, to assist you. The focus of Chapter 10, "Getting the Help You Need," is on putting together a team that you can afford and that will ultimately help you achieve success.

While you might not be in a position to hire full-time employees with various areas of expertise, chances are you can solicit the help of friends or family members, hire freelancers or consultants for short amounts of time, seek out the help of interns, or use other resources at your disposal to solicit assistance from others.

CALCULATING A DETAILED BUDGET

The focus of Chapter 5, "Crunching the Numbers," is on helping you create a detailed and accurate budget for your reward-based crowd funding campaign as well as for the project itself. Miscalculating funding needs is one of the biggest mistakes project creators make, and unanticipated expenses can lead to failure, either in getting a project funded or in bringing a fully funded project idea to fruition.

If you don't have the skills and experience needed to create a realistic budget for your crowd funding campaign and overall project, be sure to seek out the help of someone with a strong financial background. At the very least, someone with bookkeeping experience should be added to your team, although you'll most likely benefit from working with an accountant who can help you calculate your budget and establish the methods you'll implement to properly manage your project's finances.

NOW, YOU'RE READY TO PROCEED

Only after you've done the initial research and preplanning should you consider creating and launching a crowd funding campaign for your project idea. Each crowd funding platform has fine-tuned its approach to helping project creators create and launch a campaign. Be sure to follow the guidelines and tutorials provided by the platform you choose to work with, and populate your campaign's web page with appropriately targeted content.

Then use your knowledge about your target audience to reach out to these people as you promote your campaign. Plan on taking a multifaceted approach to your campaign's promotions in order to ensure you are able to reach the largest number of people in your target audience in the least amount of time without having to spend a fortune. Also be sure that you have a plan in place to maintain the excitement for your campaign during its entire duration. If a campaign loses steam partway through, but the project hasn't reached its funding goal, appropriate steps need to be taken. For example, you need to expand your promotional efforts, fine-tune your marketing message, and/or perhaps redefine your target audience.

However, if your campaign is performing well and you are close to reaching your funding goal before the campaign is scheduled to end, you'll want to consider implementing stretch goals in order to continue building excitement and raise even more money.

As you are doing your preplanning, consider a series of what-if scenarios and be ready to deal with various situations if they arise before and during your campaign. The more prepared you are initially, the easier it will be to reach or exceed your funding goal. Plus, during your actual campaign, you will have more time available to focus on reaching your funding goal as opposed to dealing with problems that arise due to lack of planning or foresight.

CHAPTER 5

Crunching the Numbers

In This Chapter

- Create a budget for your reward-based crowd funding campaign.
- Calculate your project's funding goal.
- Don't forget about hidden expenses.

Someone once said, "It takes money to make money," and when it comes to reward-based crowd funding, this statement is somewhat true. Prior to launching your crowd funding campaign to raise the money needed to pursue your project idea, you'll need to have at least some money on hand to launch and manage the campaign itself, during which you'll incur a variety of expenses.

It's true that most of the reward-based crowd funding platforms charge project creators nothing until money is collected from backers. However, to get to that point, you'll need to spend some money on the planning and creation of your campaign for things like the production of your promotional video, online advertising, and a public relations effort.

Beyond the capital you'll need to create and manage the actual crowd funding campaign, depending on the scope of your project, additional funds may be needed to get your project idea into a form that's worthy of being funded. For example, if you're thinking about manufacturing and selling a product, before launching your campaign you'll probably need to develop a working prototype or mock-up of the product.

There's also the time element to consider. If you have a job, preplanning, creating, and managing a crowd funding campaign is going to take a lot of time. In addition to being able to juggle the demands of your existing job with what's required for your project, consider the potential lost income you'll experience as a result of spending time on your project and not at your paying job.

This chapter focuses on developing a realistic budget for your reward-based crowd funding campaign, based on the scope of your particular project. Keep in mind, you'll need to develop a totally separate budget for your project prior to your campaign's launch, as this information is required to establish a realistic funding goal for your campaign.

DEVELOP A BUDGET FOR YOUR REWARD-BASED CROWD FUNDING CAMPAIGN

As you begin to explore the various crowd funding platforms and take a look at the various campaigns currently underway, you'll quickly discover that a lot of money, time, and effort have gone into some of the campaigns, while others are being managed on a shoestring budget. Yet, some projects within both of these categories ultimately wind up getting fully funded.

There are no specific guidelines when it comes to figuring out how much money you'll need to spend in order to create and manage your campaign and make it successful. A lot will depend on how much work you're willing to do yourself versus what you can afford to delegate to others. A lot also has to do with the scope of your project, its funding goal, the expectations of the audience you're trying to reach, and the current size of your network.

If your existing network (the people you will be inviting to support your project financially) is small, you will most likely need to spend extra time and money to build up your network, and perhaps focus more on paid online advertising and more extensive—and costly—public relations efforts, which require a larger budget.

Keep in mind that the overall image your crowd funding campaign projects will directly impact your online reputation and credibility. If you already have a large network of customers, fans, and followers, it is essential that you take steps to maintain or improve your image during the crowd funding campaign. Otherwise, you run the risk of negatively influencing your potential backers. If, on the other hand, you are trying to attract potential backers and position yourself as well-established and capable of making your project idea a reality, the overall image of your campaign will need to reflect this.

Crowd funding campaigns that aim to raise tens of thousands of dollars (or more), and that are created by individuals, businesses, and organizations that already have a reputation to live up to, often need to initially spend more in order to meet or exceed the expectations of their customer or fan base. Likewise, in most cases, the more money you are trying to raise, the more you'll need to spend on your campaign to give it a polished and professional look.

If you study campaigns that ultimately raised hundreds of thousands or even millions of dollars, you'll see that a lot of money (potentially tens of thousands of dollars or more) was spent in advance on the actual crowd funding campaign. Graphic designers, professional photographers, video production crews, writers, public relations professionals, and online marketing or advertising agencies are among the experts hired to assist with creating such campaigns. In addition, money was spent on extensive online advertising, a comprehensive public relations effort, and other high-profile marketing activities.

Conversely, if you study successfully funded projects that only sought to raise a few thousand dollars, you'll often discover that very little up-front money was spent on those campaigns.

Obviously, you want to spend the least amount of money possible to create and manage your crowd funding campaign, but at the same time, you need to ensure that it will cater to its target audience and their expectations and allow you to reach a large enough group of people so the project ultimately reaches its funding goal.

If you are looking to raise a significant amount of money through your crowd funding efforts, this is going to require an extensive, professionally executed, and multifaceted promotional and marketing campaign, which could easily cost you at least $5,000 per month to run correctly, even if you take on a lot of the responsibilities yourself. However, if you wind up investing, say, $5,000 in your 30-day campaign, and you are striving to raise $50,000 or more, that potentially represents a very good return on your investment.

The risk involved, however, is that you won't recover this initial investment if your campaign fails to reach its funding goal.

ELEMENTS OF YOUR CROWD FUNDING CAMPAIGN'S BUDGET

The budget for your reward-based crowd funding campaign will ultimately be based on what you're trying to accomplish as well as the funds you currently have available. Based on your knowledge of what your project entails, its target audience, and how many people you're trying to attract to the campaign, you'll need to allocate your money to the appropriate aspects of your campaign.

Again, how much money you'll actually need in advance to fund your campaign will be unique to your project and based on the decisions you make related to it. There is no preset formula or guideline to follow that says if you spend *X* on your crowd funding campaign, you'll automatically be able to raise a specific amount of money.

Let's take a look at some of the elements of a reward-based crowd funding campaign that can end up consuming a considerable amount of money.

DEVELOPING A PROTOTYPE

Depending on the scope of your project, most backers will be very leery of funding a project that is still in the idea or concept phase. Thus, prior to launching your campaign, you'll need to further develop your idea and bring it to the point where you have something to show or demonstrate, such as a mock-up or prototype of a product or a storyboard for a movie. Crowd funding campaigns that begin with something to actually show off or demonstrate to potential backers tend to do better than those that feature someone standing in front of a camera simply describing an abstract idea or concept.

To get around the cost of having a full working prototype of a product, project creators are often extremely creative during their crowd funding campaigns and sometimes rely on computer-generated animations, hand-drawn illustrations, and/or other tools to showcase their product idea and, at the same time, demonstrate to potential backers that they're capable of bringing their idea to fruition once it's fully funded.

Starting at the launch of your campaign, the more you can show to potential backers related to what the end result of your project idea will look like, the easier time you'll have getting your project funded.

PLANNING YOUR CROWD FUNDING CAMPAIGN

Based on what you've learned thus far from reading *The Crowd Funding Services Handbook*, you already know that to create and manage a successful reward-based crowd funding campaign requires that you quickly master a lot of different skills. To help project creators who don't yet possess all of the skills and experience necessary to create and manage a successful crowd funding campaign, an entire industry that provides support services to project creators has evolved.

Online marketing companies and individual consultants who specialize in creating and managing funding campaigns are available for hire as consultants or on a retainer basis. There are also video production companies, public relations experts, professional writers, manufacturing consultants, lawyers, accountants, and market research companies that can be hired to help you create and manage your campaign and project.

Yes, these companies and individuals have the skills and resources to jumpstart your campaign and help ensure its success, especially if your project's funding goal is rather high. However, unlike the crowd funding platforms and payment processing companies that take a commission after the money from a campaign is raised, these third-party companies and consultants typically get paid in advance, so hiring them represents an out-of-pocket expense.

You can easily spend thousands of dollars to have a company literally take over the creation and management of your crowd funding campaign, with you simply needing to provide the expertise related to your actual project. However, this approach is going to be expensive. To save money, you can certainly handle many or all of the tasks associated with planning and managing your own crowd funding campaign and hire one or more experts for just a few hours to review your plans and offer suggestions before the campaign launches. This can help you avoid common and potentially costly mistakes and can often provide you with additional ideas that could allow you to raise more money.

The best way to find experts to help with the creation and management of your campaign is to seek referrals from fellow project creators who have already achieved success. If you don't know anyone firsthand to seek a referral from, find a handful of campaigns that were successful and contact the project creators for those campaigns to ask who they turned to for the help they needed.

You can also use any Internet search engine. Within the search field, enter a phrase like "crowd funding marketing" or "crowd funding consultant." Another option is to take advantage of an online-based service, like eLance.com, to help you find and hire experienced crowd funding professionals on a less costly freelance basis. To learn more about hiring the help you may need to create and manage a successful campaign, see Chapter 10, "Getting the Help You Need."

BUILDING OR EXPANDING YOUR NETWORK

Theoretically, building or expanding your network on the various social networking services costs nothing. However, this can be an extremely time-consuming process. Thus, you might want to hire someone, either on a retainer or hourly basis, to help you build your online social media presence and expand your base of followers and online friends prior to the launch of your campaign. When doing this, it's essential that you carefully target the people you seek out to add to your network. After all, you want them to be interested in your project idea and fit within your target audience.

Instead of or in addition to hiring someone to manage your social networking activities on Facebook, Twitter, Google+, LinkedIn, Instagram, Pinterest, and/or other popular services, there are also companies you can pay to help you grow your network through the purchase of online friends or followers. These services typically charge per 1,000 Facebook page "Likes," Twitter followers, or YouTube video views, and the cost can be anywhere from $50 to several hundred dollars per thousand.

If you opt to purchase followers or online friends, proceed with caution. Make sure the companies or individuals you hire actually do the legwork and pursue followers who fit within your target audience. Some of the less-legitimate services have actually set up thousands of dummy social media accounts or have come up with ways to fake video or web page views.

When it comes to expanding your base of followers on Twitter, there is also software you can purchase and use from your computer that is designed to help you streamline the process of targeting specific Twitter users and inviting them to follow you. TweetAdder ($55 to $188, www.tweetadder .com), for example, is available for the PC and Mac. This software helps automate the Twitter account management process and is designed for individuals and companies looking to actively and relatively quickly expand their Twitter following with carefully targeted followers.

It's also possible to purchase highly targeted email lists, and then use those lists to help build your network and/or drive traffic to your crowd funding campaign's web page. Based on how the list is compiled, this, too, has its pros and cons, since you don't want to develop a reputation for using spam (unsolicited emails) to attract backers or website traffic. That said, there are email list companies that compile lists of people who want to receive specific types of emails.

To find companies that sell targeted email lists, use any search engine and enter the search phrase "purchase email lists" or "email lists for marketing." You'll quickly discover dozens of companies, like National Data Group (www.nationaldatagroup.com), Express Mail Lists (www.expressmaillists .com), Email-List.com (www.emaillist.com), Info USA (www.infousa.com), and Experian (www.experian.com/small-business/mailing-lists.jsp). How much you'll pay per valid email address will depend on a variety of factors. However, the potential drawback of being thought of as a spammer among your potential backers can't be overstated.

When it comes to utilizing email as a marketing tool, you're almost always better off organically growing your own email list that comprises customers, clients, friends, relatives, and others who want to receive your emails. Your list can also include individuals who respond to an online ad or who read an article about your project in a blog or publication and want to be included on your email list so they can be kept abreast of your project's development.

If you opt to create and manage your own email list, there are fee-based PC and Mac software packages as well as online-based services that can help you handle this. For example, for the Mac there's the Direct Mail software (www.directmailmac.com) which can be used to help you manage all aspects of your email marketing, but you'll need to compile your own email list to use it. This particular software has a monthly pay-as-you-go fee structure (starting at $15 per month) or a one-time payment plan that offers unlimited use of the program for $19.

iContact (www.icontact.com), MailChimp (www.mailchimp.com), GoDaddy Email Marketing (www.godaddy.com/business/email-marketing .aspx), and Constant Contact (www.constantcontact.com) are a small sampling of fee-based online email list management and email marketing services.

When it comes to quickly building your network, you can easily throw tens of thousands of dollars at the problem and take shortcuts to grow your network. However, you'll most likely discover that by investing more time (as opposed to money), you'll be able to organically grow your network and ensure that it's composed of people who want to be in contact with you, who fit within your target audience, and who potentially will want to help fund your project.

Ultimately, once you begin reaching out to people outside of your inner circle, don't expect a conversion rate of higher than 3 to 5 percent. In other words, for every 100 people who visit your crowd funding campaign's web page, only between three and five of those people will actually help to fund your project, and the average amount pledged to your project will typically be between $25 and $100. So, when you do the math, to successfully reach a funding goal of $10,000, $100,000, or even $1 million, your promotional efforts will need to successfully drive tens of thousands or even hundreds of thousands of people to your campaign's web page.

PRODUCING YOUR PROMOTIONAL VIDEO

Producing a promotional video for your crowd funding campaign is another thing you could potentially accomplish on a shoestring budget, or you could easily spend $10,000 or more to hire a professional video crew and create a slick, professional-looking production. Again, the approach you take comes down to what you're trying to accomplish and the image you want to convey to your potential backers, as well as your own skills as a videographer.

Project creators looking to raise less than $10,000 typically produce their own promotional videos in-house and spend just a few hundred dollars (or less) to accomplish this. For this type of video production, you can typically get away with using a consumer-quality video camera to shoot the video and then edit it on your PC or Mac. The goal, however, must be to create a video with the highest production quality possible. This means the high-definition video images and sound quality should be crystal clear.

Thanks to the video editing software available for personal computers, it's possible to easily add titles, animations, transitions, background music, and other production elements that will enhance the professional quality of your video. However, first and foremost, the content within your video should be a priority when you're working with a limited production budget.

When it comes to creating higher quality video, you can rent professional-quality cameras, lights, microphones, and editing tools and save money by learning to use this equipment yourself and relying on your in-house resources. Alternatively, you can invest the money to hire a professional videographer, production crew, and video editor. You might also consider hiring a professional scriptwriter.

The cost to hire individual video production specialists will vary greatly, but plan on spending at least $50 to $200 per hour, per person. It's often a good idea to negotiate a day rate or an overall project rate with these people. There are also video production companies that specialize in producing promotional videos for crowd funding campaigns. These companies often charge $10,000 or more to produce a truly professional video that runs under three minutes in length.

Keep in mind, you always have options for saving money while pursuing a high-quality video. One option is to contact a college or university with a television/movie production department or one that offers an advertising major, and look to hire a group of skilled college interns who are looking to expand their professional portfolios and gain valuable real-world experience. You might also have friends or family members who already own top-quality video production equipment that you can borrow or know people with video production experience who might volunteer their time to help you produce your project's promotional video.

Think carefully about the approach you want to take with your video and the production quality you're striving for. Then, figure out what producing the video you envision will actually cost using the different options at your disposal.

When it comes to allocating money for your video's production, plan on spending as much as you can afford in order to achieve the best production quality possible based on your available resources. For example, if spending a few hundred dollars extra to purchase or rent a high-quality microphone will allow you to offer much better sound quality in your video, this is a worthwhile investment as is hiring a video editor who will be able to take your raw video footage and develop it into an attention-getting and informative one- to three-minute video.

ONLINE AND TRADITIONAL ADVERTISING

How much you spend on paid advertising to promote your crowd funding campaign is another optional and extremely flexible expense based on what you're trying to accomplish. Without a doubt, using targeted online Facebook advertising as well as keyword advertising on Google, Yahoo!, and other search engines will help you drive targeted traffic to your campaign's web page.

These online advertising opportunities charge per click not per view. So, you only pay when someone clicks on a link and actually visits your web page. How much you pay per click will be anywhere from a few cents to several dollars, however.

Learning to effectively use keyword advertising is a skill unto itself. Invest the time needed to understand how each keyword advertising service works, and how you can spend the least amount of money in order to generate the highest possible response. You can get started by reviewing the tutorials offered online by Google AdWords (www.google.com/adwords) and the Yahoo/Bing Search Marketing Service (http://yahoobingnetwork.com).

One great thing about online advertising using Facebook or keyword advertising on the popular search engines is that you can create and launch a campaign very quickly. So, within an hour or two, you can begin driving traffic to your campaign's web page. Starting at around $50 to launch a campaign, you can then spend as much or as little as you want per day to drive a predetermined level of traffic to your web page.

To generate the best possible results, however, you'll need to allocate at least several thousand dollars over a several-week period to an online ad campaign on Facebook and/or using search engine–based keyword advertising like Google AdWords.

If you start your crowd funding campaign with a small network, one way to quickly compensate is to use paid online advertising in order to drive more traffic to your campaign's web page and build your network. The drawback, however, is that the funds needed to pay for the ad campaign will be an out-of-pocket expense, which you may not be able to recover if your project fails to get fully funded.

Traditional advertising in the real world, whether it's on television, radio, in magazines, or in newspapers, tends to be a lot more costly and less targeted than online advertising, and for many types of reward-based crowd funding campaigns, it won't generate the same results as online advertising.

Plus, these traditional ad campaigns need to be planned and paid for well in advance of the campaign's launch.

Chapter 8, "Promoting Your Campaign," focuses more on the various online advertising opportunities that can help drive traffic to your campaign's web page. What you'll most likely discover is that Facebook advertising, when combined with an active Facebook page for yourself, your project, or your company, can be an extremely useful tool. Additional information about the paid advertising opportunities available through Facebook can be found at www.facebook.com/advertising.

DEVELOPING AND RUNNING YOUR PUBLIC RELATIONS EFFORT

The goal of a public relations effort is to capture the attention of journalists, editors, bloggers, and producers and get them to feature you, your company, your project, and/or your crowd funding campaign within their respective media outlets for free.

As you review successful crowd funding campaigns on the various platforms, you'll discover that many of the most successful ones received a significant amount of media coverage. Project creators, in turn, will typically highlight this coverage on their web pages as a way to boost their projects' credibility and further entice potential backers to support their projects. A well-organized and executed public relations effort is what gets the media coverage ball rolling.

The benefit to receiving free publicity is that you can grow your network, gain potential backers, and broaden the reach of your campaign to people who might not otherwise have learned about it. Receiving coverage from a well-respected media outlet or blog will quickly enhance your reputation, give you credibility, and build your audience.

The drawback to relying on public relations efforts is that you, as the project creator, have no say in terms of when you receive the media coverage or what is actually said or written about you and your project. When using paid advertising, you control the message, when it appears, and who is exposed to it. Public relations does not give you this level of control, although in Chapter 8 you will learn strategies for sharing your marketing message with the media so that when your project does receive coverage, the right information is shared.

While as the project creator, you don't pay a media outlet for the coverage or educational attention you receive, there are costs associated with creating and managing a successful public relations campaign. You'll need to create professional-quality press materials (a press kit and press releases, for example), compile a targeted media list, incur the cost of reaching out to the various media outlets that might be interested in sharing your story, and then cater to the needs of those media outlets. This might include traveling to participate in an interview, sending out free product samples, and/or the printing and mailing of press kits.

Just as people who work at advertising agencies spend years fine-tuning their skills, the same is true for public relations specialists. Sure, you can create and launch a public relations campaign on your own on a shoestring budget, but chances are it won't be anywhere near as effective as if you were to hire a public relations firm or a freelance public relations professional to create and manage your campaign and use their established media contacts to help you generate publicity.

Realistically, if you want to hire an experienced public relations firm to create and implement a full-fledged public relations campaign for your crowd funding project that will potentially allow you to receive national or international media coverage from well-respected media outlets, you'll need to spend anywhere from $2,000 to $10,000 per month, and you will need to keep the agency working for at least two to four months.

A less costly option is to hire a single public relations specialist on a freelance basis to help you create and manage your campaign's public relations activities.

Whether you use public relations and how much money you invest in the creation and implementation of a public relations campaign is entirely up to you. However, if your funding goal is high and not achievable simply by reaching out to your existing network, you'll probably find that having a public relations campaign as part of your overall promotional plan is a worthwhile and much-needed investment.

SET A REALISTIC AND APPROPRIATE FUNDING GOAL FOR YOUR PROJECT

At the time you publish your campaign, you'll need to set a funding goal. This is the total amount of money you want or need to raise. For a variety of reasons, it's important that this dollar amount be as accurate as possible and allow you to cover all costs associated with completing your project once it's funded.

As you're calculating what your funding goal should be, be sure to take into account the commissions you'll need to pay to the crowd funding platform you work with as well as the fees charged by the payment processing service. These two fees alone will require you to add between 8 and 10 percent to the amount you determine is needed to actually make your project a reality.

Beyond these fees, be sure to calculate into your overall budget any money you've initially invested into the early stages of your product's development as well as the out-of-pocket costs associated with your crowd funding campaign that you'd like to recoup once your project gets fully funded.

Another set of expenses you'll definitely want to build into your overall budget include what you'll need to pay to the third-party companies, consultants, or freelancers who will be hired to assist with various tasks associated with your crowd funding campaign and/or the completion of the project itself. Don't forget about legal and accounting/bookkeeping fees you'll most likely encounter, as well as any taxes you may be responsible for paying.

If you are offering rewards to you backers as part of your crowd funding campaign, another commonly overlooked expense is the cost associated with sending the rewards to your backers. In addition to the cost of the reward itself, you'll need to cover shipping charges as well as shipping materials. For successful campaigns that wind up attracting thousands of backers, the costs associated with fulfilling the project's reward obligations are significant.

Reward-related shipping and handling charges should be a separate line item in your budget, so these required funds don't wind up coming out of the budget you have allocated to actually complete your project. As you're creating your rewards, try to come up with some rewards that can be sent electronically or downloaded as opposed to shipped to backers. This is particularly important for rewards in the $1 to $25 price range.

You'll also find it very beneficial to pad your budget by 10 to 20 percent, to allow for unexpected problems, costly delays, and expenses you didn't initially consider. This is particularly important if you're designing and ultimately manufacturing a product or need to work with overseas suppliers.

When establishing your funding goal and the budget for your project, you'll need to keep your expenses as low as possible. If you wind up exceeding your funding goal, you will have more money to work with. But until the campaign is almost complete you won't know for sure if you'll be able to exceed the initial funding goal, so you shouldn't count on being able to exceed your original budget.

Investing the time and money needed to sit down with an accountant or experienced finance expert as you're developing your budget is definitely worthwhile, especially if the financial specialist has experience with crowd funding and/or working with projects that are similar to yours. Starting off with an accurate and realistic budget will help you avoid a wide range of problems later, such as running out of money before your project is completed.

Once your funding goal has been tentatively set, make sure that it's actually achievable. Take a look at the successfully funded projects on the platform you plan to work with and see if your funding goal is in line with them. Then, do some basic math to determine if your core network is large enough to help raise a significant portion of that funding goal.

When you look at the success rate of Kickstarter projects, for example, you'll see that about 74 percent of all successful campaigns had a funding goal of $10,000 or less, and that only 44 percent of projects published on Kickstarter actually reach their funding goal.

Thus, it's important to have realistic goals in regard to what's actually possible using reward-based crowd funding. It's equally important to set an accurate funding goal for your project, making sure that you'll be able to complete the project with the money that's raised if you reach your funding goal.

CHAPTER **6**

Targeting Your Backers and Supporters

In This Chapter

- Learn how to rally your inner circle.
- Define your target audience.
- Expand your network.

The term crowd funding can be a little bit misleading. When you think of the word *crowd*, you might think of a large group composed of people in the general public. In reality, when it comes to getting your project funded using reward-based crowd funding, the majority of your backers will most likely come from your "inner circle," which includes personal friends and family, as well as people in your existing social network—not the general public.

Based on your funding goal and the scope of the project, you'll probably need to reach out to four distinct audiences during the course of your crowd funding campaign. To reach each of these groups and get them excited to support your project, you'll need to take a tailored approach that's carefully crafted and designed specifically for that particular audience.

The four distinct groups of people that comprise your overall network include:

1. **Your Inner Circle.** This includes your family members and close friends—people who are easy for you to get in touch with, who know you, hopefully respect you, and who will be willing to help support you and your project. You should be able to pick up the phone and call any of the people in this group or easily converse with them via email. This group should all be in place long before your crowd funding campaign kicks off.

   Even if you can't rely on a high level of financial support from people within this group (because they're not wealthy), these are the people who you want to be the most active in terms of sharing or forwarding details about your project and its campaign to their own networks at the appropriate time.

2. **Your Friends and Acquaintances.** This group of people is composed of individuals you know in real life. It could include friends from work, your church or temple, your country club, past and present coworkers, current and past customers or clients, members of an association you belong to, past classmates, and anyone else you can personally reach out to who will be receptive to hearing about your project and potentially support it. Ideally, you want to be able to reach the people in this group through personalized email. This group should also be in place long before your crowd funding campaign kicks off.

To easily converse with this group, take advantage of email marketing software that allows you to create separate databases composed of email addresses and then send out personalized email to people on various lists. You'll discover that using personalized email to reach out to this group in advance of your campaign, once your campaign kicks off, and then again with updates during the campaign, will be highly effective.

Be sure to maintain a friendly tone in these emails and always take a soft-sell approach in them. You don't want to come across as if you're spamming your friends, demanding or begging for money, being overly repetitive, or wasting their time by sending too many email messages in a short period of time. Once again, even if your friends and acquaintances are not in a position to support your project financially, make it easy for them to share details about your project and campaign with their own networks via Facebook or Twitter, for example. When it comes to managing a successful crowd funding campaign, positive world-of-mouth advertising is always a powerful and effective tool.

3. **Your Social Network.** These are people you know from cyberspace (or who follow you or your organization via social media), including Facebook friends, Twitter followers, people who read your blog, your YouTube channel subscribers, and people you communicate with almost exclusively through social media.

By regularly posting details about your project using various social media services before and during your campaign, you encourage the people in this broader group to visit your crowd funding campaign's web page and pledge their financial support. Keep in mind, the majority of the people in the group will know who you are, but they may or may not fit into your project's target audience. How to define your target audience is covered later in this chapter.

As you take steps prior to your campaign to expand your social media presence, be sure to focus on your project's target audience as much as possible, so that when you begin talking more about your crowd funding campaign using social media, a large percentage of people you're reaching out to will have a strong interest in what you're raising money to accomplish.

Ideally, by the time you are ready to kick off your crowd funding campaign, this part of your overall network will number in the hundreds or thousands, depending on the scope of your project.

4. **A Targeted Audience within the General Public.** The people in this group are basically strangers. They're people who will stumble upon your crowd funding campaign, respond to your ads, read about your project in the media, learn about your project through word-of-mouth exposure from others, or encounter your campaign's broader marketing and promotional efforts.

The advertising, marketing, promotional, and public relations activities you utilize during your crowd funding campaign will be what attract most of this group to your project. This group might also comprise repeat backers on a particular platform, meaning that they visit a platform, such as Kickstarter, spend time viewing the various campaigns, and then choose which ones to support. Perhaps they originally visited the platform to support another campaign and then wound up stumbling upon your campaign's web page because it was featured somewhere on the platform.

If your project requires raising a lot of money or preselling a product, for example, the group of people in your target audience whose attention you capture will probably represent the largest percentage of backers you attract to your project. However, if your funding goal is low and does not require more than a few dozen or maybe one or two hundred backers, reaching this group will be far less important. Instead, you'll want to focus on marketing your campaign mainly to your inner circle, real-life friends, and the people in your social network.

Once you get people from your target audience to visit your campaign's web page, you should present them with three calls to action: support the project financially; share details about the project with their own networks; and agree to allow you to stay in touch with them (either via email, by having them subscribe to your project's blog, or by liking your project's Facebook page, for example).

Even if a person from this group is unwilling or unable to financially support your project when your campaign launches, his circumstances may change before your campaign ends. At the very least, such an individual may be willing to help you promote your project and then be among the first to buy your product once it's released to the public, attend your show, download your music, see your movie, or read your book.

Each of these four groups within your network will ultimately play an important role in getting your project funded. For example, prior to your campaign's launch, and then during the first few hours or days of your campaign, your goal should be to get your inner circle, as well as your friends and acquaintances, to quickly support your project by becoming backers. This will give your campaign an initial surge of support and funding and help it get off to a positive start.

Upon seeing the positive momentum of your campaign, the people from your social network will hopefully come aboard and pledge their support. Prior to the launch of your campaign, invest the time necessary to help the people in your social network get to know and respect you, while at the same time, work hard to expand your network on the various services like Facebook and Twitter, so your network includes people who fall directly into your target audience.

Become active in various online forums, special interest groups, Facebook pages, and online communities that relate in some way to your project or area of interest. Your goal should be to get noticed online in a positive way and to be accepted as someone who is highly knowledgeable about topics related to your project, polite, respectful, and an active participant in these forums and online communities.

Be willing to respond to peoples' posts and answer their questions about topics related to your project, share what this audience perceives as valuable information, and focus on getting people interested in your project using a casual, soft-sell approach. Your objective should be to entice people to visit your campaign's web page where the hard sell will take place. When using social media you should always be casual and less sales-oriented.

Once the people in your social network know you and respect you through a series of public messages and perhaps private invitations through the social media services, you should be able to drive a significant level of traffic to your crowd funding campaign's web page, which will hopefully include the content needed to transform these visitors into financial backers.

For some types of crowd funded projects that are not seeking too much money, at least 80 percent of the funding you receive will come directly from your inner circle, personal friends, and your social network. Knowing the value of these real-life and online relationships, you'll want to cultivate them over time. Especially when it comes to people from your social network, allow them to get to know you, and work toward building a positive online reputation so that when you reach out to these people asking for their financial support, they'll be more apt to offer it. These people need to believe you have what it takes to complete your project successfully before they'll consider helping to fund it.

At least some percentage of the funds raised through your crowd funding campaign will come from the general public (i.e., total strangers). However, instead of reaching out to the mass market, you'll want to better utilize your available resources and focus your advertising, marketing, public relations, and other promotional efforts related to your campaign on reaching people in your target audience.

Keep in mind, if you opt to run an equity-based crowd funding campaign, you'll proceed in a somewhat different manner from pursuing a reward- or presale-based campaign. For example, instead of reaching out to your inner circle—friends, acquaintances, and your social media network— you may need to focus your efforts on reaching prequalified, credited investors using methods that have been deemed acceptable—and legal—by the Jumpstart Our Business Startups Act.

DEFINING YOUR TARGET AUDIENCE

Convincing total strangers to support your project will be a challenge. However, if you carefully target people who you know will share an interest in or passion for your project once they learn about it, then achieving success simply becomes a matter of sharing your message with the right group of people.

Spending your time, money, and resources trying to promote your crowd funding campaign and project to the mass market is probably a major waste of all three, as is trying to make your campaign go viral and, in the process, ignoring the people who you can more easily and effectively reach out to. Most crowd funding campaigns do not need to go viral in order to meet or exceed their funding goals. In fact, unless you have a huge budget to invest in your campaign and you're an expert marketer, you cannot force a campaign to go viral. Even with vast resources, creating a campaign that goes viral is very challenging, which is why so few campaigns actually do.

By carefully targeting your advertising, marketing, and public relations efforts and message to cater to the people you predefine as your target audience, you'll have much more success driving traffic to your campaign's web page and then converting those targeted visitors into financial backers. Ideally, the people in your target audience should already have a want or need for your project idea or be very interested in what you're trying to accomplish with your project.

For example, if you're a country music artist and you're trying to raise money to record an album, the people in your social media network will probably be your existing fans. However, if your music or your appeal as an artist overlaps with the fans of another popular country artist, such as Carrie Underwood, your primary target audience will be your own fans, and your secondary target audience will be Carrie Underwood's fans and country music fans in general.

Likewise, if you're raising money to invent a specific type of Apple iPhone accessory that would allow people to take better digital photos using the cameras built into their smartphones, your target audience would be people with an interest in iPhone photography, while your secondary target audience would be avid iPhone users looking for new ways to enjoy and utilize their smartphones.

The target audience for your particular project and its crowd funding campaign can be any group of people who you determine will have a strong want or need for whatever it is your project is offering. Your target audience can be defined by any of the following criteria:

- Age
- Gender
- Race
- Income
- Where they live (geographic location)
- Marital status
- Whether they have kids
- Religion
- Weight (or height)
- Sexual orientation
- Occupation
- Level of education
- Shopping and spending habits
- Social media habits
- Type of car they drive
- Groups or associations they belong to
- Where they work (geographic location)
- How technologically savvy they are
- Whether they use a smartphone or tablet
- Vacation habits
- Hobbies
- Special interests
- Pets
- Any other defining characteristics

In fact, when defining your target market, you can mix and match various criteria to really pinpoint the type of people you want and need to reach.

You may determine that your target audience is composed of middle-aged women who are college educated, employed, live in a major city, are currently married, and earn at least $50,000 per year.

Maybe your target audience comprises guys in their 20s who are recent high school or college graduates, play video games, are active on Facebook, and frequent nightclubs at least once per week.

The more clearly you can define the target audience for your project the better. After all, these are the people who will be the most excited about your project and who will want to support it either right away as project backers or as early customers or clients once the project is completed.

By really focusing on your project, its appeal, and what it offers, you should be able to define a clear target audience for it. Then you will want to invest the time needed to get to know everything you can about that target audience, including what they're passionate about, what challenges they're facing, and how you can best convey your marketing message to them. As you are getting to know your target audience, put yourself in their shoes, and make creative decisions about your crowd funding campaign and the project's development based on how you believe your target audience will react to your decisions.

One common mistake project creators fall into is making creative decisions about their projects and campaigns based on their own taste as opposed to what will appeal to their target audience. This happens most often when the project creator does not fit at all into the demographic of his target audience. For example, the project creator might be a middle-aged businessman, while the target audience for his project is young women in their early 20s. As a male businessman, he might never consider using the color pink when choosing the color scheme for the campaign's web page, yet this is a color that his target audience will most likely find visually appealing. This is one reason why it's important to put yourself into the shoes of your target audience when making creative decisions about your project and its crowd funding campaign.

If you determine that your target audience isn't computer savvy and spends little or no time surfing the Internet, or isn't comfortable making online purchases, for example, there's a good chance that this group of people will not support any crowd funding campaign, so relying on these people to fund your project will lead to major disappointment. However, if you determine that the majority of your target audience is unfamiliar with crowd funding, but they are active on the Internet and comfortable making online purchases, you'll have a much easier time converting them into backers of your project.

Ultimately, every aspect of your project, as well as your crowd funding campaign—from its title and text description to the promotional video, the rewards being offered, and the call to action you include within the campaign—should all be crafted specifically for your target audience. You want to address their wants and needs, their concerns or trepidations, and provide the information that will help them get excited about your project.

Once you know who your target audience is, you'll have a much easier time choosing the appropriate wording and vocabulary when describing your project, and you'll have a good idea about what color scheme and font to use on your web page that they'll find visually appealing and/or what type of background music will work best in your promotional video. You'll be able to clearly explain how your project can in some way enrich their lives, and you'll know the best way to reach them with your messaging.

Knowing everything you can about your target audience will also make it easier to brainstorm awesome rewards to offer as part of your crowd funding campaign and help you set appropriate price points for those rewards that will be affordable for the people you are targeting. Likewise, if you are using a presale approach to crowd funding, you can make more intelligent decisions with your pricing based on what you know your target audience can afford and will be willing to spend.

When it comes to developing the paid advertising for your campaign, once you know your target audience you'll be able to determine when and where the ads should appear in order to get the best response. Plus, when you're targeting media outlets to provide editorial coverage for your project, you'll better be able to pinpoint specific publications, blogs, radio shows, and/or television programs that cater specifically to your target audience.

When seeking out publicity, keep in mind that while coverage in general interest publications will be useful and help to expand your reach while boosting your credibility, in reality only a small percentage of a general interest publication's readers will likely fall within your target audience. Thus, the percentage of people who actually visit your campaign's web page and become backers as a result of this type of publicity will be very small.

However, if you obtain editorial coverage in a special interest publication or within a blog that specifically caters to your target audience, the vast majority of those readers will be inherently interested in your project and will react favorably when they read an article written by a journalist or blogger whom they highly respect. Thus, even if the special interest publication or blog has a much smaller audience or circulation than a mainstream, better known media outlet, the percentage of people who will respond to that coverage, visit your campaign's web page, and ultimately become backers will be significantly higher. Plus, you'll have a much easier time getting media attention from smaller, special interest media outlets and blogs than you will from major daily newspapers and general interest national magazines.

As you more thoroughly develop your project idea, you may determine that it will appeal to several distinct target audiences. This is a good thing, but it will also mean you'll need to develop separate marketing messages, ad campaigns, public relations efforts, and other activities in order to reach these distinct groups. In this case, determine which of your target audiences is composed of the largest group of people who will be the easiest and most cost-effective to reach, and start by focusing your overall marketing efforts on that group. Then, as time and resources allow, expand the reach of your overall marketing, advertising, and promotional efforts to reach out to your secondary target audience.

Once you flesh out your project idea, you'll be in a better position to pinpoint your target audience and secondary target audience. After this is accomplished, you can begin focusing on developing all aspects of your crowd funding campaign to appeal to these audiences.

Producing Your Promotional Video

The process of transforming an individual into a financial supporter (backer) for your project is a multiple step process. First, you need to pinpoint the people who you believe would be interested in your project. Next, you must direct those people to your campaign's web page. At this point, the content of that web page (which is typically hosted by the crowd funding platform you opt to use) needs to tell your story, build excitement for your project, and convince people to become backers.

Perhaps the most powerful tool at your disposal to sell your product idea and explain to your target audience what it's all about is the promotional video that can—and should—be included on your campaign's web page. Based on how you shoot the video and its content, the same video, or an edited version of it, can also appear on your primary website, Facebook page, blog, and/or YouTube channel. You can also use it to presell your project concept and drive traffic to your campaign's web page.

You already know that people surfing the Internet have a very short attention span, and once people visit your campaign's web page, you literally have just seconds to capture their interest and get them to click the play button and watch your video. The first few seconds of that video need to draw in the audience and make them want to watch the video in its entirety.

Once someone is watching your video, you have between one and three minutes to introduce and demonstrate your project, discuss its benefits, and seal the deal by getting viewers to financially support the project. The video needs to be concise, informative, engaging, and entertaining, and at the same time, feature a production quality that meets or exceeds your audience's expectations and that lives up to your image and reputation.

Even for the most experienced videographers, scriptwriters, and marketers, the video production aspect of a crowd funding campaign is typically the most challenging, time-consuming, and potentially expensive part of creating the overall campaign. After all, second to the actual project idea, it's typically the campaign's promotional video that causes the viewer to decide whether to financially support a project.

Just as there is no formula to follow or template to customize when it comes to creating a successful reward-based crowd funding campaign, there are very few rules to adhere to when creating the promotional video for the campaign. According to Kickstarter's website, however, "A video is by far the best way to get a feel for the emotions, motivations, and character of a project. . . . Projects with videos succeed at a much higher rate than those without."

TWELVE ELEMENTS THAT MAKE FOR A SUCCESSFUL PROMOTIONAL VIDEO

As you're developing the concept for and then producing your promotional video, the only proven guidelines to follow involve incorporating the following 12 elements into the production:

1. Keep your video short—under three minutes.
2. Present a clearly stated and easy to follow call to action at least several times within the video. Emphasize the call to action again, in a compelling way, at the very end of the video. In the previous chapter, you learned that every reward-based crowd funding campaign should include three primary calls to action. In your promotional video, the one call to action to focus on is asking for the financial support of the viewer by explaining exactly what they need to do to become a backer and why this is essential to your project's success.
3. Ensure that the video's high-definition (HD) footage is clear and in focus.
4. All of the sound in the video, whether it is people talking, voice-overs (people heard speaking who are not seen), sound effects, or background music, needs to be heard clearly and be properly mixed. The music should never overpower people's voices or take attention away from what's being said. While background music can and should be used, the

music must be appropriate. You'll also need permission to use it, unless it's music you have composed and recorded yourself or it is offered by the copyright holder on a royalty- and license-free basis. In other words, you cannot download your favorite song by a popular band or recording artist and use it in your video without permission.

5. Where the video is shot should be relevant, but whatever is in the background should not be distracting or confusing to the viewer.

6. The project's creator(s) should be prominently featured in the video. Avoid using a paid spokesperson. That said, if additional people (who will be seen but not heard) are needed to help demonstrate a product, professional models whose appearance will appeal to the target audience can be used as "supporting characters" not "featured presenters" in the video.

7. The video should quickly explain the project idea, discuss its benefits, and focus on how it will positively impact the viewer and the public, if applicable. It should also demonstrate the product or offer a preview of what the completed project will look like or entail.

8. The video should appeal directly to its target audience. In other words, the concepts, vocabulary, and imagery should all be easily understandable by your target audience, with no time-consuming explanation required. One of the worst mistakes you can make is using a video that needs to be viewed two or three times to be fully understood. In reality, potential backers will not sit through multiple viewings. By the midway point during someone's first viewing of your video, the viewer should be sold on and truly excited about your project idea.

9. Creativity is absolutely essential.

10. Make your video easily viewable on any size screen. Some people will be watching your promotional video on a large, flat-screen HD television set, some will be viewing it on their computer screens, while a signification percentage of viewers may be using their smartphones or tablets to view your video. With this in mind, avoid using a lot on-screen titles or captions that will be impossible to read on a smartphone or tablet screen, and avoid visuals that include too much detail that could be missed if viewed on a smaller screen.

11. When possible, focus on people's emotions and heartstrings, but only in a way that will help your objective. Avoid begging and using words like "donate" within your video. By becoming backers, people should feel as if they are doing something good by supporting your cause, that they're joining a movement, or that they're getting directly involved in making your project a reality. If someone supports your project, the benefits to that individual, the community, the world, and, to a lesser extent, you (the project's creator), should be made crystal clear.

12. Keep your video as simple as possible. This includes the overall production, the content, core messages, and the visuals and audio. Avoid anything that could distract, confuse, or bore the viewer, or that is not directly related to the video's core messaging and objective. Flashy animated graphics, sound effects, animated scene transitions, and other video production elements should be used sparingly, and only when absolutely needed and appropriate.

This list was compiled by viewing hundreds of videos associated with successful reward-based crowd funding campaigns, borrowing from extensive research conducted by crowd funding platforms, and listening to the firsthand experiences of the many crowd funding experts who are interviewed in the final three chapters of this book.

Of course, this list should be seen as a general guideline. Based on the focus and scope of your particular project, some of these elements might not be appropriate, and you may discover that other elements will work much better when it comes to achieving your goals.

CONDUCT MORE HANDS-ON RESEARCH

Remember, one of the best things you can do as a project creator when it comes to brainstorming ideas for your promotional video is to visit the various crowd funding platforms and watch dozens, or better yet, hundreds of videos yourself. Most of the crowd funding platforms allow you to view web pages from the most successful campaigns ever hosted on the platform as well as successful campaigns that fit into specific categories. You can also view campaigns currently underway on any platform.

Start your research by viewing the all-time most successful campaigns, even if the scope of these projects is totally unrelated to what you're trying to accomplish. This will give you a good idea about the types of videos that work well and the production quality that was utilized. Next, focus on campaigns that were targeted to the same audience you are trying to reach. Try to determine exactly why the videos were appealing to the audience, and what aspects of the video caused viewers to ultimately back the projects.

Also, review campaigns and associated promotional videos that relate to projects similar to your own. Again, try to ascertain why those videos worked. Finally, review videos for campaigns that are currently underway and that are close to ending. (Most platforms offer an option for this.) Try to select campaigns that are still far away from their funding goal with little time left to reach it. From these campaigns and videos, try to figure out what went wrong. Chances are, you'll begin seeing a pattern in which the same mistakes were made repeatedly in terms of the promotional video's approach, content, or production value.

There are a number of almost universal elements shared by successful promotional videos for reward-based crowd funding campaigns, including that they all introduce the viewer to who the project's creators are; they briefly tell the story behind the project and its current state; they boldly ask for the support of viewers; they may mention the rewards being offered at various funding levels; they discuss the importance of the campaign reaching its funding goal; and they thank the viewers for their interest and support.

CONSIDER YOUR PRODUCTION BUDGET AND GOALS

As you brainstorm ideas for your promotional video, envision what you want it to look like, and consider how you want it to be perceived by viewers, it's easy to come up with ideas that will cost a fortune to actually produce. After all, we're all accustomed to watching flashy commercials, music videos, Hollywood blockbuster movies, and expertly produced network television programs.

In most cases, the promotional video for your project does not have to share those same top-quality professionally produced production values. In fact, you're often better off avoiding them. Again, there are no rules about how much you should spend producing your video. But, when you consider the overall budget for your crowd funding campaign, the cost of the video's production will probably represent a significant expenditure.

Speaking in general terms, if you've set your project's funding goal at $10,000 or less (give or take a few thousand), a low-budget, do-it-yourself, grassroots production approach to your video will most likely work just fine. As long as you can create a video that is in focus, well lit, sounds good, and conveys your messaging effectively, you'll be in good shape. These low-budget videos can be produced using a consumer-grade video camera and can typically be edited using inexpensive software on your desktop or laptop computer.

Even if you're taking a low-budget, grass roots approach to producing your video, the messaging needs to be expertly crafted and nicely communicated. Hiring a professional writer who has experience writing scripts for reward-based crowd funding promotional videos will be a good investment. However, you'll still need to work closely with the scriptwriter to ensure your personality and your fundamental messaging about your project is incorporated appropriately. After all, nobody will be more familiar with and have a greater passion for your project than you. This is also why you, the project creator, should be featured in the video.

For projects with higher funding goals, the production budget for the promotional video should increase. How much you ultimately invest in your video should depend on the image and level of professionalism you need to convey to your audience, and that, in turn, should be based on your perception of what that audience expects.

For example, if you are already well-established as the project creator, and you are looking to raise $250,000 or more, you'll probably already have a large following of customers, clients, or fans, and those people will have high expectations for your project. Thus, you'll need to produce a video that's in line with those expectations and pay for a professionally produced video. This will typically require hiring a professional video production crew, including a writer, director, cameraman, sound engineer, video editor, and supporting crew members. The production cost for your video will probably be at least $10,000.

Obviously, there's a big gap between a funding goal of $10,000 (or less) and $250,000 (or more). This is all a gray area in terms of video production, and a lot will depend on your available resources, overall goals, and your target audience. If your project's funding goal falls within this middle area, you may find it necessary to rent higher end video production equipment (a professional-quality HD video camera, lighting, sound equipment, and editing tools, for example), and hire one or more freelance video production experts so that your video is of the quality necessary for your project.

Again, by studying the videos of successful campaigns that are similar to yours, defining your own goals, and understanding the expectations of your target audience, you should easily be able to figure out the level of professionalism and production quality that will work best for your particular promotional video.

CREATE YOUR VIDEO'S SCRIPT AND STORYBOARD

Producing a one- to three-minute video may sound like an easy task, but depending on what you're trying to accomplish, things can get complicated fast. For example, even if your plan is to feature nothing but a talking head standing in front of a basic background, speaking directly into the camera, to keep the video visually entertaining, you'll need to utilize multiple camera angles and shooting perspectives and switch between them frequently. For example, if you watch any television program or news show, you'll notice that multiple cameras are used, and the same shot is rarely used for more than five to 10 seconds.

When it comes to producing your promotional video, start by drafting a script and creating a storyboard. The script should describe exactly what's being seen and heard during every second of the video. Ideally, you'll want to hire a professional scriptwriter to help you create or fine-tune your script, since every word that's said needs to have meaning and play an important role in educating your viewers, while also convincing them to become financial backers of your project.

Of course, you can use any word processor to write your script. However, you may find it easier to use specialized scriptwriting software that's available for your PC, Mac, or tablet. Script It, for example, is available for purchase and download from the WritersStore.com ($49.95, www.writersstore.com/script-it). Final Draft ($249.99, www.finaldraft.com), Celtx ($9.99 per month, www.celtx.com/products.html), and Scripted ($9.95 per month, http://scripted.com) are a few other software programs and online script writing tools.

In addition to a script, you'll also find it useful to create a storyboard for your video. This is a graphical representation of every shot or scene in your video that is drawn out in a series of sequential boxes. A storyboard can be sketched out on paper, or you can use specialized software to create a storyboard.

StoryBoard Pro (free, www.atomiclearning.com/storyboardpro), Story Board Quick ($249.00, www.powerproduction.com/storyboard-quick-software.html), and Story Board Pro ($399.00, www.toonboom.com/products/storyboardpro) are among your software-based options.

PRODUCTION ISSUES TO CONSIDER

Regardless of your budget, every video requires core production elements that you'll need to consider, and the equipment you use will directly impact the overall production quality of your presentation. These elements include:

- The HD video camera you'll use to shoot the video
- Background and shooting location(s)
- Lighting
- Sound quality
- Who will be featured within the video and what do they look like
- Background music and sound effects
- Editing

CHOOSING THE BEST HD VIDEO CAMERA TO SHOOT YOUR VIDEO

Your video should be shot in 1080p high-definition quality. Think about where and when you'll be shooting your video and under what conditions the video will be shot. In addition to the camera, will one or more external microphones be needed to capture sound? Will you require artificial lighting in order to properly light what's being featured in your video?

Based on your anticipated needs, what special camera features will be useful? For example, will you be shooting in harsh environments and require a camera that's waterproof or temperature resistant? Will you be shooting action shots from a first-person perspective, requiring a camera to be mounted on someone's head, vehicle, or on special equipment?

If your video will feature people, will they be seated, standing still, or in motion? Will the video also incorporate some type of product demonstration that requires detailed close-ups? Once you've developed a basic script and storyboard for your video, you can determine the type of HD video camera or cameras best suited to shoot the raw video footage that's required.

Again, for low-budget and simple video productions, a consumer-grade video camera that can capture HD-quality video will probably be sufficient, as long as you can attach one or more external microphones to the camera in order to capture higher quality sound. For higher budget and more elaborate productions, it's probably in your best interest to rent or borrow a professional-quality video camera, and hire a videographer who knows how to expertly use that camera.

For example, if you need to capture "action" footage, the GoPro Hero3+ camera is priced around $400.00, is extremely compact, offers extremely high resolution, and can be mounted almost anywhere, allowing its user to capture stunning video footage in extreme conditions. The GoPro camera offers many advantages for a videographer on a tight budget. To learn more, visit www.GoPro.com.

Companies like Adorama (www.adorama.com) and B&H Photo-Video (www.bhphotovideo.com) specialize in selling new and used video equipment. These websites also offer online tutorials for learning about video cameras and what types of cameras work best for specific kinds of shooting situations.

Companies that rent video equipment, including cameras, lighting, and microphones, include:

- ATS Rentals (www.atsrentals.com)
- Borrow Lenses (www.borrowlenses.com/category/Video)
- HD Rental (www.hdrental.com)
- LensRentals.com (www.lensrentals.com/rent/video/cameras)
- Radiant Images (www.radiantimages.com)
- VER Video Equipment Rentals (www.verrents.com)
- Zacuto (www.zacuto.com)

There are also local companies in every major city that rent professional-quality equipment by the day. You'll find them online or listed in the Yellow Pages. However, if you wind up hiring a video production crew or videographer, chances are they'll have their own equipment.

You can find and hire freelance video production crew members, such as writers, directors, and camera operators from services like:

- Crew Connection (www.crewconnection.com)
- eLance (www.elance.com)
- Freelance Directory (www.freelancedirectory.tv)
- Indeed (www.indeed.com/q-Freelance-Video-Crew-jobs.html)

In addition to the camera itself, based on the type of video you'll be shooting, a tripod or Steadicam® (or another image stabilization system) may also be required to ensure the camera is kept steady while you're shooting.

SELECTING YOUR BACKGROUND OR SHOOTING LOCATION

There are two schools of thought when it comes to selecting a shooting location for your video. If the video will feature a talking head (the project's creator) discussing the project, a solid color, plain background can be used so the primary focus remains on the person speaking. However, another option is to use a background that reveals a specific location that's directly relevant to the project.

Depending on the background or shooting location you select, a variety of different sound and lighting challenges will arise. For low-budget productions, selecting an indoor location and using a plain background gives you the most control over your shooting environment. Shooting in a specific location or outdoors, for example, requires you to deal with environmental issues, such as sunlight, wind, and other ambient sounds.

Wherever you wind up shooting, you need to be able to control the ambient sound. This means either avoiding or being able to get rid of unwanted noises from nearby traffic, airplanes flying overhead, air conditioners, machinery, and other potential distractions. Always select a background or shooting location that's either very simple visually, or that will help convey your overall message, without distracting or confusing the viewer in any way.

Using a basic studio lighting setup when shooting indoors and a solid color background will probably provide the least number of challenges, but unless you mix and match your shots and do something interesting with how you shoot the video, you run the risk of it being visually boring. A basic backdrop can be made from seamless paper, vinyl or cloth. They're available from video and photo specialty stores in a wide range of colors, patterns, and sizes. Two such stores that offer a wide range of inexpensive, but professional-quality backgrounds are Backdrop Source (www.backdrop source.com) or Backdrop Outlet (www.backdropoutlet.com).

LIGHTING CONSIDERATIONS

Again, regardless of your production budget, it's essential that your video be well lit and devoid of any unwanted (and unprofessional looking) shadows. Your primary light source should be positioned in front of your video's subject, so that light is shed evenly over your subject.

If you are shooting indoors, inexpensive professional lighting systems can be purchased or rented. For example, a basic three-light system can be purchased for as little as $300 to $400, while professional lighting setups that are more extensive and flexible can be purchased for thousands, or rented by the day for a few hundred dollars.

Artificial indoor studio lighting allows you to adjust the intensity, color, and positioning of your primary light source as you're shooting. Similar lighting can also be used outdoors, but you'll have the added challenge of dealing with sunlight.

When shooting outside, you can redirect natural sunlight using reflectors, or reduce the intensity of sunlight and help to avoid unwanted shadows by using deflectors. Both reflectors and deflectors come in a wide range of styles and sizes, and some have very specific uses. This equipment can also be acquired from a video specialty retail or online store.

SOUND QUALITY CONSIDERATIONS

Most video cameras have a built-in microphone. In almost all situations, however, the quality of this microphone is poor, and because it's built into the camera, it's designed to pick up and record all audio that is present in the shooting location—not just the person speaking. Thus, using the microphone that's built into your video camera means you will also pick up the sound of the air conditioner in the room, any noise the crew makes, airplanes flying overhead, and anything else that's present when you're shooting.

To dramatically improve the quality of the audio you record as you're shooting video, connect an external, professional-quality microphone to your video camera. This applies even if you're shooting your video with an iPhone's built-in camera or a low-end consumer-grade video camera.

For a few hundred dollars, you can purchase a professional-quality microphone to use in conjunction with your video production. However, most places that rent higher end video equipment also rent compatible microphones and related audio equipment.

When you start learning about professional-quality microphones, you'll learn that there are several distinct types of microphones, which are designed for recording different types of audio in various settings. For example, if you'll be recording a talking head video featuring one or two people speaking, you might best be served using lapel microphones that clip onto your speaker's shirt or jacket. These can be corded or wireless microphones.

The trick is to select the right type of microphone for the recording task at hand. Thus, if you will be shooting in different locations, this might require using different types of microphones in order to capture the best audio quality possible. After you determine your audio recording needs, consult with an expert who can help you choose the right microphone(s) for your particular situation.

Once you've acquired the right microphones for the job, make sure they are positioned correctly on your set. As you are shooting your video, be sure to properly manage the audio input levels.

SHOWCASE THE RIGHT APPEARANCE: WARDROBE, HAIR, AND MAKEUP CONSIDERATIONS

You already know that featuring the product creator(s) in your crowd funding video is a commonly used practice that tends to help viewers more quickly relate to a project. As the producer of your promotional video, it's your job to determine who will appear in the video, and equally as important, how these people will present themselves.

In addition to the words people in your video say, what they wear, their hairstyles, their poses or positions, what props they use, their body language, their location, and their facial expressions should all encourage viewers to quickly develop a positive impression of them. Details matter a lot!

Remember, in the very first few seconds of your video, you need to make a fast and positive impression and capture the attention of viewers. The appearance of the presenters featured in your video is an important consideration, and it is something that should be carefully planned and well thought out, keeping your target audience in mind.

If the person in your video is wearing an article of clothing that blends in too much with their background or that clashes with the rest of her outfit, this will immediately distract viewers. Likewise, when people wear flashy jewelry (such as a necklace, bracelet, or earrings), a wristwatch that reflects light, or eyeglasses that don't have an antireflective coating on the lenses, these are all potentially major visual distractions that you want to avoid.

Once you've pinpointed the target audience for your video and know who will be featured in your video, consider working with a stylist to select an appropriate outfit for them. Then, work with a hairstylist and makeup artist to make sure that the people in your video look good and appropriate. Again, make sure the appearances of the people featured in your video will be deemed acceptable and appropriate by your target audience.

Ideally, the person or people featured in your video are experts on the topic they'll be speaking about and know all there is to know about your project. In a perfect shooting scenario, the people featured in the video will memorize their lines and be able to talk in a calm, casual, and easy to understand way that appears totally natural. If this isn't possible, you may wind up needing to use cue cards or a teleprompter to keep your talent focused.

The drawback to using cue cards or a teleprompter is that if the people speaking are not accustomed to using them, they will appear to be reading or simply reciting something. Their timing and speech pattern will not appear natural, and this can be a huge turnoff for the audience.

UTILIZING BACKGROUND MUSIC, VOICE-OVERS, AND SOUND EFFECTS

Incorporating background music into your video is often useful. It can help to quickly set a mood, excite your viewers, and keep the upbeat momentum of the video going. That said, it is essential that you choose background music that's appropriate, and play it at a reasonable volume so that it doesn't impede the viewer from clearly hearing what's being said.

Entire music libraries that you can purchase the rights to use are available online. There are also libraries consisting of royalty- and license-free music that can be used at no cost and with no restrictions. Using any search engine, enter the search phrase "video production music" to begin browsing through libraries of music available to you for your production. You can begin your search for the perfect background music by visiting these Kickstarter-recommended sites:

- ccMixter (www.ccmixter.org)
- Free Music Archive (www.freemusicarchive.org)

- SoundCloud (www.soundcloud.com)
- Vimeo Music Store (www.vimeo.com/musicstore)

Whatever background music you opt to include in your video, make sure you have permission to use it, or you could find yourself a defendant in a copyright infringement lawsuit.

Another useful audio element that can be incorporated into videos is the voice-over, which is words that are spoken by someone who isn't seen on camera. In other words, while a product is being demonstrated, or while a chart or graph is being shown, someone can be explaining what is going on while the camera remains focused on the product.

If the person who is being featured on camera is male, you may find it useful to use a female for your voice-overs in order to make the audio portion of your video more interesting for viewers. How you utilize voice-overs is purely a creative decision on your part. To add a touch of professionalism to your production, in addition to featuring your project's creators in the video, you might consider hiring a professional voice-over actor to record some voice-over content. You can find professional voice-over actors, like Jeff at Radio Voice Imaging (www.radiovoiceimaging.com), using any search engine.

Depending on what you're presenting in your video, you may find it useful to mix in various sound effects. Again, there are several schools of thought about doing this. On the plus side, appropriate sound effects can make whatever content is being presented come across as more realistic or authentic. However, if overused, sound effects can also become a major distraction. So, if you're going to use sound effects, use them sparingly, in a realistic way, and in a manner that won't distract your audience from what's being said or showcased.

THE PROS AND CONS OF ADDING MORE PRODUCTION ELEMENTS

Thanks to the advanced capabilities of even the most basic video editing software, it's easy to incorporate flashy animated titles, captions, and scene transitions into your video. Unless these added elements are specifically needed to help convey an important piece of information, avoid adding elements that will simply serve as eye candy and that could become a distraction. Once again, what's appropriate to use in your video will depend on what you're trying to accomplish, your target audience, and your own creativity. However, when it comes to adding optional production elements to a promotional video, the theory that less is more is usually a good one to adhere to.

EDITING YOUR VIDEO

By the time you're done filming, you may have accumulated several hours' worth of raw video footage that now needs to be edited down into a one- to three-minute promotional video. Hopefully, you've captured every scene in your video using several different camera angles and/or shooting perspectives. This will allow you to pick and choose the best take for each shot.

For basic video editing on your PC or Mac, both Microsoft and Apple offer video editing software. For example, there's Microsoft Movie Maker for Windows and iMovie for the Mac. However, if you need more professional and advanced video editing tools, there's Apple's Final Cut Pro and Adobe's Premier Pro.

Many professional video editors and television producers use Avid video editing and production software (www.avid.com/US/products), but these tools are costly and require specialized training to fully utilize.

As you're editing your video and putting the finishing touches on your production, make sure that the video:

- Caters to your target audience.
- Presents your core message clearly, quickly, and concisely.
- Includes an easy-to-understand call to action that's repeated multiple times, including at the very end of the video. For example, a statement like, "We need your help to make this happen," is very compelling.
- Doesn't look like or sound like a television commercial or infomercial.
- Has a length of between one and three minutes, no longer.
- Nicely sums up exactly what your project is all about in a way that will encourage and excite viewers to become backers.

Every scene, image, sound, and spoken word featured in your video should help to achieve one or more of these objectives. If any content is overly redundant, confusing, irrelevant, or misleading, it should be edited out of the final production.

Consider utilizing the following video editing strategies to help you fine-tune your promotional video production:

- Make sure the video flows smoothly from one scene to the next.
- The audio quality and levels should be consistent throughout the video.
- Don't use talking head shots for more than 5 to 10 seconds at a time. Vary your shots by switching camera angles or shooting perspectives often.
- When using text for titles or captions, make sure they're easily readable, even for someone watching your video on a smartphone.
- Ensure that there's nothing that's distracting within your video.

- Make sure you state and then restate your call to action in several different ways.
- Review the video's content carefully, and make sure there is nothing that people might find objectionable or offensive.
- Adhere to the video production tips and guidelines provided by the crowd funding platform you'll be utilizing. For example, if you'll be using Kickstarter, visit www.kickstarter.com/help/school#making_your_video. Indiegogo users should visit http://support.indiegogo.com/entries/20514218-what-makes-a-campaign-successful, and RocketHub users should visit http://rockethub-media.s3.amazonaws.com/rockethub-success-school.pdf.
- From a technical standpoint, make sure the video is exported into the correct file format and that it's within the file size limitations specified by the crowd funding platform you'll be hosting it on. For example, a Kickstarter video must have a file size of five gigabytes or less and be saved in the MOV, MPEG, AVI, or MP4 file format.

The process of editing your video may take several full days or even weeks to complete. Keep working until you are 100 percent confident that you've gotten everything right, and that the video is ready to become part of your reward-based crowd funding campaign. Because you've already invested a lot of time and effort into the video's production, at this point, you may be too close to the project to have an unbiased opinion about it.

Before publishing the video online as part of your campaign, show it to coworkers, friends, family, and/or a small group of people in your target audience, and solicit their unbiased and honest feedback. Keep in mind, it's very common for project creators to reshoot or reedit their videos multiple times before they're confident that they are complete and that they meet their objectives. Then, once the video does go live, track its viewership carefully. Determine if people are, in fact, watching it from start to finish, or if they're exiting out of the video early. You may discover it's necessary to further fine-tune your video while your campaign is underway in order to increase its effectiveness.

CHAPTER 8

Promoting Your Campaign

In This Chapter

- Discover ways to drive traffic to your reward-based crowd funding campaign's web page.
- Use online advertising to promote your campaign.
- Learn how to take advantage of social media.
- Reach out to the mainstream and online media using public relations efforts.

Hopefully by now, you realize that if you simply come up with an awesome project idea and then publish a reward-based crowd funding campaign for it, absolutely nothing is going to happen unless you actively and continuously promote the campaign to drive a steady flow of traffic to your campaign's web page. In addition, the traffic needs to be composed of people from your target audience who will have a want, need, or interest in your project idea, and will get excited enough about the project to become financial backers.

As with just about everything else related to a reward-based crowd funding campaign, there's no preset marketing, advertising, promotions, or public relations formula to follow that will guarantee success. Instead, a lot will depend on the scope of your project, your own creativity, how much time and money you have to invest in this aspect of your campaign, your target audience, and your ability to effectively reach your target audience in ways that get them to visit your campaign's web page.

Once you get to know your target audience, what you'll probably discover is that to drive a continuous flow of traffic to your campaign's web page, you'll need to take a multifaceted approach. In other words, you won't be able to rely on just email marketing, social media, online advertising, paid advertising, or another form of marketing or advertising. Throughout the length of your entire campaign, you'll need to use several of these activities simultaneously, and in real time continuously monitor and fine-tune your efforts based on the results you're achieving.

Thus, what you need to understand right from the start is that planning, executing, and managing a multifaceted marketing plan for your crowd funding campaign is going to take up a lot of your time and resources, and it's probably going to cost money. These are funds that you'll have to invest in advance, but you may be able to recoup if your project reaches its funding goal and you've built these preliminary expenses into your project's budget.

The final three chapters of this book contain in-depth interviews with a handful of crowd funding experts from a wide range of backgrounds. When each of these experts was asked about the biggest misconception they had about crowd funding as they were getting started, it was almost unanimous that they underestimated how much time and effort they needed to spend on marketing their campaigns from start to finish and how much preplanning was required to create a well-thought-out and appropriately targeted campaign.

Again, depending on the scope of your project and its target audience, starting before the campaign launches and extending until it ends, you will need to dedicate between 3 and 12 hours per day actively marketing and promoting your campaign, interacting online with potential supporters, and providing attention to your newly acquired backers. This interaction is important to keep them excited about your project and campaign and to solicit their assistance in promoting your project and campaign by sharing details about it with their own social networks.

When putting together your marketing campaign, all of your core messaging and imaging should remain consistent and synergistic with all of your other real-world and online endeavors. As much as possible, use the same color schemes, fonts, logos, slogans, and wording. Consistency is essential for building your brand, boosting awareness, and keeping people from becoming confused by your messaging and goals. Keep your messaging and calls to action simple and consistent.

TAKE AN ORGANIZED APPROACH TO YOUR MARKETING PLAN

Knowing that the marketing, advertising, promotions, and public relations activities for your crowd funding campaign are going to require you to carefully plan your approach and then juggle a wide range of responsibilities simultaneously to ensure all of your activities are successful, start off by developing a comprehensive and well-formulated plan.

Figure out what resources you have, your overall budget, your available time, and the specific activities you'll want to utilize before, during, and after your campaign. Then create a detailed, overall marketing plan. This plan can be written out, or you can utilize project planning tools to help keep all of the plans, activities, to-do tasks, and related deadlines organized.

One useful tool is the LivePlan application from Palo Alto Software (www.liveplan.com). This is an online application (prices start at $11.66 per month) that allows you to easily create and organize a comprehensive plan for almost any type of project or activity. In addition to using LivePlan to brainstorm, organize, and manage your campaign's marketing, advertising, promotions, and public relations efforts, you can also use it to plan and manage your entire project—from conception to completion.

In addition to the easy-to-use LivePlan application, Palo Alto Software (www.paloalto.com) also offers the best-selling Business Plan Pro software for creating detailed business plans, the Sales and Marketing Plan Pro software that you can use to plan and organize your sales and marketing efforts, as well as Email Center Pro, which is powerful email marketing and management software. These are all PC- and Mac-compatible applications that are sold separately.

Remember, weeks or even months before your crowd funding campaign launches, you should actively begin creating and planning your marketing, advertising, promotions, and public relations efforts that will be used to drive traffic (potential backers) to your campaign's web page once it's published online. Taking a well-organized approach to these efforts allows you to best utilize your time, resources, and available funds to generate the best possible results.

Once your crowd funding campaign actually launches, you'll need to spend your time managing that campaign and interacting with potential supporters and backers, not scrambling to get organized and trying to figure out how to drive traffic to your campaign's website. At this point, it will be too late to fully utilize many of the most powerful and least expensive tools available to you.

THERE ARE MANY WAYS TO DRIVE TRAFFIC TO YOUR CAMPAIGN'S WEB PAGE

Based on the time and resources you have available, as well as your budget, there are many ways to help drive a steady flow of traffic to your campaign's web page. As you'll discover, it's a bit more challenging to ensure that the traffic you generate aligns with your target audience. However, simply driving random traffic to your campaign's web page is a waste, because most of these people probably won't have an inherent interest, want, or need for your project. Thus, they probably will have no interest in backing it financially. In other words, your efforts are better spent finding and reaching out to fewer people who are actually in your target audience than trying to reach as many people as possible in the general public.

This chapter focuses on a handful of proven strategies that thousands of project creators have used (and are currently using) to promote their reward-based crowd funding campaign just before it launches and once it's underway.

Four core strategies, which consist of email marketing, social media outreach, paid online advertising, and public relations, are just a small selection of options available to you, but each of these tends to work well when promoting a broad range of project types.

USE EMAIL MARKETING TO REACH PEOPLE WITH A PERSONAL MESSAGE IN THEIR INBOX

When promoting a crowd funding campaign, reaching out to your inner circle, friends, and acquaintances, as well as your customers, clients, fans, and followers, using personalized email is an extremely powerful tool. There's a big difference, however, between using personal email to reach out to people you know (and who know you) and utilizing spam.

Spam refers to sending out unsolicited email to strangers that is not wanted by the recipient. Spam is often associated with online scams and should be avoided, since the response rate will be low, and this activity can tarnish your credibility and online reputation.

For people you know, who know you, and/or who have opted into your email list, email marketing can be effective. It allows you to compose and send personalized messages to select groups of people and target your message accordingly. Using software or email marketing tools, it's possible to create separate databases with contact details for specific groups of people, and then target each group with a separate set of carefully composed email messages.

So, as you're gearing up for your crowd funding campaign, reach out to your inner circle via a personalized email to tell them about your project and crowd funding plans, and personally ask for their assistance. Prior to the campaign's launch, these initial emails should be informational and used to motivate and rally your friends and family to support you and your project's campaign once it kicks off.

Then, as soon as the campaign launches, direct email to your inner circle (as well as your friends and acquaintances) should use personalized messages to ask that they be among the first to back your project, so they can help to create that initial surge of financial support. At this point, also ask that they help promote your project's campaign to their own social networks. Since the recipients of these emails are people close to you in real life, the tone of the message should be highly personal in nature.

Also, once your campaign launches, use direct email to reach out to your broader group of friends, acquaintances, customers, clients, fans, and followers. You'll want to compose a different assortment of email messages to address these recipients, since they know you but are not as close to you as your inner circle. In these emails, you may need to remind the recipients of your credentials or background, how they know you, why they should support you, and highlight details about your project and its relevance to them.

As your campaign progresses, use personalized email to stay in touch with your backers, keeping them updated on news related to your campaign and your project and thanking them for their support. You can also use direct email to introduce backers (and people who have opted into your email list) to your campaign's stretch goals, for example, and to build additional excitement about your campaign if you experience a lull. Sharing details about project-related successes is a wonderful use of direct email.

Chapter 9, "Interacting with Your Backers Using a Blog," focuses on additional ways you should stay in touch with your backers and supporters, both during the campaign and once the project is fully funded and the process of developing and creating the project begins.

There are a few email marketing strategies that tend to work well for project creators. First, write as many of your email messages as you can before your campaign launches. Determine when, in the time leading up to the campaign and after it has launched, each email message should be sent. This gives you plenty of time to compose well-thought-out and highly targeted messages.

Also, create a group of separate email list databases, and compose separate messages for each group. Some of the separate email list databases you might create and manage include:

- People in your inner circle
- Friends and acquaintances you know in the real world
- Customers, clients, fans, followers, and other individuals who know you, but with whom you don't have a personal (real-world) relationship
- People who learn about your campaign and opt into your email list (meaning they provide you with their email address and grant you permission to send them promotional emails)
- People who become financial backers of your project during the course of the crowd funding campaign

Using email marketing software or online tools, it is easy to create and manage as many separate email lists as you need, and then to compose messages that will be personalized for the intended recipient and later sent when you deem appropriate.

When composing each of your email messages, remember your goal is to drive traffic to your crowd funding campaign's web page, encourage recipients to become backers of your project, and solicit the recipients' help in promoting your campaign to their own social media networks. The following strategies will help you compose appropriate emails:

- Make sure each email message is targeted specifically to its intended audience.
- Don't write your emails to people on a list. Each message should be written as if it were directed to a single individual.
- Compose each message's subject line so it is attention getting and to the point yet will pique the reader's curiosity. Don't try to be too clever, however. The message should appear to be personal in nature, and not come across as a sales solicitation or spam.
- Use powerful and upbeat vocabulary that your target audience will understand and relate to. Keep the messaging simple. The Boost Blog Traffic blog featured an article that listed 317 "power words" that can be highly effective in a marketing email. To view the article, "317 Power Words That'll Instantly Make You A Better Writer," visit www .boostblogtraffic.com/power-words.
- Keep your overall email messages short and directly to the point. The overall length should be just a few paragraphs, and each paragraph should be no longer than two or three sentences. Don't waste the reader's time.
- Focus the content of your emails on the benefits of your project and how the project will help the reader, the community, or the world. Stress the important role the reader can play in your project's success.
- Invite readers to become supporters and join your movement. Make them feel like they're doing something positive and amazing. Again, don't beg for money or use words like "donate" (unless the campaign is for a charity and you are fund-raising).
- The tone of the emails should be friendly, upbeat, and personal. Avoid taking a hard-sell approach. Instead, provide enough information about your project and campaign to get readers excited, so they want to visit your campaign's website. Pique their interest in a positive way using email.
- Include a call to action in the email, and make it very easy to understand and follow. Tell the readers exactly what they need to do next and why. Create a sense of urgency.

community whenever and wherever you happen to be. Plus, as you receive incoming messages or posts on your Facebook page, or as people direct message or reference you on Twitter, for example, you can be alerted instantly on your mobile device. At the same time, your audience can interact with you and your other followers and learn about your project and campaign directly from their mobile devices, when and where it's convenient for them.

Another benefit to using social media to communicate with potential supporters, backers, followers, fans, and others is that you can adopt a highly personal approach, and give people access to you, without investing the time needed to communicate with people individually. Project creators have discovered a wide range of ways to use social media as a powerful marketing tool for their crowd funding campaigns that are designed specifically to cater to their target audience. So, as you visit each of the popular crowd funding platforms and study campaigns, also take a look at how social media is or was being used by other project creators.

One of the best strategies for developing a large online following on any social media platform is to become extremely active on that platform. Again, this is something you want to start doing long before your crowd funding campaign kicks off. Using social media effectively is free, but it can be time-consuming and it requires dedication on your part. Unless you take steps to grow your Facebook or Twitter following, for example, it will not expand on its own. This is another situation where neither the "if you build it, they will come" or the "built it and then ignore it" approach will work.

What most project creators discover is that social media is ideal for boosting awareness about a project, building a brand, and communicating with potential supporters and backers, but the conversion rate among people who are Facebook friends or Twitter followers and who will actually visit your campaign's web page and fund your project is often relatively low. Instead, social media can be used to build your opt-in email list, for example, and then personalized emails can be used to drive interested and prequalified traffic to your campaign's web page.

Sure, some project creators have used social media exclusively to promote their project and get it successfully funded. However, the vast majority of project creators have utilized social media as just one component in their overall marketing, advertising, promotions, and public relations campaign.

DRIVE TRAFFIC TO YOUR CAMPAIGN'S WEB PAGE USING PAID ONLINE ADVERTISING

If your crowd funding campaign requires you to reach out beyond your existing network in order to attract backers (or presales), one of the least

expensive and most targeted tools for accomplishing this is online advertising on Facebook, as well as paid search marketing/keyword advertising on
Google, Yahoo!, Bing, and their content partners.

All of these paid advertising options work basically the same way. Each
allows you to set your daily ad spending limit and reach a highly targeted
audience using a pay-per-click model. These services allow you to launch an
ad campaign within an hour or two, so you can drive traffic to your campaign's web page quickly. The amount of targeted traffic you'll receive will
be based mainly on your budget and how well you set up and customize
each campaign.

To create and launch a Facebook ad campaign, click on the Create Ad
option that's found at the bottom of the main screen or click on the gear-
shaped menu icon that's displayed near the top-right corner of the Facebook
screen.

As you begin creating a campaign, you'll be prompted to choose your ad
campaign's overall objective. Your options include: Page Post Engagement,
Page Likes, Click to Website, Website Conversions, App Installs, App
Engagement, Event Responses, and Offer Claims. If you're promoting a
reward-based crowd funding campaign and looking to drive traffic to your
campaign's web page, select the Click to Website option.

When prompted, enter the website URL for your campaign's web page.
The next steps involve selecting and uploading an image to accompany your
ad (such as a logo or product shot), composing the headline and text for your
ad, selecting your target audience, and then choosing your campaign details,
which includes setting the dates your campaign will run, as well as your budget.

One feature offered as you compose your Facebook ad is the ability
to display a Call to Action button in the lower-right corner of the ad. Your
Call to Action button options include: Shop Now, Book Now, Learn More,
Sign Up, and Download. However, you can also opt to skip displaying a button altogether. If you're running a reward-based crowd funding campaign,
you'll probably find that the Learn More button is appropriate. However, if
your campaign's focus is on presales, displaying the Shop Now button will
probably work best.

Every Facebook ad includes a headline (up to 25 characters) and text
(up to 90 characters). The headline should be short and immediately capture
someone's attention. The text within the ad allows you to include one short
sentence that more clearly explains what you're promoting or selling.

When it comes to defining who will see your ads, you can determine if
the ads will be displayed as part of someone's Desktop News Feed, in the
right column of the Facebook screen, and/or as part of their Mobile News
Feed (seen on their smartphone or tablet when they access their Facebook
account).

After composing your ad and previewing exactly how it will look, scroll down to the Audience section of the Advertise on Facebook page. Here, you can choose the target audience that will see your ad. You're asked to customize the Location, Age, Gender, Language, Interests, Connections, and Related Categories options. Each should be customized for your own target audience.

One of the great things about Facebook is that all users are encouraged to create detailed profiles about themselves. It is information within these profiles, as well as their online activities, that Facebook is able to utilize when it comes to helping advertisers target highly niche audiences.

Once you define your target audience for the Facebook ads, an Audience Definition summary will be displayed. Next, you'll be prompted to select your budget and schedule. The budget can be per day or lifetime (which is the entire length of the campaign, which you select). When prompted to select your ad's schedule, you can choose to run it continuously, starting on the day it's created, or you can set a specific start and end date range.

The last set of options you'll need to set relates to how much you'll pay when someone sees or responds to your ad and clicks on it. With Facebook advertising, you can choose to Bid for Clicks or Bid for Impressions. If you choose to Bid for Clicks, and then click on the Manually Set Your Maximum Bid for Clicks, you'll be prompted to enter your maximum bid per click, and will be presented with a suggested minimum bid that will help you effectively reach your target audience.

Click on the Place Order button to process your ad purchase. Then, use Facebook's own ad tracking tools to see the effectiveness of your campaign in real time and, if necessary, fine-tune your ad's content or settings to maximize its impact. The charges to run your campaign will be billed to the credit or debit card you have on file in conjunction with your Facebook account. If no credit card information has been provided for your account, you'll be prompted to enter it.

Once your ad is approved, which typically happens in a matter of minutes, it will start appearing on the Facebook service and will be seen by the people you've targeted. As you'll discover, Facebook offers a variety of powerful tools to help you more effectively reach your target audience. For example, if you have an email database you're using for email marketing, you can use one of Facebook's tools to see if each email address is associated with an existing Facebook account, and if so, arrange to have your ad displayed to those people as well. To learn about and access the online tools for managing a Facebook ad campaign, visit www.facebook.com/ads/manage/campaigns once your initial campaign is created.

Beyond using Facebook advertising to find people in your target audience and drive them to your campaign's web page and/or your project's

Facebook Fan Page, it's also possible to use similar advertising tools, often referred to as paid search marketing, in conjunction with the Google, Yahoo!, and Bing search engines, for example, in order to target people using these popular search engines to search for specific keywords or phrases. (In addition to the search engines, these ad services display your ads on the web pages of participating content partners.)

To learn more about Google AdWords, visit www.google.com/adwords. To learn about the advertising opportunities offered by the Yahoo! and Bing combined network, visit http://advertise.bingads.microsoft.com. As with Facebook ads, you can set your maximum daily spending limit to adhere to your budget and get started running a campaign for as little as $50.00.

For unbiased advice and tips for creating and managing an online ad campaign, access the Search Engine Watch website (www.searchenginewatch .com), which is updated with new articles and tutorials on a regular basis.

When it comes to online advertising, Facebook ads, Google AdWords, and the paid search marketing services offered by Yahoo! and Bing are only a small sampling of what's possible. Based on your budget, there is a wide range of other online advertising opportunities available on popular websites, search engines, content provider services, and through affiliate marketing services.

TAP THE POWER OF THE MEDIA USING PUBLIC RELATIONS EFFORTS TO EXPAND YOUR AUDIENCE

Another piece of your overall crowd funding campaign's marketing efforts should include public relations. The goal here is to compile a targeted list of editors, journalists, show hosts, and producers, among others, who work for media outlets that reach your target audience. By providing these media people with press releases and other information, you want to entice them to feature information about your project and/or campaign within their editorial coverage.

Beyond just getting your project or campaign featured in an article, for example, you could also try to get your product reviewed, and/or get your project's creator(s) interviewed as experts in their field. Using public relations techniques, you can reach out to newspapers, magazines, radio shows, television shows, news-oriented websites, online publications, and other traditional media outlets.

In addition to focusing their public relations efforts on traditional media outlets, project creators have achieved incredible success reaching out to bloggers and getting their projects covered within popular blogs. Some blogs have larger readerships and more dedicated audiences than mainstream newspapers or magazines. In addition, there are blogs that cover just about every topic imaginable and that cater to every possible target audience.

To discover blogs that cater to specific topics or audiences, visit one or more blog directories and do some basic research. Blog Catalog (www .blogcatalog.com), Blog Hub (www.bloghub.com), Technorati (http:// technorati.com/blogs/directory) and BlogTopSites (www.blogtopsites.com) all offer easy-to-search blog directories. Of course, you can also use any search engine to find popular blogs about a specific topic. For example, to find blogs about sailing, you can use the search phrase "sailing blogs" when using Google, Yahoo!, or Bing.

If you are not familiar with how public relations works, seriously consider hiring a freelance PR specialist, one who has established media contacts and who can help you reach your target audience. A more costly option is to hire a public relations firm to create and manage your entire PR campaign, but this will cost between $2,000 and $10,000 per month, and to generate the best results you'll need the PR campaign to run for at least two or three months.

Just about everything you'd hire a freelance public relations specialist or PR firm to handle on your behalf, you can do yourself. But you'll need to take the time to learn the right skills, develop your media list, and then reach out to targeted media professionals.

At the core of every public relations campaign is one or more well-written press releases. A press release is typically a one-page news announcement that follows a very specific format. It provides journalists with the essential facts. A press release needs to be targeted to the media outlet it's being sent to, and it needs to be well-written and informative. It should convey the appropriate information (i.e., who, what, where, when, why, and how) in the most attention-getting but concise way possible.

At the top of a press release is a catchy and to-the-point headline. Immediately below that is contact information for the person, company, or organization sending out the press release. This is followed by a few short paragraphs that contain the core message. If a press release is well-written, a journalist will have all of the information needed to include details related to the announcement within their media coverage, or at the very least, be enticed to contact the issuer to schedule an interview or request more information.

It's absolutely essential that the press release be formatted correctly and then sent to appropriate members of the media. Free information about how to write and format a press release can be downloaded from PRWeb (http://service .prweb.com/learning/article/how-to-write-a-press-release),PublicityInsider.com

(www.publicityinsider.com/release.asp), or CBSNews.com (www.cbsnews
.com/news/how-to-write-a-press-release-with-examples).

Beyond just issuing stand-alone press releases, a PR campaign might
involve creating and distributing more elaborate press kits to select media
outlets. A press kit will include press releases, a company backgrounder,
biographies of the project creators, clips from recent media coverage, and
other pertinent information. For PR campaigns designed to generate hype
for a new product, it's common to send out free product samples or review
units to select media outlets, in hopes of getting reviews of the product
incorporated into a media outlet's editorial coverage.

In addition to creating well-written and attention-getting press releases
and PR materials, another challenge related to creating an effective public
relations campaign is compiling a targeted media list and contacting the
appropriate journalists, editors, reporters, show hosts, producers, or bloggers. To help with this aspect of a PR campaign, you can purchase media
directories, which are customized lists of media outlets as well as specific
media professionals that cover specific topics.

Some of the companies that sell media directories or media lists include:
Cision (www.cision.com/Media_Lists), Bulldog Reporter's Media List
Builder (https://listbuilder.bulldogreporter.com), Easy Media List (www
.easymedialist.com), and Handle Your Own PR (www.handleyourownpr
.com). There are also press release distribution services, like PR Newswire
(www.prnewswire.com) and Business Wire (www.businesswire.com), that
can help get your press release into the hands of journalists.

Another way to begin building your targeted media list is to browse
through crowd funding campaigns on the various platforms that cater to
the same target audience you hope to reach. Many project creators boast
about the media attention their project has received and often include links
to articles, for example. Determine what media outlets covered these other
campaigns, and specifically which journalists at those media outlets did the
reporting, and start by contacting those people. From this research, you'll
find that some media outlets, including many online news services and
publications, frequently cover interesting, highly successful, or cutting-edge
crowd funding campaigns.

Meanwhile, if you're looking to get yourself booked on talk radio shows
to promote your project and your crowd funding campaign, you can contact
program producers at radio stations that cater to your target audience, or
you can run a paid ad in the *Radio and Television Interview Report* (www
.rtir.com), which is a monthly publication that gets mailed to thousands of
talk radio show producers, and serves as a sourcebook for talk show guest
ideas and recommendations.

As you learned from the previous chapter, running a public relations campaign allows you to receive free media coverage and potentially boost awareness about your project, campaign, and/or company. The drawback is that you, as the project creator, don't control when your media coverage will run, and you don't have control over the exact message that's published. Journalists are free to write or say whatever they want about your project.

However, if you carefully craft your press releases and the content within your press kit, provide quality images, and then target media professionals whose audience is similar to your own target audience, you'll discover that journalists will often rely heavily on your press materials when creating their coverage. Thus, your core messaging could be reproduced word-for-word, or at the very least, the main concepts behind your core messaging will be conveyed within the editorial coverage you receive.

When dealing with the media, it's important to understand that every media outlet runs on a lead time and works under specific, nonchangeable deadlines. Become familiar with the schedule of your targeted media outlets prior to making contact, and then plan your PR campaign accordingly.

It's also important to understand that journalists working under tight deadlines have a job to do, and are constantly being approached by people, companies, and organization seeking free publicity. Thus, it's important to cater to the needs of journalists you work with and avoid harassing them.

CONSIDER MEETING POTENTIAL BACKERS IN PERSON

In addition to the other methods discussed within this chapter, another often successful approach for attracting higher level or more generous backers is to plan meet ups, parties, and/or live (or web-based) seminars, and invite people to informal presentations where you share details about your project in person. This method tends to work best if your target audience lives within a certain geographic area. Otherwise, to do this effectively will require a lot of travel and planning on your part.

However, if you can get groups of 25, 50, or several hundred people from your target audience into a room, and then spend 30 to 60 minutes telling them all about your project and answering their questions, you should be able to convince a large percentage of these people to back your project right on the spot. After all, instead of using a short promotional video, you're taking the opportunity to interact with people on a personal level for an extended amount of time, and you're giving those people the opportunity to interact with you, get their questions answered, and have their concerns addressed.

If you opt to pursue this in-person approach to soliciting backers, seriously consider having at least some of the rewards you're offering in conjunction with your campaign on hand to present to backers on the spot as a thank-you for their support. At the very least, offer a limited edition T-shirt or something extra for attending your seminar. This creates a sense of immediate gratification and helps to boost the loyalty of those new backers.

Interacting with Your Backers Using a Blog

Much of this book has focused on preparing for and then managing a reward-based crowd funding campaign. As your campaign gets underway, hopefully you'll attract a large number of backers and supporters. It then becomes your added responsibility to stay in touch with these people throughout the rest of your campaign and to keep that dialog going once the campaign ends.

Some of this ongoing communication should be via email. For example, as soon as people become backers, they should receive a personalized email thanking them for their support. The call to action within this thank-you email should be to get the backers to share details about your project and campaign with their own social networks. Word-of-mouth promotion is highly effective, especially when someone is sharing details about something in the form of an endorsement with their friends.

Later, when it is time to ship out rewards and/or products related to your campaign, another personalized email should be sent to each backer, telling how and when to expect the reward. If possible, include shipment tracking details.

If you're using Kickstarter to host your campaign, in addition to publishing updates on your campaign's web page that are accessible by the general public, all backers, or specific groups of backers, you also have the option to send a direct message (instead of a traditional email) to one or more backers at a time. To send a specific backer a direct message, access your list of backers from the Creator Tools sidebar. Select a backer, and then click on the Send Message link. Alternatively, you can click on the Message All option to send a direct message to all of your current backers. Similar functionality is also available on most other crowd funding platforms.

Beyond the individualized communications with your backers, you'll want to address this group as a whole on a regular basis, keeping them up-to-date on the campaign's progress, as you achieve various milestones and successes. You'll also want to keep your backers in the loop as you release details about stretch goals during your campaign, if applicable. Once the campaign draws to a close and work begins on the actual project, you'll want to keep your backers informed every step along the way.

While direct messages can be used to share important information directly with backers at least once per week, you'll also find it useful to publish some type of blog that offers a behind-the-scenes look at your project and its crowd funding campaign. A blog is basically an online diary that's available via the Internet either to the general public or to a select group of invited individuals. The blog itself is composed of a series of individual blog posts, which are displayed in chronological order (with the newest entries first) based on the time and date each is published. A blog entry can include text, photos, video clips, links to a website or online articles, and/or other multimedia content.

When it comes to creating and populating a blog with content, you have a variety of options. Virtually all of the crowd funding platforms allow you to publish updates about your project and campaign (using a blog-style format) directly on your crowd funding campaign's web page. These updates can then be read by your backers and by anyone else who is curious about your project and its current status.

In addition to the updates you can publish directly on the crowd funding platform as part of your campaign's web page, many project creators opt to create a stand-alone blog. This can be done for free, using a social media service, such as Facebook or Tumblr, or it can be done using a blog creation and hosting platform, such as WordPress.com or Blogger.com. The benefit to using a stand-alone blogging service is that you can select a professionally designed template for your blog, customize that template, add widgets to add more functionality, and then compose your content using a set of tools that are available for free from the blogging service.

Another very useful aspect of running a stand-alone blog using Word Press.com, for example, is that each new blog entry immediately becomes searchable on the popular search engines, including Google. Thus, by creating a keyword-intensive title for each entry, and then populating each entry with appropriate keywords, tags, and phrases, details about your campaign are more apt to pop up in someone's search engine results, which can lead to generating new traffic on your campaign's web page.

This strategy also works when you publish new videos on YouTube. Any video content you create in conjunction with your crowd funding campaign or project should be published on your own YouTube channel, which you can create for free. YouTube has become the second most popular Internet search engine in the world after Google. When you publish a new video on YouTube, it becomes searchable both on YouTube and other popular search engines.

Knowing this, it makes a lot of sense to repurpose your project's promotional video so it can be a stand-alone YouTube video that drives interested viewers to your campaign's web page. In addition, future videos or video clips you publish as updates for your backers or as part of your blog posts should also be published separately on YouTube (on your branded YouTube channel) to increase the free search-related traffic your project and campaign will benefit from.

No website design skills or programming knowledge are required to create and manage a professional-looking blog or YouTube channel. When you use a blogging service, or when you create a channel on YouTube, you have the ability to customize its appearance and layout using your existing logo and branding.

Plus, the popular blogging services, such as WordPress.com and Blogger .com, all support widgets, which are mini programs that can add specialized features and functionality to a blog. Adding a widget to a blog is simply a matter of copying and pasting specific widget content into your blog's template. Meanwhile, YouTube allows you to incorporate links within your videos, as well as make those links part of a video's "About" description.

Both stand-alone blogs and YouTube channels can include Share buttons, which make it easier for readers or viewers to instantly share a link to the blog (or a specific blog entry or video) with their social networks.

If you, your company, or your organization already maintains its own website, you can easily incorporate a blog into that website. To do this, instead of using the tools offered by WordPress.com, for example, you'd use a separate set of free blogging tools offered by WordPress.org that get installed onto your web page's server. This approach is a bit more complicated to set up initially, but it offers more creative control over the blog and integration with your existing online presence.

Whether you publish updates on your campaign's crowd funding web page or in a blog, you can also reach out to your backers via Twitter or Facebook and announce when each update is published. To maintain the maximum level of engagement with your backers, with the least amount of time-consuming one-on-one interaction, publishing at least one new blog entry per week is advisable. You should start posting updates as soon as the campaign begins and continue at least until the project is complete and perhaps on an ongoing basis thereafter, depending on the scope of your project and the relationship you want to maintain with your backers.

ESTABLISH A STAND-ALONE BLOG

A stand-alone blog, created using a blogging service, such as WordPress.com or Blogger.com, can be created in a matter of minutes for free. You can then invest as much time as you want customizing the appearance of the blog, populating it with original content on an ongoing basis, and promoting it.

When you use a blog hosting service such as WordPress.com or Blogger .com, the blog you create is stored and hosted on a remote server operated by the blog service. All of the tools needed to create the blog, manage the blog, and create and publish new blog posts are made available online, and can be accessed using any web browser. Many of the blogging services also offer proprietary apps for popular smartphones and tablets, so you can create blog content and manage your blog from virtually anywhere.

To create a new blog, go to a blogging service's website, such as WordPress .com or Blogger.com, and click on the Get Started button. Right on its home page, WordPress.com offers a tutorial video, plus a Discover WordPress option, which allows you to quickly learn more about this popular blogging platform.

Once you opt to create a new blog, you'll be prompted to create a title for your blog and provide additional details about it, including a short description, and a list of keywords that describe it. The blog will then be assigned its own URL (website address). This will most likely be a rather long URL. To keep things simple for your backers, consider registering a short and easy-to-remember domain name (using a domain registrar, such as GoDaddy.com), and then use a free domain forwarding feature to automatically forward your custom domain name to the blog's original URL.

Part of the initial blog creation process includes selecting a template or theme for your blog. This is a professionally designed layout, which ultimately determines the appearance of your blog. Most templates/themes can be fully customized, so you can incorporate your own color scheme, fonts, and branding. The majority of popular blogging services offer vast libraries of templates/themes to choose from. Some are offered for free, while a small, one-time licensing fee applies to others.

You only need one theme or template per blog, but it's important to choose the right one to help you achieve your goals. There are also many third-party WordPress-compatible template/theme services that you can access on the Internet to increase your selection of potential templates. TemplateMonster (www.templatemonster.com) offers more than 1,800

WordPress-compatible, premium (fee-based) themes and templates to choose from. Elegant Themes (www.elegantthemes.com) also offers a collection of themes starting at $39.00 each, and ThemeFuse (http://themefuse .com) offers an extensive premium theme selection. Using any search engine, use the search phrase "WordPress themes" to find more.

Part of the theme customization process can include adding widgets to your blog template. There are thousands of widgets to choose from that allow you to add individual and customizable features to your blog, such as the ability to conduct polls, display your Twitter feed, or present an animated slideshow of images. First select a theme that's most appropriate for your project and target audience, and then select widgets that add features and functions you and your backers and supporters will appreciate.

Once the blog is created, the blogging service offers easy ways to compose and format posts using what looks like a word processor that's accessible from a web browser (or from a smartphone/tablet app). So, if you can surf the web and do basic word processing, you have the skills needed to become a blogger.

To speed up the process of creating a professional-looking blog, consider hiring a freelancer who is a WordPress expert and who can help you select a theme and customize it to meet your needs, typically within a few hours. Much of the learning curve associated with becoming a blogger relates to setting up and creating the initial blog. Once this step is done, creating and publishing posts is very easy. eLance.com (www.elance.com) is an excellent resource for finding WordPress or Blogger.com experts, whom you can hire for a flat-fee or on a per-hour basis to help you quickly establish your project's stand-alone blog.

Creating your own YouTube channel is also very easy. To do this, visit www.youtube.com and click on the Sign In button. You can create an account for free from scratch or use an existing Google account to create a YouTube channel. Once you've customized the main channel page, you can populate it with videos as often as you'd like. Your YouTube channel page will have its own URL, as will each of your individual videos. To start learning about how to create and manage a YouTube channel, visit www .youtube.com/yt/creators/index.html.

HOW TO PUBLISH UPDATES TO YOUR CROWD FUNDING CAMPAIGN'S WEB PAGE

When you use Kickstarter to host your crowd funding campaign, you can post updates exclusively for your backers or for the general public. To do this, from the Creator Tools sidebar (displayed on the left on your project page), click on the Post an Update option. After you compose an update, you can select who will be able to see it. Your options include all backers, select-tier backers (people who have committed to a specific level of support to your project), or the public.

Making updates available only to your backers creates a sense of exclusivity. You are sharing insider information with the elite group of people who have chosen to help support your project. When people become backers, even if they commit at the lowest funding level, they can automatically receive access to your For Backers Only updates.

Using this update tool is highly recommended, and you'll find similar functionality offered by virtually all of the crowd funding platforms. If you opt to also manage a blog, you can either publish separate updates on your campaign's web page, or publish updates on the campaign's web page first and then share that content with the general public via your independent blog a week or two later. Another option is to create your own stand-alone blog that is accessible only by your backers.

Your options for composing and formatting updates on Kickstarter and other platforms are more limited than what's possible using a stand-alone blogging service, but they do allow you to easily share quick tidbits of information with your backers throughout your campaign and after its conclusion.

Project updates published on the crowd funding platform can be used to thank backers, share progress reports, and post content in the form of text, photos, or video clips. Use updates as a way to quickly share timely information with your backers and to celebrate successes.

INFORMATION TO SHARE WITH YOUR BACKERS

Coming up with informative and entertaining weekly content for your blog and/or project updates may at first seem like a daunting task, but when you think about all of the potential types of information and content you can share with your backers, it becomes more a matter of deciding what information to share and when. Keep in mind, each update can be just a few sentences long, and may be accompanied by one or more applicable photos or video clips. You don't need to compose pages upon pages of fresh content each week.

In fact, when you remember that your backers are busy and have very short attention spans, you'll want to focus on keeping your blog posts and updates as short as possible, while making sure the content is always relevant and of interest to your backers.

Here are a few suggestions about what you can include in updates for your backers and the approach each update should take:

- Share a new piece of information, such as when your campaign or project reaches a milestone, the creation of a stretch goal, or details about an important new person joining your project's team.
- Thank your backers for their support and participation, and share details about what else they can do to help keep your project moving toward completion.
- Maintain your backers' excitement for your project. One way to do this is to share links to articles about your project that appear in the media or to share other positive information, such as how close you are to reaching your funding goal, or how many preorders you've received within the past week.
- Put a positive spin on whatever developments you have to share. Projects almost always experience some type of hiccup. Details about delays or problems should be shared with your backers, but anytime you share negative information, you also want to share something positive or put a positive spin on the negative information. For example, explain exactly what you're doing to address the problem and how those actions will benefit the project. Talk about what you learned from a mistake and the positive impact that knowledge will have. Focus on how long it will take to fix and when everything will be back on track.
- Encourage some type of additional engagement. For example, as the project creator, you can seek out feedback or suggestions, challenge people to answer trivia questions, or have backers participate in quick polls or surveys that are related to the creation of stretch goals and/or the development of your actual project.
- Include some type of call to action (which will change, based on where you are in your campaign or the project's development cycle).
- Share more details about how your project will impact the lives of your backers. For example, if your project is product-related, talk about innovative features of the product, or ways it can be used to save time, save money, enhance someone's life, or to solve a problem. Discuss aspects of the product or project that people might not have otherwise considered.
- Introduce them to members of your project's team using interviews, behind-the-scenes photos, and other content that will help your backers get to know who is involved in the creation of your project and what their areas of expertise are. Humanize your project's team, so backers get to know your team members as people.

When communicating with your backers, you always want to take an approach that's targeted to your audience, and at the same time, keep all of your messaging and branding consistent. Think about why your backers opted to support your project to begin with, and provide them with an ongoing flow of information that capitalizes on those positive thoughts or emotions. As the project creator, you're caught up in the day to day developments pertaining to the project. Take the time to put yourself in your backers' shoes; think about what they'd like to know, and provide that information in an entertaining and concise way.

Use your ongoing communications with your backers to further personalize your project. Offer a behind-the-scenes look at the project itself, as well as the project's creators. This can be done with candid photos, first-person diary entries, and by sharing details about major events that occur that allow the project to move forward. Provide anecdotes and more detail about the origin of the project, and where you see it going in the future.

Once again, take a look at other successful campaigns and see how those project creators utilized updates and blog entries to stay in contact with their backers. Focus on extremely successful campaigns, as well as campaigns that got fully funded but that ran into problems during the project's creation or development process. Use these examples to help you brainstorm ways to effectively interact with your own backers when problems arise or unexpected delays are experienced.

USE UPDATES AND BLOG POSTS TO GENERATE HYPE FOR STRETCH GOALS AND REFUEL BACKER SUPPORT

You already know that stretch goals can and should be used if your reward-based crowd funding campaign is going well in terms of reaching its funding goal, but you still have plenty of time before the campaign comes to an end. Or, in some cases, if the campaign has officially ended, there's still a lot of support and momentum among new backers.

There are several ways you can use updates and blog entries to support stretch goals within a campaign, including:

- If you determine your campaign could benefit from one or more stretch goals, ask your backers to participate in a poll and vote between three potential stretch goal options they'd most like to see.
- Once you've selected a stretch goal, inform your backers about it and encourage them to back your project with more financial support in order to acquire the new reward that's associated with the stretch goal.

Focus on the benefits or rewards that backers will receive if the new stretch goal is met.

- Encourage your backers to once again share details about your campaign with their own social networks to help ensure the new stretch goal is met. Perhaps this time, you can encourage your backers to share details about your campaign with their friends via email, as opposed to a Facebook post or tweet. If you take this approach, consider providing backers with a draft of an email they can easily copy and send to their friends.

The more active you are in developing awesome stretch goals and rallying your existing backers around them, the more money your crowd funding campaign will raise above and beyond the campaign's initial funding goal. Updates are the best way to get existing backers excited about stretch goals.

KEEP THE LINE OF COMMUNICATION OPEN

Regardless of how you plan to stay in touch with your backers throughout the length of your campaign and beyond, make sure it's part of your plan to maintain a consistent and open line of communication with the people who have chosen to financially support your project. Use the tools available to you to solicit questions and comments, allow backers to voice their concerns, and to share a continuous flow of information. As a project creator, you should be vocal, consistent, forthcoming, and totally honest with your backers at all times. Of course, if you need to share negative information, put a positive spin on it. You'll find that your backers will be much more supportive and understanding when problems arise if you're proactive about sharing information.

If you're ever at a loss about what information to share, reach out to your backers and ask them what they want to know. Invite them to post questions for the project's creator, and then publish answers to those questions on your blog or in campaign web page updates.

If you maintain a positive relationship with your backers, they'll be more apt to help you promote your current campaign and help your project succeed. They may even opt to support your campaign with more money in exchange for a better reward, for example. If you launch additional crowd funding campaigns for new projects in the future, this group of original project backers will most likely be among your biggest supporters for those future endeavors.

Communicating with your backers should be one of your priorities as a project creator, not something that can be ignored or put on the back burner because you're too busy or caught up in other details related to your project. Remember, your backers are the people who have made your project possible from a financial standpoint. At the very least, you owe it to them to continuously communicate with them by posting updates or blog entries. Unfortunately, this is one area where many project creators fail, and this leads to backers having regrets about their decision to support projects.

CHAPTER 10

Getting the Help You Need

In This Chapter

- Pinpoint the help you may need to plan and manage your reward-based crowd funding campaign.
- Learn where to find skilled and experienced people to help you.
- Identify pitfalls to avoid when hiring freelancers and specialists.

By now, you should fully understand that creating and managing a successful reward-based crowd funding campaign is no small undertaking, and that to reach or exceed your funding goal, you are going to need to master a wide range of different skills, successfully juggle a variety of responsibilities, utilize the resources at your disposal in the best possible way, and avoid taking any shortcuts.

If your funding goal is $10,000 or less, seriously consider handling most or all of the tasks associated with creating and managing your crowd funding campaign yourself or dividing up the responsibilities among people already on your team. Chances are, it won't be within your budget to hire freelancers or pay experts to assist you in any meaningful ways. However, a lack of budget should not stop you from seeking out people willing to help you for free or at least wiling to offer their advice related to their area of expertise.

The free help you need could come from friends and family, volunteer organizations such as SCORE (www.score.org), or by working with college interns, for example.

For projects with a funding goal above $10,000, your potential backers and supporters are probably going to expect more from your campaign than a do-it-yourself, grassroots effort, especially when it comes to things like the production quality of your campaign's promotional video, the quality of your digital photography (if applicable), and the quality of writing that's showcased throughout the campaign's web page.

To achieve this higher level of overall quality and professionalism, and to save yourself valuable time, you might consider hiring experienced free-lancers and experts to handle various tasks associated with the planning and managing of your campaign. Before hiring specific people to handle various responsibilities, think about the skills and time commitment involved to handle each specific task. Then ask yourself if you have the experience, knowledge, and wherewithal to handle that task yourself successfully.

Next, consider the value of your time. Determine if it makes more sense for you to hire someone who is an expert at performing the task at hand, paying them to do so, and ensuring it gets done properly versus you taking the time to learn how to handle the task yourself, running the risk of doing just an average job, and utilizing some of your time that you could otherwise spend performing tasks that you know you can do well and that require your attention. Consider doing a basic cost-benefit analysis when considering if you should handle a task yourself or hire an expert to help you.

EIGHT QUICK TIPS FOR HIRING FREELANCERS

Regardless of the type of freelancer you're looking to hire, these eight tips will help you hire and ultimately put your trust in the right person for the task(s) at hand:

1. Determine exactly the type of help you need from each freelancer. What expertise should they have, and exactly what tasks will they be handling for you? When working with a freelancer, it is essential that you are able to communicate exactly what work needs to be done and what your expectations are. Miscommunication or misunderstandings will result in work that does not meet your needs or quality standards.
2. Put someone in charge of managing each freelancer. Someone from your core team, such as one of the project creators, should be responsible for working with and overseeing the work being done by freelancers, con-tractors, and/or consultants.
3. Make sure you do your due diligence before hiring freelancers. Look at their portfolio of past work, check their references, talk to past clients, and if available, read reviews from past clients. If the freelancer claims to have a specialized education or license or an affiliation with a profes-sional association/organization, check this out and confirm it.
4. If you are hiring freelancers who will work remotely, be conscious of language barriers and time differences that can impact your ability to

communicate with them. It may be cheaper to hire people from overseas, but you typically wind up getting what you pay for. If you're not careful, miscommunications between your team and freelancers working remotely will occur frequently and can lead to costly mistakes and delays.

5. Put together a contact in writing before any work gets underway. The contract should be dated and signed and include a detailed description of the work to be done, the amount to be paid, payment terms, and a clear deadline for the work to be completed. Negotiate the payment terms. Some freelancers require a portion of their payment at the 50 percent completion milestone; others will accept payment in full at the 100 percent completion point. Avoid paying anything up front. The contract should specify the steps that will be taken if the freelancer's work does not meet expectations or the freelancer fails to meet his obligations, responsibilities, or deadlines.

6. Freelancers are considered independent contractors. Know the local and state laws where you are based to determine if there are any rules you need to follow in regard to hiring or paying these people.

7. Maintain your relationships with the freelancers you hire who work out well. You are typically better off using the same person again when more work of a similar nature needs to be done.

8. Acquire ownership of the work that is completed on your behalf. It should be made clear and in writing that you, as the project creator, own the exclusive rights to all work completed by the freelancer. This includes ownership of copyrights for content, artwork, programming, or anything else that's created on your behalf. Make clear that all work you commission that involves the creation of something must be 100 percent original and not violate any copyrights, patents, intellectual property rights, or trademarks owned by third parties.

AGREE TO TERMS BEFORE HIRING A FREELANCER, CONSULTANT, OR EXPERT

There are some tasks related to creating and managing a reward-based crowd funding campaign that require skills that experts literally spend years perfecting. Sure, you can learn to handle these tasks yourself, but based on what you're trying to achieve and whether you have the budget, it may make more sense to hire someone to help with these tasks and ensure they get done right the first time.

Hiring people to assist with these tasks can be done on a freelance basis, in which you pay an expert either a flat fee for accomplishing a specific task, or you pay them by the hour. In general, you are better off negotiating a flat fee per task and agreeing to the terms with the freelancer in advance.

All details and expectations related to the task(s) to be done by a freelancer should also be spelled out and agreed to by both parties. For example, if you hire a freelance graphic designer to create a logo for your project, company, or organization, the agreement should spell out that the artist will create at least five different logo concepts, allow you to select one, and then include at least three rounds of revisions and fine-tuning, before the project is completed. For any additional work beyond what's agreed to, the contract should note that the freelancer will be paid extra, based on a prenegotiated hourly rate.

If you were to hire two people who posses a specific area of expertise to handle the same task, you'll quickly discover that while they may wind up with the same end result, their work process and how long it takes them to complete a task will vary greatly. This is why paying a freelancer, consultant, or expert a flat-fee per task makes more sense than paying by the hour.

The alternative is to hire someone on a retainer basis. This may be required if you hire a full-service online marketing company, law firm, accounting firm, public relations firm, advertising agency, or some type of consulting firm to assist you. This typically costs a lot more than working with individual freelancers and should be reserved for campaigns with a high funding goal and for project creators willing to invest a significant amount of money into planning and managing a more elaborate campaign.

CROWD FUNDING-RELATED TASKS WHERE FREELANCERS AND EXPERTS CAN BE USEFUL

As with most other things, the type of experts you may want or need to hire to help your campaign will vary greatly, based on the scope of the overall project, your budget, and your own areas of expertise. Even if you cannot afford to hire a full-service agency or freelance experts to help you with the various tasks, it still makes sense to develop a plan for each aspect of your overall crowd funding campaign and then to hire an expert for just an hour or two to review your plan and offer suggestions. This can help you avoid costly and time-consuming mistakes or miscalculations and only requires a small amount of a freelancer's time.

Some of the experts you might consider hiring include:

- **Crowd funding experts**. These are people who truly understand reward-based crowd funding. They've helped to create and manage many successfully funded campaigns in the past and stay up-to-date on the latest trends related to crowd funding. These people know how to populate a crowd funding campaign's website with appropriate content, reach out to potential backers, develop rewards that backers will find appealing, and make sure that all of the different components related to a campaign are handled correctly and in a timely manner. These experts can either review a plan you've already established, help you create an overall plan for your campaign from scratch, or oversee and handle many of the day-to-day activities associated with managing a successful campaign by working continuously on your behalf and under your supervision.

- **Finance expert (accountant or bookkeeper).** As you begin work on your crowd funding campaign, it's important that your money is properly allocated and spent where it will do the most good. It's equally important that right from the start, you put the proper bookkeeping infrastructure in place to manage the financial component of your campaign and project. When it comes to preparing a budget for your project and calculating your funding goal, this is something that can best be handled by someone who has a strong financial background. As you now know, one of the biggest mistakes project creators make is miscalculating their campaign budget and/or overall project budget, which ultimately can lead to significant problems or total failure. If you're not good at creating budgets, financial projections, managing money, or bookkeeping, seek out the help you need right at the start.

- **Graphic artist.** Whether you need logos created, illustrations to showcase what your completed project might look like, a professional design for a website or blog, or help creating a visual image for your project, company, or brand, these are tasks a talented graphic artist can help with.

- **Lawyer.** Acquiring legal advice is essential if you're pursuing an equity-based crowd funding campaign, but for a reward-based campaign a lawyer can also help you establish your business as a legal entity, secure copyrights and patents, draft binding contracts, and protect your legal interests related to your project.

- **Online advertising specialist.** Again, if you need to reach out to a target audience to attract potential backers beyond your own existing network, utilizing online ads on Facebook, as well as search marketing ads, can be a cost-effective tool. While anyone can create a campaign, it takes experience to fine-tune an online advertising campaign so that you can spend the least amount of money and drive as much traffic to your campaign's web page as possible. An online advertising specialist can assist with this. The money you would spend on an ineffective ad campaign created by an amateur could easily be saved by hiring an online advertising expert who knows how to create attention-getting copy and compile the right keywords, understands the nuances of the different advertising services like Facebook and Google AdWords, and knows how to use traffic analysis tools like Google Analytics to get the most out of an online ad campaign.

- **Photographer.** In addition to producing a promotional video, you may opt to use digital photographs of people, products, prototypes, or other aspects of your project in order to effectively tell your story. These photos should be of professional quality: in focus, well-lit, and showcasing as much detail as possible. Thus, hiring an accomplished photographer with high-end equipment will be beneficial.

- **Professional writer/editor.** Someone who specializes in creating up-beat promotional copy can help you compose all of the text needed for your crowd funding campaign's web page, your project's blog, and the marketing materials and other text-based communications that will play a huge role in attracting and securing backers for your project. If you are not an eloquent writer, this is one area where a freelancer can make a huge positive impact on the professional image your campaign conveys. Keep in mind, spelling mistakes, punctuation errors, and/or the misuse of words are not acceptable in any text that appears on your campaign's web page or in any communication between you and your backers.

- **Public relations specialist.** The impact that a well-orchestrated public relations campaign can have on your project in terms of reaching its funding goal cannot be overstated, especially if you'll need to reach backers beyond your inner circle and core group of friends, family, fans, and followers. Being able to effectively reach out to targeted media with well-written press materials is important, and hiring someone with established media contacts and the ability to cater to the needs of the media will be a huge asset to your project. The more positive media and blog coverage you can get for your project before and during your crowd funding campaign, the better.

- **Social media expert.** Developing a strong presence on social media services and staying active on these services is essential for building a dedicated network composed of potential backers. However, to manage a social media presence on Facebook, Twitter, and other services requires time—and if you want to attract a highly targeted audience—a certain level of expertise. You can either hire someone to help you establish and brand your social media presence and then manage it yourself on a day-to-day basis, or hire an expert or online marketing agency to handle this entire component of your campaign for you. This same person or agency can also help you create and manage a project-oriented blog and/or YouTube channel and make sure everything you do online is synergistic.

- **Videographer.** The promotional video that serves as the centerpiece of your reward-based crowd funding campaign needs to offer production quality and content that will appeal to your target audience. Working with an entire video crew is a worthwhile, but costly, investment. Working with an experienced videographer who can help you shoot and edit your video will be less expensive and still help to ensure that you pack as much quality content into your one- to three-minute video as possible.

WHERE TO FIND EXPERTS TO HIRE

One of the tricks to hiring the right experts to help you with various aspects of your reward-based crowd funding campaign is to find people with related experience handling the tasks that need to be done. For this reason, even if you hire an expert to handle one or more aspects of your campaign, as the project creator, you'll still need to work with that person and oversee her work, since you will know and understand the scope of your project and your target audience better than whomever you hire. As you are seeking out people to work with, take time to interview them. Then, consider testing them out by hiring them to handle a small task. See if they're a good match for you and your project before expanding their role and spending a significant portion of your budget on hiring them.

Ideally, you want to hire people who come highly recommended by people you know and trust. If this isn't possible, take a look at the expert's portfolio of past work, speak with a few of his past clients, and spend the time to find people who you believe will be a perfect match for your project.

To find these people, perform a search using your favorite search engine. You can also run "help wanted" ads online (using Craigslist.com or another service), and/or run ads in traditional print publications (i.e., local newspapers and/or industry-specific trade publications). Yet another option is to use an online service such as eLance.com (www.elance.com).

eLance.com, Guru.com (www.guru.com), or Freelancer.com (www .freelancer.com), and many services like them help people, companies, and organizations find freelancers with very specialized skills. Odesk (www .odesk.com) is another example of a service that can be used for finding web development, software development, writing, design and multimedia, sales, and advertising and marketing specialists.

With eLance, you publish a help wanted ad that describes exactly what you're looking for, the scope of the project or work that needs to be done, and a budget. Once this is published, within a very short time you'll receive bids from experts who are willing to do the work. As you receive each bid, you can review that freelancer's online portfolio and read reviews from past clients. You can also communicate with the freelancer through the eLance service to get questions answered and iron out details.

eLance.com works with freelancers from many different fields. However, to find specific types of freelancers, such as accountants/bookkeepers, graphic artists, web page designers, photographers, videographers, and so forth, there are similar services that cater only to promoting freelancers with specialized skill sets. For example, to find a freelance accountant or financial expert, you can use the iHireAccounting service (www.ihireaccounting.com). You can find similar specialized freelance services using any popular search engine.

Another useful resource for finding experts is the LinkedIn social networking service (www.linkedin.com). Unlike Facebook, for example, LinkedIn is targeted specifically to entrepreneurs, small business operators, and business executives. In addition to offering an online directory, the service offers an open forum for people to post very specific, work-related questions and have experts answer them for free. LinkedIn focuses on networking and developing business-to-business relationships, so if you're looking for someone with a specific area of expertise in your immediate geographic area or someone you can work with remotely, chances are you'll be able to find the right person using this service.

Professional associations or industry-specific organizations are another resource for finding experts in their field to hire as consultants or freelancers. Many of these groups offer online-based referral services. For example, if you need to hire a lawyer with a specific area of expertise in your immediate area, contact your state's bar association.

Another option is to contact a local college or university and establish an internship program. Figure out in what areas you need help, and then look for paid or unpaid interns that possess the skills you need. College interns earn college credit for their work and are able to gain real-world work experience and/or expand their portfolios. Interns sometimes require more supervision or guidance, but they do possess knowledge and skills that could be useful, and they're often willing to work hard for little or no pay.

As a project creator, you're probably on a tight budget. Be sure to figure out in advance what tasks you can handle yourself, and then seek out only the experts you need to round out your skill set and available resources. Bring the necessary people aboard before your crowd funding campaign launches, so there's ample time for the freelancers to learn about your project, build a positive working relationship with you, and ultimately help you reach out to your target audience in the best ways possible. The more time you have to accomplish this, the better, so plan accordingly.

You've Reached Your Funding Goal—Now What?

In This Chapter

- Learn how to collect the money you've raised.
- Send out rewards to your backers.
- Get your funded project underway.
- What to do if your campaign fails to reach its funding goal.

Your reward-based crowd funding campaign will come to an end after a predefined number of days. Hopefully, you will have reached your funding goal, or better yet, exceeded your goal by perhaps utilizing one or more stretch goals. Then, depending on which crowd funding platform you used, once the funding goal is met and your campaign ends, the funds you've raised will soon be transferred to your bank account (minus the commission charged by the crowd funding platform and the fees associated with the third-party payment processing company). Now, you'll be ready to get your project underway.

If you used a crowd funding platform that doesn't use an all-or-nothing approach to dispersing funds raised, after your campaign ends you're entitled to receive whatever funds were collected during your campaign, whether or not its funding goal was met. In fact, some platforms forward funds to you as they're received. If your funding goal is not met with one of these platforms, you'll typically wind up paying a higher commission to the crowd funding platform and higher fees to the payment processing company, but you'll still receive some of funds you were hoping for.

Whether or not your project was fully funded, if you accept any funds, you're responsible for sending out the promised rewards to the backers who supported your campaign, so have a plan in place to accomplish this.

Kickstarter and many similar reward-based crowd funding platforms have an all-or-nothing funding model in place, so to receive any money as a project creator, your campaign's funding goal must be met. Then, once the campaign ends, the real work begins. It's now your responsibility to get your project underway and make it a reality.

When you read the fine print associated with many crowd funding campaigns, you'll see there's up to a 14-day window between the time your campaign ends and when funds are ready to be deposited into your bank account. Once the funds transfer is initiated, it could take an additional three to five business days for the money to become accessible in your account, so plan accordingly.

In situations where your crowd funding platform provider waits until the end of your successful campaign to process the credit/debit cards from all of your backers at once, you need to plan for the fact that, for whatever reason, some of your funds will be uncollectible. For example, some of your backers' credit cards may be declined. Thus, you'll need to wait until all of the transactions have been processed and the commissions and payment processing fees have been deducted before you'll know exactly how much money you'll be receiving.

Depending on the types of rewards you promised your backers, any rewards that can be sent out upon the completion of the campaign should be shipped as quickly as possible. You'll be expected to provide an expected delivery date to your backers. If the rewards depend on your project being completed, you'll need to begin this pursuit, and as soon as you've achieved your project's goals, then immediately ship the promised rewards.

SHIPPING REWARDS TO BACKERS

By the time some campaigns end, they've attracted hundreds or even thousands of individual backers, who are now anxiously waiting for their reward(s) to be shipped. This alone can be a daunting task for project creators. To handle this in the most efficient way possible, collect each backer's shipping details from your crowd funding platform and sort them based on the reward(s) they're entitled to receive.

If you're using Kickstarter, for example, you can create a short survey for your backers in order to gather their shipping addresses and the other pertinent information you'll need in order to process and ship their reward(s), such as their T-shirt size or any special inscription they want added to their autographed photo, CD cover, or poster, for example. The information you'll need to collect will depend on the types of rewards you've offered. Kickstarter offers a survey tool as part of its Creator Tools sidebar to accomplish this task.

Now, figure out how many packages you need to ship out for each type of reward that was promised, and start gathering the rewards themselves and the required shipping materials. Determine the exact size and weight for each reward package, and figure out the most cost-effective way to ship these packages using a method that includes package tracking, insurance, and/or signature confirmation, depending on your needs. At the very least, you need to be able to track the packages you ship.

Based on the size and weight of the package, and how many similar packages you need to ship at once, you may discover it makes the most sense to use a flat-rate Priority Mail envelope or box from the U.S. Postal Service. When you choose this option, the envelope or box is supplied for free, and whatever fits within that package can be shipped for a flat rate. To make things even easier, you can set up your computer to be able to generate postage and shipping labels from your home or office and then simply drop off the packages at the post office when they're ready to ship (or arrange for a free pickup).

To learn more about using flat-rate Priority Shipping from the U.S. Postal Service, visit www.usps.com/business/business-solutions.htm. To be able to purchase and create postage stamps from your computer, sign up for a service like Endicia (www.endicia.com).

Alternatively, based on your shipping requirements and the quantity of packages you'll be shipping, you may discover it's more affordable and efficient to use FedEx or FedEx Ground (www.fedex.com) or UPS (www.ups.com), to ship rewards to your backers. Depending on the option you choose, shipping boxes and/or labels may or may not be provided for free.

Once you know how many similar reward packages you need to ship for each reward category, acquire all of the shipping materials you'll need, including boxes, packing tape, package stuffing (such as bubble wrap), shipping labels, and invoices. Keep in mind, the cost for these materials, as well as the postage or shipping charges, are your responsibility and will come out of the money you've raised from your campaign.

You'll discover that these charges can add up quickly, especially when it comes to shipping packages overseas. Let's take a look at one possible scenario. If you have 2,000 reward packages to ship out domestically, and you're able to use a medium flat-rate shipping box from the U.S. Postal Service, as of early 2014, the flat-rate shipping charge was $12.34 per box, plus added fees for package tracking, signature confirmation, and/or insurance. Thus, in postage charges alone (without any the extra fees for added services), you're looking at an expense of $24,680.

If you need to acquire all of your own shipping boxes, as well as additional shipping materials, be sure to purchase everything wholesale from a shipping supply company, such as Uline (www.uline.com) or PackingSupplies .com (www.packagingsupplies.com), in order to save money.

After figuring out the exact size and weight for each category of rewards you'll be sending out, do your research and figure out the most efficient and lowest-cost shipping option. For shipping small quantities of packages, UPS or FedEx, for example, may be more expensive than the U.S. Postal Service. However, if you need to ship hundreds or thousands of similar packages, all of the shipping companies offer significant corporate discounts.

Between the campaign management tools offered by your crowd funding platform and your own resources, try to automate as much of the reward fulfillment process as possible, and keep detailed records. For example, collect as much information as you'll need from your backers, and then retain records about when and how their reward(s) were shipped.

Various software packages are available for managing databases that link directly with FedEx, UPS, and/or the U.S. Postal Service, so you can generate labels, invoices, and other necessities, track packages, and keep all of the details pertaining to each backer in one place. Once your crowd funding campaign ends, dedicate your efforts to shipping all of the rewards as quickly as possible, and then start focusing on your actual project. Obviously, if the reward(s) you've promised are based on the completion of your project, get right to work on the project.

As soon as your campaign comes to an end, send out a personalized email or direct message to each of your backers, once again thanking them for their support. This email should include either a survey to request the additional information you require or make reference to a survey that will soon follow. The email should also outline your timeline for what happens next in terms of the progression of your project. Discuss exactly when your backers can expect to receive their rewards and when work on your project will get underway.

Based on what you learned from Chapter 9, from this point forward, it's absolutely essential that you stay in regular contact with your backers and keep them apprised of the project-related progress you're making.

EXPECT TO TAKE ON MANY MORE RESPONSIBILITIES IN THE DAYS AND WEEKS AHEAD

Beyond just sending out the promised rewards, based on the remaining funds you now have available, rework your budget and come up with a more accurate and realistic plan for pursuing and completing your project, using the resources you now have available or that you can realistically now afford.

Keep in mind, unless you've established your business as a not-for-profit entity, there's a good chance that the funds you've raised and received from your crowd funding campaign will be subject to taxes. At this point, it's a really good idea to sit down with an accountant to discuss your particular tax responsibilities, and what you can deduct as legitimate business and project-related expenses.

If you've used Kickstarter as your crowd funding platform, be sure to visit www.kickstarter.com/help/taxes for more information about your potential tax liabilities. Keep in mind, as details pertaining to the Jumpstart Our Business Startups Act are finalized by the federal government, the tax implications related to reward-based crowd funding campaigns (and/or presale-based campaigns) will likely change. Thus, it's important to work with an accountant or tax advisor who is familiar with crowd funding.

It is very possible that a percentage of the money you've raised through crowd funding will need to be paid as a state and/or federal tax, so once again, this expense should be built into your initial budget and your funding goal.

You've probably surmised, a lot of hard work still lies ahead. The more detailed and accurate your plans and budget are, the better off you'll be moving forward. Now is a good time to sit down and create a detailed business plan for your project, and then, based on your objectives, create a legal entity for your business or endeavor.

The Business Plan Pro software ($79.95, www.businessplanpro.com) or online-based LivePlan tools ($19.95 per month, http://specials.liveplan .com/create-your-plan), or another software package or online tool that walks you through the process of creating a business plan will be useful if you've never done this before.

The Small Business Administration offers a free online resource for creating business plans (www.sba.gov/category/navigation-structure/starting-managing-business/starting-business/how-write-business-plan), as well as a free 25-page guide for creating a business plan, which can be downloaded (http://archive.sba.gov/idc/groups/public/documents/sba_homepage/pub_mp32.pdf).

Consider sitting down with a business attorney who can help you establish yourself as a legal business, whether it's a DBA (doing business as) or some type of corporation such as a limited liability corporation, that may offer you personal financial and legal protection. LegalZoom (www .legalzoom.com) and Incorporate.com (www.incorporate.com) are two online services that can help you set up a DBA or corporation on your own without an attorney. These services offer no legal advice. They simple help you complete and process the necessary forms.

Hopefully, now that your project has been funded, you'll have the resources to hire the professional help you need to assist you in pursuing your project's goals. Seeking out expert advice is particularly important if your project involves manufacturing something and/or sourcing materials, and you have no previous experience with these tasks. This is one area where inexperienced project creators tend to make extremely costly mistakes that lead to delays or the ultimate inability to complete their project.

As things start to fall into place, expand your core team as needed, and establish a strong and well-organized infrastructure for your project (business). After establishing yourself as a legal business entity, if you decide to do so, open a bank account, and begin using financial software (such as Intuit's QuickBooks, www.quickbooks.com) to keep all of your bookkeeping and financial records organized.

WHAT TO DO IF YOUR CROWD FUNDING CAMPAIGN FAILS

At the start of this book you learned that a significant percentage of reward- and presale-based crowd funding campaigns do not wind up reaching their funding goals. Thus, if you're working with a crowd funding platform that has adopted an all-or-nothing approach and your project fails to reach its funding goal, you receive no money whatsoever at the conclusion of your campaign (and the credit or debit cards belonging to the people who chose to support your project are never charged).

There are many reasons why some crowd funding campaigns fail, and it's absolutely essential that you figure out the reason(s) why your particular campaign failed before trying to figure out what to do next. Whatever the reason(s), try not to get too upset, frustrated, or embarrassed. Instead, if you're truly passionate about your project, take a step back, regroup, refocus, and consider trying again, but with a fine-tuned or modified approach.

The top 10 most common reasons why a campaign fails include:

1. The project idea itself wasn't viable.
2. The target audience composed of people interested in supporting your project idea wasn't big enough. In other words, there is not sufficient demand.
3. As the project creator, you didn't successful communicate details about your project idea on your crowd funding campaign's web page, in your promotional video, and/or in your other marketing materials or efforts.
4. You didn't present a professional enough image to potential backers or convince these people of your ability to successfully complete your project if it got funded.

5. Your crowd funding campaign was ineffective at reaching the right audience or didn't successfully reach enough people. Perhaps your various calls to action weren't clearly stated, or you focused too much attention and too many resources on trying to reach the wrong audience.
6. Your funding goal was unrealistic.
7. Your overall network wasn't well enough established resulting in not enough people initially supporting your project.
8. You adopted the fatal "if you build it, they will come" mentality, and by doing nothing after your campaign was published online, nowhere near enough potential backers magically found their way to your campaign's web page.
9. The crowd funding platform you chose to work with wasn't a perfect fit for your project idea or its campaign.
10. The money you invested into your campaign was not used correctly, so you wound up spending too much money on advertising, marketing, or promotional activities that were ineffective. For example, if you tried search marketing advertising, perhaps you associated a poorly selected list of keywords with the campaign, or you didn't create an attention-getting headline for the ad.

As you read this list, hopefully you can identity one or more areas where things did not go as planned or where mistakes were made, and you can fine-tune those aspects of your project or campaign before attempting to try again.

Once your campaign fails and it's come to an end, you have several options. Based on why you believe the campaign didn't work, your options now include:

- Give up and walk away from the project altogether.
- Fine-tune the project idea.
- Redefine your target audience.
- Rethink your funding goal and figure out how you can either complete your project using less money, or break up the project into several separate projects, each with its own crowd funding campaign.
- Do more research and study other successful campaigns that targeted the same audience as your project. Figure out why those campaigns worked and yours did not. Ask yourself, what those other project creators did differently.
- Seek out traditional investors or other ways of securing some or all of the funds needed. You can then move further along with your project, and later launch a new crowd funding campaign once you've proven the project is more viable.
- Rework aspects of your campaign that clearly didn't work. For example, you could reshoot and reedit your promotional video from scratch,

adopt a different approach, or change your video's core marketing message or call to action.

- Invest the time needed to build up and expand your online social network.
- Figure out better ways to reach out to potential backers, through social media, online advertising, public relations, and/or direct email, and use these tools more efficiently in the future.
- Expand your core team and include people who posses more experience or specific skills that you now see are clearly needed to create and manage a successful crowd funding campaign.

Once you've determine what needs to happen, if you opt to try crowd funding again, you have two options. First, you can make the necessary adjustments to your project and/or campaign, and then relaunch it and try again using the same platform (after the required waiting period stipulated by the crowd funding platform ends).

Alternatively, if you opt to pursue the project, choose a different, more appropriate crowd funding platform, and launch a new campaign on that platform. Whichever option you choose, consider rereading the appropriate chapters of this book, working with additional experts, and doing more research. Brush up on the skills and knowledge needed to be successful in areas of your campaign that failed the first time.

Also, be sure to stay in touch with and continue to build your relationship with the people who did choose to support your failed campaign. These are people who are clearly excited about your project idea and who want to support you, so take the steps needed to retain their support and excitement so you can turn to them again when and if you opt to launch a new campaign.

In the final three chapters of *The Crowd Funding Services Handbook* are in-depth and exclusive interviews with crowd funding experts. Be sure to read these interviews carefully, and learn as much as you can from the advice these people share. In many of these interviews, specific tips for avoiding common mistakes and crowd funding pitfalls are discussed. Even if a featured expert comes from a background that doesn't relate directly to your project idea, chances are the advice they have to offer can still be used to help you achieve your own success.

CHAPTER 12

Get Started Using Kickstarter.com

In This Chapter

- Learn about the Kickstarter.com service and its benefits.
- Discover how to launch a crowd funding campaign using Kickstarter.
- Explore strategies for effectively using Kickstarter.

There are many different crowd funding platforms available to you that can assist in raising enough money to fund your project, launch your business, expand your business, bring an idea for an invention to fruition, or create something that others will want to experience or participate in.

While the crowd funding landscape is continuously and quickly expanding, the most popular crowd funding platform is currently Kickstarter, which launched in April 2009, with the goal of helping to bring creative projects to life. Not only is Kickstarter a pioneer in the crowd funding arena, it's also the most successful platform. As of late 2013, the platform had helped more than 60,000 separate projects get funded, which accounted for more than $930 million in pledged funding by backers.

KICKSTARTER IS FOR FUNDING CREATIVE PROJECTS

What sets Kickstarter apart from other crowd funding platforms is that it is exclusively used for funding creative projects, ranging from films and video/computer games, to music, art, and technology. In other words, when the project is ultimately funded and completed, something—a movie, book, video game, painting, album, or some other creative project—will be produced. One of the biggest misconceptions about this platform is that it's a place to fund anything.

Kickstarter organizes the projects that are published online using this platform into categories, which include: Art, Comics, Dance, Design, Fashion, Film, Food, Games, Music, Photography, Publishing, Technology, and Theater. A Kickstarter project must have a beginning and end, which is a finite and clearly defined goal. For example, writing and publishing a specific book is a viable Kickstarter project; trying to raise money to launch your writing career is not.

If you want to use crowd funding for another type of project that does not fit into one of these categories, Kickstarter is not the platform you should consider using. This particular platform is exclusively focused on funding creative projects. There are many platforms available on the Internet (discussed elsewhere in this book) that use crowd funding to help fund charitable causes, businesses, or other types of ventures. Kickstarter is not a donation platform or a place to beg for money. It's a platform for funding creative projects, and there is always a value exchange, in the form of a reward, for a project's backers or supporters.

As of early 2014, Kickstarter is open to project creators from the United States, United Kingdom, Canada, Australia, and New Zealand, but backers can come from anywhere. One thing to understand about Kickstarter, and virtually every other crowd funding platform, is that not all projects get funded. Each project is independent and controlled exclusively by the person or group that launched it.

KICKSTARTER PUTS CROWD FUNDING TOOLS AT YOUR DISPOSAL, BUT YOU'RE IN CHARGE

Kickstarter simply serves as a platform and resource. Thus, while this particular platform has more than 54,000 success stories, between 2009 and 2013 more than 70,000 projects were unsuccessful due to many different reasons, some of which are explored in this book.

As the project creator, you set your own funding goal and deadline and ultimately keep 100 percent control over and ownership of the work. However, if a project's funding goal is not achieved, the project creator receives no monies whatsoever, and the backers that did pledge wind up paying no money. Kickstarter uses an all-or-nothing funding approach.

The objective behind Kickstarter, and many other crowd funding platforms, is that the project creator develops a project in order to raise money for a specific creative endeavor. The Kickstarter platform is used to help convey the project idea to potential backers and then manage those backers and the financial transactions associated with them.

When using Kickstarter, a project backer is not an investor, since backers receive no equity or ownership in the project they're supporting. What backers do receive, however, is the chance to be among the first to purchase or participate in the project, plus depending on how much they pledge, they receive some type of tangible reward, benefit, or value in exchange for their support.

In other words, before the project is produced or created, backers pre-purchase the product or the opportunity to experience it, because it's something they're excited about and want to support. Using Kickstarter, project creators can determine if there is sufficient interest in their idea before investing a lot of time and their own money in it, plus raise some or all the money that's ultimately needed to make their creative project a reality.

DISCOVER WHAT SETS KICKSTARTER APART AS A CROWD FUNDING PLATFORM

Beyond the creative project focus, there are a handful of things that differentiate Kickstarter from other crowd funding platforms. To begin, it's currently the largest crowd funding platform in existence. The service provides a world stage on which someone can showcase their idea. Kickstarter also has a huge community of repeat backers, many of whom spend time on the service looking for multiple projects to support.

As a result, while a project creator must promote her own project and drive potential backers to her Kickstarter page, there is a population of over 1.5 million repeat Kickstarter backers that may stumble upon your campaign and want to support it. It's this growing community of repeat backers who support multiple projects that makes Kickstarter appealing to many project creators.

Kickstarter's all-or-nothing funding model also sets this platform apart from its competition. What this means is that as the project creator, you determine how much money you want or need to raise, the duration of the project, and the scope of the project. (The duration of a crowd funding project published on Kickstarter can be between 1 and 60 days; however, 30 days is the most popular option.)

For example, if you're a musician, singer, or recording artist and you publish a project on Kickstarter that aims to raise $10,000 to record an album, and you opt for a 30-day campaign, at the end of those 30 days, if you've raised $10,000 or more from your backers, you receive all of the money (minus Kickstarter's fees and the third-party credit card transaction fees). At the end of the 30th day, Kickstarter will charge the credit/debit cards of all of your pledgers simultaneously.

However, if, at the end of the 30 days, your campaign fails to raise the $10,000, even if you are just $1 short of your goal, you receive nothing, and your pledgers'/backers' credit/debit cards will never be charged. No money changes hands and everyone walks away as if the project on Kickstarter never happened.

This all-or-nothing approach helps to protect the project creators, because if they don't raise enough money (based on their own budget) to create the project, they are not obligated to move forward without enough funding. Because of this, creators can experiment with their ideas, use Kickstarter to conduct free market research, and, if necessary, fine-tune their idea before being obligated to complete it.

At the same time, the all-or-nothing approach protects backers, because they know that if they pledge money on Kickstarter, they'll only need to pay that money if the project is fully funded, and theoretically, the project will be completed as promised. The risk of losing the money they pledge is greatly reduced.

Also, while a Kickstarter campaign is actually taking place, the all-or-nothing approach creates a sense of urgency, since everyone knows that if the project does not get fully funded, nothing will happen. Thus, the project creators are more apt to work hard on the promotion and marketing of their campaigns to solicit backers, and backers are motivated to pledge money and share the concept with their own friends in an effort to ensure that something they become excited about actually comes to fruition. Many backers become emotional stakeholders in the projects they pledge to support, and they're willing to rally behind them by utilizing their own online networks to help get the word out.

Kickstarter's own research shows that if a campaign reaches 30 percent of its funding goal early on, there is then a 90 percent chance that the campaign will get fully funded. This is, in part, thanks to the emotional connection backers who rally behind the project feel, and their subsequent efforts to share the project with their own networks.

With this all-or-nothing approach in place, it becomes the sole responsibility of the project creator to develop an accurate budget for the project in advance, so that they're confident in their ability to produce or create the project if they reach their funding goal.

A fully funded project can still falter if the initial budget is inaccurate. If the project creator determines he requires $10,000 to complete the project, but due to inaccurate research, fails to understand the project will actually cost $15,000 to complete, Kickstarter will still award the funds because the project creator successfully met his funding goal. The campaign winds up getting into trouble because it now has dozens, hundreds, or even thousands of backers who are expecting results, but the project can't move forward because it's not adequately funded.

To prevent this situation, it is essential to sit down in advance with an accountant or someone with a strong knowledge of finance who can assist in the creation of a realistic project budget. It is also highly recommended that the project creator include a 15- to 20-percent financial cushion in her budget, allowing for unexpected expenses, delays, hurdles, or miscalculations.

Ultimately, if a hurdle does arise after a successful Kickstarter campaign, Kickstarter recommends that the project creator remain fully transparent by keeping backers well informed every step of the way—both when milestones are achieved and when hurdles arise. Research shows that most backers are very understanding when they are kept well informed.

Kickstarter refers to people who support a project financially as backers or pledgers—not as donors, investors, or customers. People who support projects on Kickstarter are not donating money nor are they making traditional investments that would result in them obtaining some form of equity or ownership in the project or business. Nor are they making purchases like a traditional customers at a retail store.

KICKSTARTER BACKERS ALWAYS RECEIVE A TANGIBLE REWARD

Kickstarter pledgers or supporters are pledging money to help bring a creative project to life. In exchange for that pledge, they receive something of value beyond just an altruistic feeling of helping. For example, if a backer supports a Kickstarter campaign for the creation of a computer game, when that game is completed, the backer becomes one of the very first people to receive a copy of the game and have a chance to play it. In essence, because the backer is excited about that game, he is purchasing a copy of it months or maybe a year or longer before it actually exists.

Beyond just allowing for the prepurchase of a product or experience, Kickstarter provides the opportunity for project creators to be extremely creative in terms of how they reward their supporters. In fact, it's often the reward that backers will receive that entices them to support a project in a bigger way than simply the opportunity to prepurchase something.

Project creators use this reward system to develop a much closer relationship or connection with their backers in a way that's never before been possible. Often backers receive a behind-the-scenes look at the creation of the project from start to finish. In some cases, backers are allowed or encouraged to provide feedback along the way.

Beyond this closer connection with the project creator, Kickstarter backers are often able to purchase some type of exclusive experience related to the project they support. For example, in the case of a computer game, backers who pledge a particular amount may be given the opportunity to have a character in the game named after them or be developed to look like them. The creative and unique ways project creators choose to reward their backers often plays a critical role in a campaign's success.

When it comes to developing the rewards for their campaigns, project creators should focus on several considerations. For example, across the board the most common pledge on Kickstarter, regardless of the project, is $25. The average pledge is $70. Knowing this, the project creator should set reward levels at or around these dollar amounts when possible.

All rewards should be priced fairly and realistically, based on their actual value. Someone will not pledge $100 for something that would otherwise cost $10. According to the online Kickstarter School, "Projects without a reward of $20 or less succeed 28 percent of the time, while projects with a reward of $20 or less succeed 45 percent of the time."

In general, according to Kickstarter's research, the rewards that are the most compelling are the ones that narrow the distance between the project creator and the backer. This includes offering unique experiences or one-of-a-kind rewards for those who commit to higher pledges. Every project should have a handful of rewards at different price points, starting at a $1 or $5 entry point (for someone who wants an emailed thank-you and wants to follow the project, but doesn't have the disposable income to support it more fully).

While it may be counterintuitive to offer some type of minor reward for just $1, many project creators have used supporters at this level to their advantage. In exchange for an automated emailed thank-you note and access to a behind-the-scenes blog, it's often possible to get those $1 backers to reach out to their own online networks and promote your project. This can help project creators find and solicit many more backers, some of whom may be able to provide higher levels of financial support.

There should also be at least one reward that results in the backer receiving a copy of the item that's being made, such as a DVD copy of the movie being produced or a copy of the computer game being created, plus rewards that allow people to receive some type of unique experience or reward in exchange for a higher level of financial support. For example, many project creators offer exclusive, limited-edition T-shirts to backers as a stand-alone reward or as part of a reward package for higher levels of support.

In addition to brainstorming your own ideas for ways to reward backers, do your own online research. Explore the Kickstarter platform for yourself, look for projects that are somewhat similar to your own, and discover what successful rewards other project creators have offered in exchange for various levels of support.

As you are developing your list of rewards, be careful not to overcomplicate the decision making process for your potential backers. Offer a handful of rewards at different price points, but don't offer so many reward options that it becomes confusing or difficult for a potential backer to make a decision. Ultimately, the rewards that will work will be unique to your project, appeal to your target audience, and reflect your creativity and your willingness to provide exclusive or unique opportunities for your supporters.

DETERMINE WHAT RESULTS IN A SUCCESSFULLY FUNDED PROJECT ON KICKSTARTER

Just about anyone with a computer that's connected to the Internet can create and launch a Kickstarter campaign relatively quickly and for free. But, if you want your project to be successful, you must be willing to do extensive research and planning and have the dedication and the willingness to take a proactive role in promoting and managing the campaign.

The Kickstarter platform allows you to view thousands of other projects that are currently active, plus you can also access free research and tutorials to help you plan and execute your own project. Part of your advance research should include determining exactly what makes campaigns like the one you're considering successful on Kickstarter.

As you conduct your research and look closely at other successfully funded projects, you'll find many common components. For example, your project should have a well-produced, informative, and concise promotional video that's targeted to your backers. On Kickstarter, videos are not required, but they're strongly encouraged. The video should be used as a tool to educate people about the project, but more importantly, get them excited to participate in making that project a reality.

The video should clearly articulate exactly who you are, what you're trying to accomplish, and at the same time, humanize the project. The video should also be less than three minutes in length, allow viewers to see and get to know the project creator(s), and make clear exactly how potential backers/supports can become part of the project. It should include a clear call to action with a benefit attached to that action.

Some of the biggest mistakes project creators make are producing videos with low production quality, poor sound quality, and/or that are too long. The attention span of people watching any type of video content online is extremely short, even if the content is of direct interest and engaging.

Be sure to review Chapter 7 to discover what you need to know about writing, producing, and editing your video. Ultimately, the length and content of your video will be determined by the story you need to tell and how you go about telling it. Every project has its own story. In some cases, the backstory behind the conception of a project is important. For other projects, making the project's creator the focus of the video will be more effective, especially when it comes to humanizing the project for the intended audience.

As for a video's production quality, you don't need to spend thousands of dollars to create a slick video production, when devices like an iPhone are capable of shooting high-definition video. What is important, however, is good audio quality and how you utilize production elements, like background music, within your video. If your video simply showcases you looking into the camera and clearly articulating the scope of the project and what you are trying to accomplish, this is often adequate.

Keep in mind, the overall production quality of your video impacts how someone perceives your project and professionalism. If the quality of the video is poor, this can easily create a negative perception. A more professionally produced video, on the other hand, will help boost a backer's confidence in you, your company, and/or your project.

Developing and offering well thought out and enticing rewards for supporters that bring them closer to the project is also an essential ingredient for a campaign's success. Offering that exclusive, up-close-and-personal or behind-the-scenes look at the project and its creator(s) is highly effective. Backers should be made to feel that they are doing something positive to help bring a project that they've become excited about to life.

A third component is a well thought out promotional and marketing campaign for the project that allows you to identify, reach out to, and solicit potential backers. Even if you have an awesome idea for a project, and you know it will be of interest to a particular audience, your campaign will fail if you are not able to effectively reach those potential backers, drive them to your Kickstarter page, and then successfully encourage them to support your project. Simply publishing a campaign on Kickstarter will not result in success. People will not magically find you and throw money at you.

With this in mind, the people you promote your Kickstarter campaign to should include your family and friends, your online friends (who are part of your broader online social network through Facebook, etc.), the target audience for your project, as well as others who are active on the web.

Anytime you see a successful campaign on Kickstarter, you can be sure it is supported by a detailed, preplanned, and often multifaceted marketing, public relations, and/or advertising campaign that uses real-world and online tools and resources in a cost-effective way. For many project creators, getting the word out about a Kickstarter campaign is the most time-consuming and difficult part of the process, but it is also absolutely essential.

ACQUIRE THE SKILLS YOU NEED IN ADVANCE

Creating, launching, and managing a successful crowd funding campaign on any platform, including Kickstarter, requires that you have a core set of communication, storytelling, writing, video production, sales, marketing, advertising, self-promotion, and public relations skills. As you create your Kickstarter campaign, not only do you need to capture the attention of potential backers/supporters, you need to quickly and effectively inspire those people to financially support your project and potentially help you promote it to their online networks.

This means that having the ability to tell your story using text, video, photos, and other multimedia elements is as essential as having an awesome idea for a project to begin with. Being a good storyteller is helpful. Being able to empathize with your potential backers/supporters, so you understand what backers will respond to on an emotional level, is another useful skill.

Kickstarter has worked hard to develop a platform that anyone can use effectively, without having to pay for expensive third-party experts. In fact, out of the more than 60,000 projects that have been successfully funded using this platform, only a small percentage of those project creators have hired outside support services to provide professional assistance in creating, launching, and managing their campaigns.

That said, based on your unique project, your funding goal, and your personal skill set, you may want or need to hire a writer, public relations expert, online marketing specialist, videographer, and/or photographer to help you create, launch, and manage your Kickstarter campaign. Many successful project creators solicit the help of people they already know, including friends or family members, who posses specific skills or professional experience.

If you are not familiar with or actively using online social networking services, like Facebook and Twitter, for example, hiring an expert who can help you use these and other low-cost (or free) online tools to market and promote your Kickstarter campaign may be highly beneficial. Ultimately, what support you seek out should depend on what you are trying to accomplish, what skills and experience you already possess, and what needs to be put into place to help ensure a successful campaign.

WHEN YOU SHOULD LAUNCH YOUR KICKSTARTER CAMPAIGN

Much needs to happen before you go onto the Kickstarter platform to set up and launch your campaign. To begin, develop your idea and make sure it's viable. Next, determine the exact scope of your project, calculate exactly how much money you'll need to make the project a reality, and develop a timeframe that's viable.

Once you complete these steps, figure out your target audience, and be specific. Who should your Kickstarter campaign be targeted to, based on the potential audience for your project? Knowing this, determine how you can best reach that audience to tell them about your project and ultimately invite them to visit your Kickstarter page.

Reaching out to your target audience can be done using paid advertising (both online and in the real world), public relations, email, and by becoming active on Facebook, Twitter, Google+, LinkedIn, and other online social networking services. How you go about promoting your Kickstarter campaign should be customized specifically to your project, and the approach you take will need to be unique to your project and its intended audience.

Only after all aspects of your project and the Kickstarter campaign have been researched and planned out should you actually take the steps needed to create and launch your campaign online. Taking shortcuts or skipping vital steps will result in failure.

HOW TO GO ONLINE AND CREATE YOUR KICKSTARTER CAMPAIGN

Actually creating your Kickstarter campaign and getting it online so you can begin driving traffic (potential backers) to your page is a quick and straightforward process that the platform will walk you through, step-by-step.

Before doing this, however, invest the necessary time to explore the site and view other active projects. Also, be sure to participate in the free online tutorials offered by Kickstarter. To find these resources, visit Kickstarter.com, scroll toward the bottom of the main page, and click on one of the options listed under the Create heading. Your options include: Kickstarter School (www.kickstarter.com/help/school), Creator Questions (www.kickstarter.com /help/faq/creator+questions), and Project Guidelines (www.kickstarter .com/help/guidelines).

Before creating your first Kickstarter project, explore the service and become a backer for several other projects. Doing this will force you to research and experience how the crowd funding process on this platform works, and it will allow you to see firsthand what types of approaches are effective. First becoming a backer for several projects will also help you become part of the Kickstarter community.

To actually build your project online, go to www.kickstarter.com, click on the Start A Project button that's displayed near the top-center of the screen, and follow the on-screen instructions. Be sure the information you provide about yourself and your project is well-written, error-free, concise, informative, and that every element of your text, video, and whatever other photos or content you include all convey the right message in an easy-to-understand and honest way.

Put thought into each component of the online project, starting with its title. Your title should be descriptive, easy-to-understand, specific, memorable, and keyword searchable. Also consider your project's overall online image. This refers to how you represent yourself online. Remember, you are trying to get people to believe in and support you. It is essential that you convey an image that's credible, reliable, honest, professional, and knowledgeable.

When it comes to writing the description for your project, how you say it is as important as what you say. In other words, you need to convey your story and message using wording that is easy to understand and error-free. Spelling errors, misuse of punctuation, or incorrect word usage will dramatically deter from your ability to create a positive first impression. Once again, focus on being precise, accurate, and easy to understand when writing your project description and any supporting text that's associated with your project's Kickstarter page.

Your personal biography is another component you will need to provide when creating a project on Kickstarter. Use this to introduce yourself to your potential backers, showcase your related skills and accomplishments, build the respect and trust of your potential backers, and tell your unique story. For example, why are you pursuing this project? Why is it important to you?

One additional tool offered to project creators is the ability to preview their project before it is made public. Use this preview option to share your Kickstarter page with close friends and advisors, for example, and solicit their feedback in advance. Often, people who are not directly involved with a project will be able to provide honest and impartial advice, as well as insight related to things you might have overlooked.

Once you make your way through the project creation process and click on the Submit button, someone from Kickstarter will review your submission and make sure it adheres to the platform's project guidelines. Be sure to visit the Kickstarter Project Guidelines page to learn about these guidelines before submitting your project to avoid the unnecessary hassle and aggravation of having to rework your submission and resubmit it.

After your project goes live on Kickstarter, your work has only just begun! It's now your responsibility to drive traffic to your project's Kickstarter page and convert those online visitors into financial supporters. How long your campaign will last is a decision you will need to make in advance. The average length for a successful Kickstarter campaign is 30 days.

DISCOVER HOW MUCH RUNNING A KICKSTARTER CAMPAIGN COSTS

Some of the components related to developing, executing, and managing a successful crowd funding campaign are going to cost money up front. However, the majority of these expenses are optional.

For example, if you have no public relations experience, you'll probably want to hire a public relations firm or freelance public relations professional to help you with this aspect of your campaign's marketing and promotion. Likewise, if you determine that paid online advertising, on Facebook, for example, is an ideal approach for reaching your target audience, this, too, will cost money.

Likewise, depending on the level of production you're seeking for your project's promotional video, you may need to purchase or rent video production equipment or hire a professional production crew to produce the video on your behalf. These are all upfront costs that will be paid to various third parties based on your unique needs.

In terms of fees that you will ultimately pay to Kickstarter for hosting your campaign, you will wind up paying 5 percent of the total dollars raised. This is taken immediately and off the top from the funds actually collected from your backers once a successful campaign ends.

Above and beyond the 5 percent fee that is paid to Kickstarter, an additional fee of between 3 and 5 percent is paid to Kickstarter's credit/debit card payment processor. Obviously, you should build these fees and third-party expenses into the overall budget for your project.

One additional fee to consider and build into your budget is what it will ultimately cost to ship your product(s) and/or rewards to your domestic and international backers, taking into account all packaging, insurance, and shipping charges.

AVOID THE MOST COMMON MISTAKES MADE BY PROJECT CREATORS

The folks at Kickstarter have gone to great lengths to monitor all projects that have been published on the platform and have gathered extensive research into what works and what does not.

Some of the biggest mistakes Kickstarter sees project creators making include not putting enough thought into the goal of a project, its budget, the production of the video, or how the campaign will be promoted once it goes live. If you don't have a well-conceived plan for attracting backers during the campaign, they will not magically materialize. Taking the launch-and-forget approach to running a Kickstarter campaign almost guarantees failure.

At any given time, there are at least 3,000 other active projects on the Kickstarter platform. Being able to position your project as important, unique, and innovative is beneficial, especially if you are looking to attract media attention through a public relations effort and/or trying to solicit some of Kickstarter's repeat backers.

WHAT TO DO IF YOUR KICKSTARTER CAMPAIGN FAILS

If a Kickstarter campaign fails to reach its funding goal, the project creator is always welcome to try again. However, before immediately relaunching the campaign, figure out what went wrong and why, and make adjustments to whatever is necessary. For example, does the project idea itself need to be tweaked? Did you not properly define your target audience or your marketing message? Was your marketing message or video too long, confusing, or off-topic? Did you fail to drive enough traffic to your project's Kickstarter page?

Be sure to determine what went wrong, address and fix the problem(s), and then take the appropriate steps to relaunch a revised campaign. In other words, learn from your mistakes! As you look back at what went wrong, you may discover that Kickstarter was not the most suitable crowd funding platform to meet your needs.

Taking a second look at Indiegogo (www.indiegogo.com) or another platform may be advantageous. You might also consider seeking out alternative funding options for aspects of your project or dividing the project into several smaller projects with more readily achievable funding goals.

WHAT TO EXPECT FROM KICKSTARTER IN THE FUTURE

In the months and years to come, Kickstarter will be launched as a tool for project creators in many additional countries. The company is also on a continuing quest to fine-tune and enhance its online tools to make crowd funding opportunities available to more creative people. To truly understand how this platform works, however, there's no better way than to begin using it yourself—first as a backer for other projects and then as a project creator.

In addition to giving you the tools needed to raise funding for a project, Kickstarter provides a way to build a base of extremely dedicated supporters who, if managed properly, will remain supportive throughout the life of the initial project, as well as other projects you may pursue in the future.

THERE ARE OTHER CROWD FUNDING OPTIONS AVAILABLE

While Kickstarter is a pioneer in crowd funding, and is currently the most popular platform, there are many other platforms available. In the next chapter, you'll read interviews with executives from several of these platforms and discover why using one of them may be more beneficial, based on what you're trying to achieve.

If you determine that Kickstarter is the perfect platform for you to use in order to raise the money you need for your project, the crowd funding tips, strategies, and insight offered by the various experts featured within the next few chapters will be extremely useful. In these interviews, the various experts, who have many different and diverse backgrounds, share their real-world experiences and philosophies about how crowd funding can be effectively utilized.

CHAPTER 13

Interviews with Crowd Funding Experts

In This Chapter

- Meet a handful of executives who help operate crowd funding platforms.
- Discover crowd funding strategies from experts.
- Learn how to overcome crowd funding mistakes.

What better way to learn about something new than to hear directly from the people who are recognized experts in their field as well as those who have had a tremendous level of influence within it. As you know, crowd funding (in its current form) is a relatively new concept that is continuously evolving and making it possible for more and more people, from all walks of life, to get their projects funded so their ideas can be transformed into reality.

While Kickstarter's focus, for example, is on helping creative people fund their projects, there are many other crowd funding platforms that support more traditional business start-ups, for example, or that are better suited to be used by inventors utilizing technology. There are also crowd funding platforms that allow people to seek funding for themselves, not a particular business idea, project, or invention, as well as platforms designed specifically to help organizations raise money for charities and nonprofit organizations.

In this chapter, you'll read exclusive and in-depth interviews with executives from some of these crowd funding platforms. Even if a particular platform isn't suited to meet your specific needs, the advice, anecdotes, and information these crowd funding experts have shared may still directly relate to what you're trying to accomplish.

As you read these interviews, keep in mind that each of these executives and experts has extensive experience in the crowd funding and business arenas. Each of them shares his own thoughts and ideas about what works and what doesn't when it comes to crowd funding. Thus, in some cases, the advice offered by one person may directly contradict the advice of someone else. Yet, the advice each of these people has shared has led to their personal success, and often to the success of many others.

Thus, based on what you're trying to accomplish using crowd funding, it's up to you to gather as much knowledge and advice as you can from each of these people, as well as from your own research, and then determine what information is most applicable to you.

Some advice that was unanimously shared by all of the executives and crowd funding experts interviewed for this book is that to be successful you must do your homework, determine exactly what you're trying to accomplish, understand how the crowd funding platform you choose works, get to know your target audience, and then utilize all of the tools at your disposal to promote your crowd funding campaign by taking a continuous and multifaceted approach.

BRIAN MEECE, CEO OF ROCKETHUB, SHARES HIS CROWD FUNDING ADVICE

RocketHub (www.rockethub.com) is a fast-growing and popular crowd funding platform that caters to a wide range of different types of businesses and projects that are seeking capital. As you'll discover, one of the things that sets RocketHub apart from its competition is its partnership with the A&E television network. In this interview, RocketHub CEO Brian Meece talks about his platform, who should use it, how to best use it, and what it takes to be successful with crowd funding in general.

How did you get involved with crowd funding?

Brian Meece: "Prior to RocketHub, my background was working in creative media and the arts. I studied filmmaking in college and have been playing in bands since high school. That perspective as a creative person has served me well at RocketHub, because it's the creative community that has really pioneered the crowd funding model.

"While RocketHub can be used to fund creative projects, entrepreneurial ventures and small business ventures are currently our fastest growing categories. We are seeing a lot of people turning to crowd funding, and RocketHub in particular, to help them launch their business or to somehow grow their existing business."

What does it take for a person, company, or organization to be successful using crowd funding?

Brian Meece: "One of the things we've discovered at RocketHub is that crowd funding is a skill that people can learn, develop, and implement. We've also seen that the patterns of success are the same, regardless of what type of project someone is looking to fund using this method.

"There are basically three components to successful crowd funding. When campaigns incorporate these three components, they do well. When campaigns are missing one or more of these components, they tend to fail.

"The first thing that every crowd funding campaign needs to have is something exciting to bring to the public. Just releasing a new product or launching a new business isn't enough. The concept needs to generate excitement and personal engagement. Crowd funding is all about people funding people. If a project and the person or people behind it are not exciting and inspiring, the campaign won't generate enough interest from backers.

"Thus, the people who use crowd funding need to be expert communicators who are truly excited about what they're doing. These people need to be able to communicate clearly about what they're doing, as well as why they're doing it. Often, the folks who are ultimately funding these campaigns are just as excited about the why as they are about the what. People are funding people, not necessarily just the business, product, or project. They're also funding the stories behind the people involved in the business, product, or project.

"The second thing every crowd funding campaign needs is the concept of social capital. This is the ability to motivate, reach, and influence folks, and get people to fund and share your project. Crowd funding is very much a community phenomenon. These campaigns all start within their own communities, because that's where social capital is built up.

"If you're an existing company that has existing products out there and a large following of happy and loyal customers, for example, you're a great fit for crowd funding. If you're a community leader who is out there moving and shaking and promoting who you are and what your mission is, you, too, are a good fit for crowd funding.

"Crowd funding today is Internet enabled. Most of the funding that comes in is a result of your outreach within the various online communities and social networking services. If you have a strong online presence, you're already successfully using social media, or you're savvy using the tools available to you for communicating online, you, too, are a good fit for crowd funding. Crowd funding is all about utilizing your network and engaging your communities using social capital.

"The third thing every crowd funding project needs is a well-conceived reward system for backers. What will the backers receive in exchange for their support? On RocketHub, we refer to these rewards as 'the goods.' Backers get to feel good about supporting a project they, too, become passionate about it, but they're also rewarded for it.

"We have seen all sorts of creative ways crowd funders use rewards to give back to the backers in order to get them even more excited about their participation. These rewards can come in the form of exclusive goods or experiences, for example."

You refer to RocketHub as a movement. What do you mean by that?

Brian Meece: "A movement is something that has significant impact and that ultimately changes communities and ultimately the world. That's exactly what we're seeing with crowd funding and with RocketHub. The movement is that there's no longer a need to pursue traditional funding practices to get funding for a project, product, or business, for example. We're basically democratizing the entire process. Someone looking to raise money no longer needs to associate themselves with high net worth individuals or traditional financial institutions, for example, to fund their projects."

What would you say is the biggest misconception people have about crowd funding?

Brian Meece: "The biggest misconception is that people think their ideas are so great that they're going to sell themselves. It's that 'if you build it, they will come' mentality. People think they can slap up a project, publish it online, and then the money will come pouring in within 30 to 90 days. This is not the case at all.

"Crowd funding is a contact sport. It's a proactive exercise in communicating and promoting that needs to be done very well to achieve success. As an entrepreneur, business person, or creative individual who wants to use crowd funding, the two skills you'll need to develop are the ability to communicate well and use promotion, both online and in the real world."

What sets RocketHub apart from other crowd funding platforms?

Brian Meece: "We look at crowd funding as a movement and put a lot of emphasis on education. On the RocketHub website, you'll discover what we call our Success School. This is an online-based program designed to educate people who want to raise money using crowd funding, as well as potential backers. Our biggest differentiator, however, is our partnership with the A&E television network.

"A&E takes our online community and opens it up to a national television audience. Integrated into some of A&E's highest rated programs are vignettes that showcase RocketHub projects and campaigns. This broadens our potential audience of backers to the more than 100 million people with television sets who have access to the A&E television network.

"This partnership began in summer 2013, and it's been evolving ever since as A&E Project Startup, as well as through direct integration between the projects RocketHub has helped to fund and specific programs airing on A&E, such as *Duck Dynasty*."

Who is the core user of the RocketHub platform when it comes to raising capital via crowd funding?

Brian Meece: "This thing started off with artists and creative people, which is the same pattern that social media followed. It has very quickly gone into new verticals, such as science, entrepreneurship, and traditional small businesses. We have seen at least 30 percent growth on our platform month after month since our launch. We are seeing a ton of new businesses and project creators come to RocketHub.

"I am getting really excited about the volume of new projects launching on our platform every month. We are launching 600 to 1,000 new projects per month. We don't judge projects based on how much money they raise. We measure them on the impact they have within their communities, and how many projects we're enabling as a result of crowd funding."

If someone wants to use RocketHub, how does the process work?

Brian Meece: "The first thing I recommend that everyone does is check out our Success School [www.rockethub.com/education]. It takes a proactive approach to be successful using this funding model, and people should understand how it works before trying it for themselves. People should do their homework and educate themselves.

"Actually launching a project on RocketHub is a very easy, quick, and straightforward process. Once you know what you want to say and how you'll say it, a project can be created and published in 15 to 20 minutes. We've made the process as easy as creating a listing to sell something on eBay.

"Projects have to be authentic. Before a project goes live, we verify that the person or organization is who they present themselves to be. We also make sure the project is legal, tasteful, and won't be offensive to anyone. We don't curate. We are an open platform that offers a self-serve model to crowd funding."

What are the costs involved with using RocketHub to host a crowd funding campaign?

Brian Meece: "One of the beauties of crowd funding is that there is a very low barrier to entry. It's free to launch a project on RocketHub. You can set your funding goal for whatever you want or need within your time frame. If you hit or exceed that goal, we charge a 4 percent fee. If you raise funds, but don't reach your goal, you still get the funds, but we charge an 8 percent fee.

"We incentivize you to set realistic and achievable funding goals. There's also a 4 percent credit card merchant fee that does not go to RocketHub. Those are the only mandatory fees. In terms of other costs, project creators can spent whatever they want to produce their video, as well as to advertise and promote their campaign.

"When it comes to video production, however, one thing we stress is that authenticity trumps slickness. What I mean by that is that the video should tell a great story and that the people featured in the promotional video should be very personable and credible. The video does not need to be a mini-movie with Hollywood-quality production values. Use the resources that are available to you, within your immediate community. We have seen folks raise $50,000 to $75,000 using a video created with a low-end web camera.

"The video needs to be well lit and have good quality sound, but it's the content of the video and the story it tells that's the most important. We've also seen project creators spend a fortune on video production but not achieve their funding goals, perhaps because their story wasn't compelling, or they didn't handle the promotion element of their campaign correctly.

"Keep your costs low, but relative to where you are. For example, if you're an established company with a professional image and a broad customer base, and you're looking to use crowd funding in order to expand the business or its product line, a higher level of production quality in terms of the video is expected by potential backers."

Obviously, a promotional or pitch video is a key component to a crowd funding campaign's success. What are the key elements needed to create and shoot a successful video?

Brian Meece: "We have found that the best videos to promote a crowd funded project are between one and three minutes in length. The video should showcase who you are as an entrepreneur, what you're doing, and why you're doing it. The video should also have a clear call to action, which is for potential backers to fund this project and share this project with their own networks.

"Nobody likes to watch commercials. Therefore, the video should tell a story. Why are you pursuing this project? What will be the value to the community? If applicable, showcase the product you're trying to create, and demonstrate its benefits. We have found that backers love to fund good stories and the stories behind the ideas, not just the ideas themselves."

At what point should someone pursue crowd funding in a project's lifecycle?

Brian Meece: "This is different for every project. There are no hard and fast rules about when you should reach out to your community for funds. There are, however, general guidelines. The better you can communicate the idea or concept, in terms of showing pictures, mock-ups, or prototypes, the better off you'll be, because the potential backers will have more faith that you'll be able to deliver on what you're proposing. If it's just you standing in front of a camera talking about a grandiose idea, backers will be more hesitant to fund just a raw or abstract idea related to a product or business."

What are the benefits of crowd funding?

Brian Meece: "Using crowd funding allows project creators to spend very little upfront, but achieve three main benefits: funding, awareness, and feedback. The cost of running a crowd funding campaign is miniscule compared to the cost of manufacturing a new product, launching the product with an advertising campaign, and then figuring out through customer feedback if your target audience wants or needs that product after the huge investment has been made.

"A crowd funding campaign allows you to solicit feedback from your customer base before you've made that huge investment. Most project creators who have launched successful crowd funding campaigns that ultimately got funded look back and see one of the biggest benefits of crowd funding as being the feedback they received from their backers.

"In addition, the awareness that's built up by a successful crowd funding campaign can generate enough sales, in advance, to make the company, product, or project launch an immediate success. This is a beautiful side effect of crowd funding."

How should someone go about setting realistic goals for a project?

Brian Meece: "I would say do some self analysis and plenty of research. Make sure that what you decide to do is actually possible and realistic based on the skills, experience, and resources you have available. Consider, for example, how many backers you believe you'll be able to attract for your campaign, and how much money you believe you'll be able to receive on average from each backer, based on your project.

"On RocketHub, the average for what you can expect to receive from a backer is about $75. So, for every 100 backers you successfully attract, you can generate $7,500. When deciding how much funding to seek out, consider carefully how many backers you believe you'll be able to attract, based on your communication and promotion skills. Will you be able to attract hundreds, thousands, or tens of thousands of backers?

"Look to your own community as the first group of potential backers. This might include friends, family, current customers, or people who are already excited about your project. Then, be prepared to reach out to a broader community. We have found that in terms of business ventures, consumer-oriented businesses that use crowd funding tend to do better than business-to-business-oriented companies, although that's just a general guideline, not a hard and fast rule. Also, projects that have a product associated with them tend to do well on RocketHub. These are the projects that tend to go viral the fastest."

What are some of the biggest crowd source funding pitfalls to avoid?

Brian Meece: "Don't set a funding goal that's way too high and impossible to achieve. Also, make sure your funding goal is achievable based on your bandwidth for being able to manage a successful promotional campaign for the project. If you don't have the time and resources to actively promote your campaign, you won't attract enough backers to it. Also, if you don't understand how online social media works, for example, unless you're willing to bring on people with this area of expertise, don't expect to effectively use online social media to promote your campaign. That being said, using online social media is an essential component to running an effective promotional campaign or a crowd funding project. Again, communication and promotional skills are essential. It's all about telling and sharing a great story, not just asking for money."

How important is it to have a traditional business plan in place before utilizing crowd funding?

Brian Meece: "For our flavor of crowd funding, which involves attracting backers and rewarding them with goods, a traditional business model is not necessary. What is important is having a clear vision for your project, and being able to communicate that vision. A traditional and detailed business plan can serve as a useful internal alignment document, but it's not needed to pursue crowd funding. Most backers will watch a one- to three-minute video and decide whether or not to back a project. They will not read through a 50-page business plan."

In terms of fine tuning a compelling story for a project, is there information that should or should not be disclosed?

Brian Meece: "At RocketHub, we believe in transparency. Project creators should be open and honest about risks, challenges, or potential obstacles they could encounter when making their project idea a reality. When selling anything, your campaign should be backed by confidence, passion, and excitement.

"Running a crowd funding campaign is a time-consuming process. Once the campaign goes live, you'll need to invest time each and every day in order to reach out to potential backers and promote the project using all forms of online social media and also promote it when applicable in the real world. You'll also want to engage in a comprehensive public relations campaign in order to reach out to the media. Plan on spending at least several hours per day managing a crowd funding campaign and promoting it."

What advice can you share about choosing rewards for backers?

Brian Meece: "Think of the rewards as part of a menu. On the menu, you want something that's available in the low range, medium range, and high range. Develop creative and compelling rewards at each of these levels, allowing your backers to decide how they want to engage with the project. The rewards should offer something that can't be acquired elsewhere."

GET CROWD FUNDING ADVICE FROM DAVE GIROUARD, FOUNDER OF UPSTART

While working at Google for eight years as president of Google Enterprise and vice president of apps, Dave Girouard met with many young people who were about to graduate or had recently graduated from college or graduate school and who wanted to pursue some type of entrepreneurial career path that involved significant financial risk. However, for a variety of reasons, many of these people chose to pursue a safe, plan B career path, which involved taking a stable job with a large company.

One reason these people often choose to take the safe career path is because they're burdened with student debt and/or credit card debit, so they're forced to take jobs that will allow them to reliably pay off their debt and meet their other financial responsibilities.

Seeing this trend, Dave Girouard developed a crowd funding platform that lets young people with an entrepreneurial spirit and a proven academic track record seek funding for themselves as individuals to relieve some of the financial pressure after graduation and allow them take more risks with their career paths and pursue their professional dreams.

After leaving Google, Dave Girouard and a handful of his former coworkers founded Upstart (www.upstart.com), which has evolved into a very unique crowd funding platform. In essence, Upstart allows recent graduates to raise money in exchange for a small share of their future income over a 5- to 10-year period. The backers invest directly in an individual, not in a particular business or idea, and at the same time, have the opportunity to stay in contact with the individual they're supporting and possibly serve as a mentor.

Dave Girouard left his position at Google in April 2012, and launched the Upstart platform in November 2013. By early January 2014, the service had funded 208 people with a total of more than $2.6 million, more than 5,000 people had created profiles to seek funding, and more than 5,000 backers had signed up so they could invest in individuals. As a result, about 7 out of 10 people who seek funding using Upstart wind up getting funded.

For certain types of people, including recent graduates, using Upstart's crowd funding approach and platform is very appealing.

What exactly does Upstart offer to recent graduates?

Dave Girouard: "In essence, recent graduates are able to use Upstart in order to borrow from their future earnings and bring those funds into the present in a way that would give them more decision making freedom when it comes to pursuing an entrepreneurial career path."

How did your experience at Google lead to you founding Upstart?

Dave Girouard: "At Google, we were very data and algorithm driven in terms of how we hired, particularly when we hired young people just out of college. Basically, we created an algorithm that could accurately predict someone's success at Google; I thought to myself, why couldn't we create an algorithm that could predict someone's success in the larger economy—which is ultimately what we've done at Upstart.

"By building an algorithm that will predict how much someone is likely to earn over the next 5 to 10 years, we allow people to borrow a small fraction of that and obtain those funds today, when it can have an immediate impact on their career path decisions. Upstart's formula for paying back the money received from backers is based on how much someone earns over a 5- to 10-year period, [it is] not based on a fixed amount that needs to be paid back every month regardless of what happens in their life.

"Upstart funding is what we call an 'income share agreement.' That's the generic term for what we do. Recent graduates receive money, and in return they pay a very fixed and defined fraction of their actual earnings over a period of either 5 or 10 years. By definition, this income share agreement is always affordable. If someone commits to sharing between 1 and 7 percent of their income with Upstart, in exchange for the money they receive, they know exactly what they'll need to pay back each month based on their earnings. What participants can feel comfortable knowing is that what they need to pay back is always affordable to them, which is why income share agreements are so interesting and attractive."

Upstarts promotes its crowd funding model as a new way for people to access capital. Do you use this slogan because you believe the old ways no longer work?

Dave Girouard: "Essentially, for people in a certain age group, there is very, very little access to capital with any kind of reasonable terms. If you're in your 20s, your access to capital is typically credit cards or a rich family member. Access to capital is generally based on how much someone is currently earning and what assets they have. That's the simple formula for getting a loan. Instead of looking at what someone is earning today, Upstart looks at someone's earning potential over the next decade and offers capital based on that."

Is Upstart considered a crowd funding platform?

Dave Girouard: "Yes, Upstart is a crowd funding platform. A potential participant would visit our website and create a profile. Part of the profile would state how much money they are seeking, their chosen payback time period, which is between 5 and 10 years, and the percentage of their future income they're willing to dedicate to paying back their debt. Then, potential backers can review a profile and decide how much they'd like to invest in that person.

"Unlike some crowd funding platforms that seek backers or supporters who receive no equity in whatever projects they're investing in, what we offer to our backers is an actual, regulated investment opportunity with upside and downside potential. As a result, our backers are all credited investors.

"Currently, to be a backer on Upstart, someone needs to have at least $1 million in net worth, or have earned at least $200,000 per year for each of the last three years. These are U.S. Securities and Exchange Commission guidelines. At Upstart, we are looking to remove this restriction for potential backers over time, and we hope to eliminate it sometime in 2014 or 2015.

"We have designed a platform that offers smart investment opportunities, in terms of risk and return, for our backers, who, in this case, really are investors."

On the recipient side, who is the perfect candidate to use Upstart?

Dave Girouard: "The first notion we had, which represents about half of the people on the platform, includes recent graduates who are very entrepreneurial. These are people who want to build their own business and work for themselves. They do not want to graduate from college or graduate school and become part of the corporate grind. So far, we have funded people doing tech start-ups, one guy who opened an ice cream shop in Brooklyn, and people working as consultants, for example.

"We have also seen a lot of interest among people who want to learn new skills that they didn't acquire in college but that would prepare them for a new or higher-paying career. We are seeing a lot of people looking for the money needed to pay for the additional classes or training they require, so that upon completing the classes, they have much higher earning potential.

"The common denominator among our participants on the recipient side of Upstart is people who are proactively looking to take control of and build their career, as opposed to taking a safe job and riding it out. Upstart is like a social network with a bank embedded inside of it. Participants don't just apply, get the money, and then run away. There is a whole online interaction between the participants and the backers, in a way that the backers become mentors and advisors."

How much can a typical recipient expect to raise from Upstart and in what time frame?

Dave Girouard: "This varies a lot based on the person. When someone applies at Upstart, we use our proprietary algorithm to calculate what we call their 'funding rate.' This includes calculating how many dollars someone can raise for Upstart's backers, based on every 1 percent of income they share over the 5- or 10-year period. Someone with an impeccable academic record, for example, might achieve a funding rate of up to $20,000 per 1 percent of their income. So, we provide a participant with their funding rate, and they come back and tell us what percentage of their income, between 1 and 7 percent, they want to share, and over what period of time, between 5 and 10 years, based on how much money they want to raise.

"Currently, the most one participant has raised through Upstart is $100,000. The average, however, is around $25,000. The funding rate we assign to someone is based on their past academic record and their work experience. We look carefully at where someone went to school and what they studied, what their grades and standardized test scores were, and use this to help predict and calculate someone's future earning potential. We also look at work history, which includes past internships and even job offers that someone didn't accept. Other things we look at are someone's credit score, credit history, and the amount of debt they currently possess.

"Our method isn't a perfect indicator when looking at an individual, but it tends to be pretty accurate. When used on a pool of people, our algorithms tend to be extremely accurate."

What is the process for a participant to use Upstart?

Dave Girouard: "The process begins by someone visiting our website [www .upstart.com] and creating a profile for themselves. This takes one to two hours. It then gets submitted to Upstart. The next step requires potential participants to provide the necessary documents to verify their information. This includes their transcripts from school, SAT scores, and so on. This is the profile and application process. Once this information is collected by Upstart, we calculate the potential participant's funding rate.

"Then, the potential participant determines how much they'd like to raise, based on the percentage of their income they want to use to pay back their backers and over what time period. Once these decisions are made, the participant clicks on a button within their profile to make it public, and it goes live for Upstart's backers to see and review.

"Once a profile is published on the Upstart platform, participants have 60 days to be funded. At this point, the process is somewhat similar to crowd funding on Kickstarter or Indiegogo, for example. After a profile goes public, participants can begin receiving offers from backers that same day. Once a participant receives at least $10,000 in backing, they can choose to accept the funds at any time and end their funding campaign, or they can continue until they receive their entire funding goal.

"One feature that Upstart offers to our participants is the ability to accept or reject an offer from any backer. Some participants are looking for specific types of backers who have a specific background or who work in a particular field, for example. It's also possible for backers to make anonymous offers, which participants can also choose to reject, although, the rejection of offers from backers doesn't happen too often."

During the funding period, what does a participant need to do to solicit and interact with potential backers?

Dave Girouard: "Right now, Upstart is a little constrained in terms of interaction between participants and potential backers until a backer makes an offer to back someone. It is possible for participants to seek out investors on their own. Most of the interactions happen after the funding is completed. This is where the participants publish updates about themselves, and backers can become mentors. They can offer advice or make professional introductions, for example. Because Upstart is currently limited only to working with credited investors, the Upstart participants are a little bit restrained in terms of soliciting their own backers, which is something we're looking to change soon."

Are the backers typically looking for a good financial investment, or are they looking to give back and serve as a mentor to young people?

Dave Girouard: "It varies, but many of our backers are looking for both opportunities. They want to make good financial investments but also want to share their knowledge, experience, and advice with others. Some backers remain quiet investors, while others make an effort to meet with the people they back and serve as an ongoing mentor."

What is the biggest misconception people have about Upstart?

Dave Girouard: "Outsiders who first hear about Upstart sometimes think that what we offer is a modern form of indentured servitude. This is not the situation at all. We have not reinvented slavery for the twenty-first century. Our goal is to liberate people and open up opportunities for them by giving them access to funds they can use to pursue their professional goals and dreams, while eliminating some of the all-too-common constraints that relate to debt.

"When someone participates in Upstart, they only owe based on what they earn during a predetermined period. The backers have absolutely no binding say over a participant's decisions or career path. They can offer advice, which the participant can take or ignore. It is very possible that participants will make career decisions that will negatively impact a backer's investment, but that's part of the game. If a backer is truly looking to profit from their investment, we recommend backing a pool of participants not just one."

Aside from giving up a percentage of their income for a predefined term, what other costs or fees are participants responsible for when using Upstart?

Dave Girouard: "When an individual gets funded, Upstart takes 3 percent off the total amount raised as our one-time fee. We also charge the backers one-half of a percent annually on the amount that they've invested, as an account management fee."

What tips can you offer to someone interested in using Upstart to raise money for themselves?

Dave Girouard: "When creating your profile, be as honest and detailed as possible about your goals. Try to provide as much specific information as you can. Focus on how you'll use the money you raise, how you'll pay off your existing debt, and what your future plans are from a career standpoint. Keep in mind, backers are investing in you, as a person, not in your business idea, for example. This is what sets Upstart apart from other crowd funding platforms."

In terms of potential participants in Upstart, who are the people that tend to get funded?

Dave Girouard: "There is no doubt that having an area of extraordinary achievement jumps out at backers. Being at the top of your class and from an elite school, for example, attracts attention. Including some information within your profile that jumps off of the page certainly helps in terms of positioning you as a unique individual.

"In addition to using text with a profile, participants can include photos or video within their profile to help tell their story. We encourage people to create high-quality videos of themselves. Making a video about yourself, as opposed to a business idea or project, can be tricky. We have seen some of our participants doing some pretty creative things on video in order to share their story. I recommend watching other peoples' videos on Upstart and reviewing their profiles before creating your own.

"In terms of pictures and video, potential backers want to see you at your vocation. Showing yourself at work or in an environment that is all about you and who you are is very useful. Be creative and showcase your personality, as well as your achievements. Figure out a way to demonstrate your drive and passion. You want potential backers to connect with you on an emotional level, plus see your potential as a financial investment.

"When creating your profile or video, don't play the sympathy card or try to create a reality show about your life. If you have overcome adversity and it somehow relates to your future and your goals, that's worth sharing. Otherwise, I recommend focusing on your achievements and not what you've overcome. For example, if you say, 'I am the first person from my family to graduate from college,' that is a strong and relevant statement.

"We have found that the participants who are the most active communicators using social media tend to be the most successful using Upstart. These people attract attention and continue to share information about themselves and their successes with backers and the Upstart community as well as the general public. Most of the people who have failed to get funded using Upstart were not good or active communicators."

How do you see Upstart evolving in the future as a crowd funding platform?

Dave Girouard: "I see two big changes occurring in the not-so-distant future. First, I would like to open up the service so just about anyone can become a backer. I believe this would allow the online community aspect of the service to grow and prosper. I also see this as becoming a more local product. In other words, backers will be able to find and invest in people from their own community, if they choose to. Backers will also more easily be able to support people looking to enter into their industry or who are pursuing a similar career path.

"Over the longer term, I would love to see the young people we're currently backing ultimately become successful and go from being participants to backers in order to give back to the community we're creating. I also see employers using Upstart as a recruiting tool.

"Within the next decade, Upstart's goal is to help people successfully launch one million new businesses. We are becoming a nation driven by entrepreneurs, and we want to help support those people starting in the very early days of their careers. We are creating a platform that is aligned with the way we believe the U.S. economy is currently going and will continue to go."

SCOTT N. MILLER, CEO OF DRAGON INNOVATION, DISCUSSES HOW TO USE CROWD FUNDING TO LAUNCH A TECHNOLOGY-RELATED PROJECT

Scott N. Miller has always been fascinated by technology. As a child, he loved taking things apart and putting them back together. Ultimately, he attended MIT to obtain his master's degree, and while there, had the opportunity to work on several cutting-edge projects, one of which was the Robo-Tuna, featured on the cover of *Scientific American*.

Upon graduating, he worked at a division of Walt Disney Imagineering R&D that was located near MIT, during which time he helped to create a life-size robotic dinosaur that was powered by a Corvette engine. After three years at Walt Disney Imagineering, he moved to iRobot, and spent a decade designing and manufacturing robots for the consumer market.

It was during this decade that Scott N. Miller learned all about high volume manufacturing. He ultimately ran iRobot's Roomba team to design and manufacture these consumer-oriented cleaning robots. During this time, he moved to China for four years, built and lead a team of more than 50 people, and oversaw iRobot's manufacturing, which included the creation of 40,000 Rumba robots per week. He was promoted to vice president of new product development for iRobot. His objective was to take what he now knew about manufacturing and incorporate that knowledge when initially designing and developing products.

In 2008, Scott N. Miller departed from iRobot and launched his own company, called Dragon Innovation (www.dragoninnovation.com). The goal of this company was to help start-up high-tech hardware companies successfully scale up from the prototype phase to the manufacturing and sale of the product. What few inventors or high-tech product designers realize is that reaching the prototype phase for a product is just the very start of what is necessary to ultimately bring a product to market.

By bringing together a team of designers and manufacturing and marketing experts, and having the ability to tap his team's vast international network, Dragon Innovation has successfully worked with hundreds of start-up, high-tech companies. A notable example is Pebble, the company that raised $10 million using crowd funding to create, manufacture, and ultimately sell one of the world's first smart watches.

More recently, however, Scott discovered the potential of crowd funding. Initially, he helped many of his clients use crowd funding campaigns on various existing platforms to raise the money needed to design, manufacture, and launch their products. However, Dragon Innovation has since launched its own crowd funding platform, designed specifically to help inventors and high-tech product designers raise the funding needed to develop and manu-facture their hardware products.

Why did Dragon Innovation launch its own crowd funding platform?

Scott N. Miller: "It just made sense for us. When I worked at iRobot, we would spend millions of dollars on the design and creation of a product, only to see it succeed or fail after the huge investment was made. I always thought it would be ideal if a company could predict a product's success before investing millions of dollars into it first. I wanted a better way to validate a product idea. It was around this time that I first started hearing about crowd funding.

"Crowd funding allows companies and inventors not just to raise capital, but validate their idea in the marketplace before making a huge financial investment. If enough people are willing to open their wallets and buy a product before it even exists, the inventor or company can be confident there will be a market for that product very early on.

"At the same time, those backers and supports can help a company or inventor spread the word about a product in a much more powerful way than using paid advertising. Crowd funding can also help a company deter-mine what inventory levels to built to, plus help raise additional financing through more traditional methods based on a proven customer base. We believe that crowd funding has changed the product development paradigm.

"We also discovered a major flaw in the crowd funding methods that already existed. Crowd funding gave start-ups the money needed to go from the design or prototype phase to the manufacturing phase, but many of these designers or inventors know little or nothing about manufacturing, which ultimately resulted in their project's failure. Over and over again, we were seeing companies that used crowd funding successfully, but didn't set their funding goal high enough to cover the true costs associated with tool-ing and manufacturing. We saw many entrepreneurs with great ideas wind up destroying themselves due to miscalculations."

What sets Dragon Innovation's crowd funding platform apart from others?

Scott N. Miller: "When a start-up wants to work with us and use our plat-form, we start out by doing what we call a deep dive on manufacturing, and use our expertise to price out all of the costs that will be associated with developing and manufacturing the product. We understand all of the hidden costs associated with domestic and international manufacturing and know how to avoid many common manufacturing pitfalls. We also know how to estimate the necessary tooling costs, so that the entrepreneur can figure out exactly how much money they'll need to raise in advance.

"By the time we're done, we develop an accurate projection related to how much money will be needed to help our client manufacture their product, so they can scale their crowd funding campaign accordingly. Part of this evaluation process also involves us running a series of what-if scenarios related to manufacturing. We work with our clients to help them save money when it comes to building a prototype and handling each aspect of the design through manufacturing process.

"Finally, we will sit down with our clients, and in conjunction with our marketing team, develop a comprehensive approach to promoting the crowd funding campaign to help ensure its success. Once all of these initial steps happen behind the scenes, only then will we publish their project's crowd funding campaign on our platform. Our goal is to make sure that if a project gets funded, the project creator will ultimately be able to deliver. This is something that's unique to our platform.

"When inventors and start-up high-tech companies use other crowd funding platforms, we have found that 75 percent of the funded projects either deliver late or don't deliver at all. Our goal is for 100 percent of our clients to be funded and ultimately deliver their product on time and on budget.

"Once a company is funded through our platform, it has the option to continue working with Dragon Innovation and utilize our expertise, which most of our clients do, or they can go off on their own.

"We primarily work with early-stage entrepreneurs whose projects are super risky and super expensive. Even if traditional investors don't see the merit of a project, it can still get funded using a crowd funding campaign and ultimately become successful. Crowd funding is a very powerful tool, but it's also very public. If a company doesn't manage their crowd funding campaign correctly, it could fail for reasons that have nothing to do with the validity of the product idea. Thus, crowd funding is a powerful tool that people want to use wisely."

How does Dragon Innovation choose which entrepreneurs, start-ups, or inventors it will work with and allow onto its crowd funding platform?

Scott N. Miller: "First, we only focus on consumer electronics hardware. Each client needs to meet with our various in-house experts to determine if their product or concept is, in fact, viable. Each step of this process takes two to three weeks. Then, as long as our team approves the project, and it comes from one or more entrepreneurs that demonstrate that they have the wherewithal to build the prototype for their product and handle a successful crowd funding campaign, we'll move forward.

"What we don't do is pick guaranteed winners. We don't care if traditional investors have turned down the project idea in the past. If a project can get through our in-house team's evaluation, we'll move forward with it.

"In almost all cases, a potential client for Dragon Innovation needs to come to us with a working prototype not just a rendering. What that does for us is show is they have the technical chops to actually build their product and grow a company around it. We also need that prototype information to do our in-house evaluation and calculate pricing for manufacturing, for example. In addition to having a prototype, we look for clients who understand their market.

"Each of the projects that go up on our crowd funding platform is assigned an in-house project manager who helps keep the campaign on track toward success. This is also something that's unique to our platform.

What are the costs associated with crowd funding using the Dragon Innovation platform?

Scott N. Miller: "Dragon Innovation charges $5,000 to analyze and prepare the campaign, and then receives 5 percent of the money collected for each funded project, with an additional 3 percent going to the credit card processing company. This takes them through the crowd funding process. If the project fails to get funded, we receive no money.

"Once the crowd funding campaign is done and the project is funded, a client can continue working with Dragon Innovation and take advantage of our expertise in high-tech manufacturing. Some clients, however, choose to move forward by themselves, but we still keep our eye on the project, since our name was on it.

"The majority of our clients work with us from the beginning of the project until we ship the goods to customers and beyond. If the client continues working with us, that is handled on a retainer basis."

Realistically, how many projects can the Dragon crowd funding platform handle simultaneously?

Scott N. Miller: "We're currently able to handle about 40 separate projects per month. We want to build companies, as opposed to overpopulating the platform with projects. We're also looking for the companies looking to raise $200,000, $500,000, $1 million, or more, not the companies that need $25,000."

What would you say is the biggest misconception people have about crowd funding?

Scott N. Miller: "Entrepreneurs are always optimistic, which is great. However, they also need to be realistic. Sometimes, expectations about how much money they can raise or how difficult it can be to run a successful crowd funding campaign are way off. Running a crowd funding campaign requires a significant time commitment every day. If you simply publish your project on a crowd funding platform and then sit back waiting for the money, that project will not get funded.

"It's absolutely necessary to keep your community excited and engaged throughout the entire process during the campaign. Another misconception is that the platform drives the traffic. In reality, the platform manages the traffic, but it's up to the project creator to drive the traffic to it."

Once a crowd funding campaign is underway, what are some of the best strategies for attracting backers?

Scott N. Miller: "The industrial design and promotional video are extremely important. However, it's equally important to drive a continuous flow of traffic to the platform. First and foremost, it's important to seek out the support of your own friends and family at the very start of a campaign in order to build up that initial hype for the project and get the funding process underway.

"Beyond that, we have found some of the paid advertising opportunities available on the Internet, such as Facebook ads, tend to be very effective. These campaigns are inexpensive, and can be very carefully targeted. Our clients have had very good results with Facebook advertising. Twitter and LinkedIn are useful tools, but we have not seen the same level of positive results from these services.

"Another useful tool is a website or blog that can be used to communicate with backers on an ongoing basis, throughout the life of the project."

You stress the importance of a promotional video as part of a crowd funding campaign. What tips can you offer on how to produce an effective video?

Scott N. Miller: "What's really important is that the company or project's founders be featured in the video. Don't use a paid spokesperson. Within the video, it's essential you get to the point quickly. Within the first 10 seconds, viewers should understand what the project is all about. The production quality is less important than the content, but the video should be in focus and have good quality audio. You'll probably want to use better equipment than the video camera built into an iPhone, but having an authentic video in terms of content is more important than production quality.

"Incorporating a call to action into the video is also essential. People need to be told what to do, how to do it, why their action is important, and what the benefit of their action will be. One of the great things about a crowd funding campaign that lasts for 30 days, for example, is that you can tweak your video along the way, based on response from backers.

"We highly recommend using analytical tools to obtain useful market research relating to your video. For example, not only can you easily determine the percentage of people who watch the video and then become a backer, you can figure out how long people are watching the video, at what point in the video people are clicking away, or what parts of a video they're watching repeatedly. If you find people are dropping off too soon, that means you are not conveying the right message fast enough.

"In terms of length, a two-minute promotional video should be enough to get the job done. That being said, many of our clients will invest several weeks producing their video to ensure every aspect of it is handled correctly. Most of our clients are able to create a really great video on a budget of $3,000 to $5,000, which includes hiring a professional videographer."

On the Dragon platform, do project creators use rewards to incentivize backers?

Scott N. Miller: "This is one thing that sets us apart from Kickstarter and other platforms. We focus on presales, not rewards, to attract backers. Our backers are able to purchase a product before it exists, and then be [among] the first to own that product once it's created. We do, however, encourage what we call early-bird specials. Our goal is to get projects at least 30 percent funded within the first week. To achieve this, during that first week of a crowd funding campaign, a product will often be sold at cost or just above cost. When we do this, we limit the quantities available.

"We also offer the option for backers to buy products in quantity, at a discount, in order to take advantage of the business-to-business angle. Because Dragon Innovation has an excellent reputation for delivering, we have many businesses as backers that will preorder products in blocks of 100 or more units.

"Having the right pricing strategy for a crowd funding project is critical. If you set the price too low, it takes too much work to reach your funding threshold. If you set the price too high, people won't buy the product. Pricing strategy is something we work closely with our clients on."

You talked about why it's important to have realistic goals. How should someone looking to use crowd funding set those goals?

Scott N. Miller: "Having realistic goals is essential. When you're trying to bring some type of product to market, you first need to understand your cost of goods sold. How much will it cost to buy the inventory? Next, you need to look at tooling costs. In our business, tooling can cost anywhere from $10,000 to several hundred thousand dollars. It's also important to understand all of the costs associated with manufacturing, including some of the less obvious costs. Our area of expertise at Dragon is manufacturing high-tech consumer electronics, so we're able to really help our clients set realistic goals.

"Once you know your costs, we have proprietary formulas we use to help our clients set a realistic funding threshold to ensure they'll have enough money to deliver the product. One of the biggest mistakes companies that don't work with us make is not setting their funding threshold correctly, so they don't raise enough money to actually create, manufacture, and ship their product on time. This is a deadly outcome for a project, even if they engage in a successful crowd funding campaign. We see this happening a lot with companies that don't do enough research and that use a crowd funding platform that doesn't offer the same level of support as ours."

How do you see crowd funding evolving in the not-too-distant future?

Scott N. Miller: "We're seeing more and more specialized crowd funding platforms launching. We're also seeing backers becoming more sophisticated and knowledgeable about how the crowd funding process works and, as a result, they're more cautious about what projects they support. This means that companies and individuals that utilize crowd funding need to do more preparation and research in advance.

"Right now, there are several different types of crowd funding. Our focus is on presales to help businesses raise money to launch a product. Some platforms allow companies to offer actual equity to their investors, and then there are charity-based crowd funding models. In the near future, these different forms of crowd funding will become more clearly differentiated and defined."

LEARN MORE ABOUT CROWD FUNDING FROM ROBERT WOLFE, FOUNDER OF CROWDRISE

Prior to launching CrowdRise (www.crowdrise.com), at the age of 21, Robert Wolfe founded a company called Moosejaw, an outdoor retailer dedicated to selling the best outdoor gear and apparel. At the time, he did everything possible to make running the company, working for the company, and being a customer of the company fun. Inadvertently, he developed a very unique way to interact with his customers.

When Robert Wolfe and his brother Jeffrey sold the Moosejaw business in 2009, they decided that their next business venture would not only be better, but that it should help to change the world. This led to them researching the charity space. What they learned from this research experience was that nobody was making fund-raising for a charity fun and that most donors were shamed into giving money to charity.

This research transformed into a goal, which was to develop innovative fund-raising opportunities that are fun and that create a positive impact. Their philosophy is that if people enjoy giving money, they will donate more, and if the fund-raisers have fun doing it, they will do it over and over again. Part of their goal was to transform the fund-raising process from being a tool into a movement.

At the time, Robert Wolfe looked at LinkedIn as a niche version of Facebook, used for posting information about one's professional life. He decided it was time to create a niche online-based crowd funding platform that would be more like Facebook, Instagram, and Twitter, in that it would be an interactive community as opposed to just an online tool, and the niche he was going to focus on was fund-raising. Read on for the story of how CrowdRise (www.crowdrise.com) works.

What sets CrowdRise apart from its competition?

Robert Wolfe: "We have created a way for anyone to have fun within an online community and raise money for just about any charity that's important to them, their business, or their organization. From a functional standpoint, every individual, organization, and charity has a page on CrowdRise, in much the same way people have a unique profile on LinkedIn that showcases their professional life."

CrowdRise is being used by both individuals and businesses to help raise money for charities they are passionate about. Who is the typical user of this platform?

Robert Wolfe: "There are lots of different types of users. It appeals to all sorts of runners, for example, who participate in marathons and who want to raise funds and awareness for a charity. We're the official fund-raising platform for many high-profile marathons. There are also many individual charities on the site, which are huge organizations, that now use CrowdRise as their official fund-raising platform. However, there are also kids giving up the opportunity to receive presents on their birthday in favor of raising money for the pet shelter that's located down the street from where they live."

How have you seen businesses utilize CrowdRise in order to boost their brand and give back to a charity?

Robert Wolfe: "This is a mass generalization, but many organizations are doing their philanthropy by taking the same approach that was used 20 years ago. For example, if a company wants to give $25,000 to a charity raising money in the environmental space, they'd donate the money, have a picture of the CEO holding a giant check taken, and that's the start and end of it. What we do is create an online-based campaign around a company's philanthropy by creating a public CrowdRise page around it. This is basically a microsite for a campaign.

"Now, instead of just giving away $25,000, a company can reach out to their community and say that through CrowdRise, instead of just giving away $25,000, we're going to do it as a match. Thanks to community engagement, that $25,000 donation becomes a $50,000 donation, and the company benefits from being seen as the driving force behind the campaign. This is just one way businesses are getting involved with CrowdRise and benefiting from the experience."

What is the process involved for an individual or business that wants to utilize CrowdRise to create an online fund-raising campaign that utilizes the crowd funding approach?

Robert Wolfe: "The process takes just a few minutes to set up online. You create an account, choose your benefiting charity, and then link your CrowdRise page to all of your online social networking accounts and email account. Then, anytime a donation is made to your charity through our platform, the person donating receives a tax-deductible receipt, and the money goes to the charity.

"Users are responsible for building their CrowdRise page, which is very quick and easy, and then driving traffic to it. We handle everything else. At CrowdRise, we take a small percentage of the total donations as our fee. There are no up-front payments. The percentage we receive depends on which type of account the various charities sign up for, and this can be 3, 4, or 5 percent, plus credit card processing fees.

"For an individual to raise money for a particular charity, that charity needs to be affiliated with CrowdRise. However, there are more than 1.6 million charities that are already registered on sites like CrowdRise, so all of those charities can be supported right away in conjunction with CrowdRise."

What's involved in driving traffic to a CrowdRise page so an individual or organization can raise money for the charity of their choice?

Robert Wolfe: "After creating their CrowdRise page, people simply need to drive traffic to that page using online social media, their website, blog, direct email, word of mouth, or any other forms of promotion. We have found that the whole concept of friends giving to friends works very well. We recommend taking advantage of as much exposure as you can get using your online networks. If your friends get an email about your campaign, there's probably a 50 percent chance they'll donate, while if you reach out to total strangers, that percentage is much lower, but you'll benefit from the exposure received for yourself and your cause.

"The best way to get exposure for a campaign is to make it fun or unique using the CrowdRise platform. This is what gets people motivated to donate and to share details about your fund-raising campaign with their own online networks. For example, if two people pick the same charity to raise funds for using CrowdRise, the person that says to their friends that they'll dye their hair blue if they reach their fund-raising goal is the person who will raise the most money the fastest.

"On your CrowdRise page, tell a personal and tangible story when soliciting donations. The more personalized your story and the more people relate to it, the better results you'll achieve. People also want to understand where their money is going. For example, if your campaign is to raise $10,000 to buy malaria nets, explain that the cost to get a net into the hands of someone who desperately needs it is $10. So, if someone donates $50, they know that they just supplied five people with malaria nets."

What is the biggest misconception people have about CrowdRise?

Robert Wolfe: "I think that the biggest misconception about the fund-raising on CrowdRise is that most people believe that having a big following on Facebook or Twitter, for example, will be an easy solution to raising a lot of money for a particular campaign. This certainly helps, but there's more work involved for the fund-raiser. We recommend using all of the social networking services at your disposal to promote your campaign, but we have found that direct email works the best in terms of driving traffic to a CrowdRise page.

"We have also found that people or organizations that incentivize people to donate have much better results. This leads back to my dying your hair blue example. Be creative and make it cool and fun for your friends, relatives, and online friends to donate to the cause you're passionate about.

"You definitely need to use direct email, engage with people using other online social networking services, and reach out to people about your fundraising campaign using other methods, or you won't drive traffic to your CrowdRise page and receive the donations you are seeking. Also, we have found that if, as the fund-raiser, you're enduring something, like participating in a marathon, this makes it easier to attract donators."

On many crowd funding platforms, having a promotional video is a powerful tool for attracting backers. Do promotional videos work on CrowdRise?

Robert Wolfe: "Most definitely. You can use text and photos to tell your story and explain the charity you or your organization is supporting, but a short video works much better as a storytelling tool. The video's production quality is nowhere near as important as using that video to tell your personal and tangible story. Producing a short video that's fun or quirky really works."

What are some of the ways a business or organization can brand its fund-raising activities using CrowdRise?

Robert Wolfe: "CrowdRise is now in the process of adding and expanding our online-based tools to allow businesses and organizations to create a more branded online experiences for their fundraising campaigns. This will allow people, organizations, and companies to help build their brand and reputation using CrowdRise, while also doing their fund-raising through a reputable and easy-to-use platform.

"We're also creating ways for companies to be able to donate a portion of proceeds from their online business transactions not just to their own favorite charities, but to allow the customer to choose their favorite charity."

BRAD WYMAN TALKS ABOUT THE FUNDANYTHING PLATFORM AS A VIABLE CROWD FUNDING OPTION

As a successful Hollywood producer with more than 30 films to his credit, Brad Wyman has helped create a wide range of major motion pictures as well as independent films. After seeing it become more and more challenging to get new movie projects funded, he began to explore other technologies and options for creating and distributing movies. By experimenting with several high-profile Internet-based streaming projects, he learned how to drive people to a web page and create compelling content. After working for Indiegogo for a while, he was invited to become the Chief Crowdfunding Officer (CCO) of FundAnything (www.fundanything.com), a fast-growing crowd funding platform that, as its name suggests, allows people to raise money for any type of project.

What made you get involved with the FundAnything crowd funding platform?

Brad Wyman: "As I was working on the various Internet streaming projects, I started hearing a lot about crowd funding, so I tried using it to fund movie projects. I wound up experimenting with crowd funding campaigns on many of the existing platforms, and over time, I got really good at using it. As a producer, my number one job is to get the money needed for each project. Crowd funding became a very viable way to fund movies.

"Based on my success, I was offered a job with Indiegogo and spent a year running their film, video, and web vertical. Due to a variety of issues, I found that Indiegogo limited me in regard to what I wanted to accomplish. I was then approached by some of the founders of FundAnything, and was asked to take on a leadership role on their platform."

As a reward-based crowd funding platform, what sets FundAnything apart from Kickstarter or Indiegogo, for example?

Brad Wyman: "A lot of things. Kickstarter does not offer flexible funding. If a campaign run on Kickstarter fails to reach its funding goal, the project receives no money. The way the transactions work is that even if you reach your funding goal with Kickstarter, you still need to wait up to a few weeks to receive your money. FundAnything offers almost instantaneous transactions. Within 24 hours after a backer supports your project, you receive the funds. We also offer better fulfillment tools, as well as tools for better interacting with backers.

"FundAnything is also open to any type of project, as long as it's not illegal or offensive. We offer customer service support that can help projects achieve success and get funded. One thing people launching a campaign with FundAnything need to realize is that it's their responsibility to drive people to their page. At the very least, someone from our campaign management team, however, looks at every campaign in advance and offers some personalized guidance."

What do you believe is the biggest misconception people have about reward-based crowd funding?

Brad Wyman: "That it's begging. People mistakenly think that you're looking for a handout. In reality, people choose to support your project, but you're required to give something back that has value. That's one of the keys to reward-based crowd funding. Thus, you better offer something that people want if you want to be successful raising money for it. Then, if you don't drive traffic to your campaign, it won't attract the backers it needs to be successful."

Who is a typical user of FundAnything, and what types of projects tend to do well on the platform?

Brad Wyman: "There is no typical user. The objective of a crowd funding platform is for people to bring their crowd to a campaign in order to raise money for a project. I recommend that before someone gets started, they read the FundAnything Handbook we created [http://fundanything.com/en/how#handbook] that explains exactly how the process works. We've divided the crowd funding process into 10 main steps that are broken down within the handbook.

"I recommend that people follow the steps outlined within the handbook to create their FundAnything campaign page. Then, once their page is created and enters the prelaunch phase, that's when our team takes a look at the project and starts working with you. My best advice is to get started and create your FundAnything campaign page. Don't just think about it."

What goes into creating a FundAnything campaign page?

Brad Wyman: "We offer extreme flexibility when it comes to page design, while other crowd funding platforms force you to do things a certain way. Start by setting a campaign goal amount and duration. I recommend between 30 and 35 days for duration, but there's certainly flexibility in that.

"Next, choose a campaign start date. You'll also be asked to supply imaging. This includes a thumbnail image for your campaign, a promotional video, as well as a catchy title. A campaign's chances of success increase 90 percent with a well-done video.

"Beyond that, you're directed to create a detailed campaign description and press release. We also guide you through the process of pinpointing your audience, who will be your initial supporters, and in linking your social media accounts to your campaign page.

"An extremely important part of any reward-based crowd funding campaign are the rewards to be offered. When creating your campaign, you'll need to set up your rewards. Make sure the pricing of your rewards is reasonable. If someone can buy the reward elsewhere for less, for example, they'll quickly lose interest in the campaign. People may want to help finance your project, but they're not looking to get ripped off."

What makes a good reward?

Brad Wyman: "Offering rewards that include some level of engagement is useful, especially if the person behind the campaign isn't typically accessible by the public. If you're a filmmaker, author, recording artist, musician, or actor offering exclusive access is a great reward. For example, a movie maker can offer a visit to the set, or a recording artist can offer special concert tickets and an exclusive meet-and-greet opportunity at a concert.

"If you're raising money to launch a product, a reward can be the opportunity to prepurchase that product at a good discount, so your backers get a bargain."

What are the fees involved with using FundAnything?

Brad Wyman: "We charge a 5 percent fee if you reach or exceed your funding goal, or 9 percent if you miss your funding goal. There's also a fee of approximately 3 percent charged by the third-party credit card processing company."

What tips can you offer for setting realistic funding goals for a project?

Brad Wyman: "Make sure you accurately reverse engineer whatever it is you're doing, so you know all of the costs involved. It's amazing how many people start off thinking they need $1 million to launch their project idea, but when they're forced to sit down and create a realistic budget, in reality they need much less money.

"It's important to understand how much money you actually need, but also to understand how much money you can realistically raise from your network using crowd funding. Figure out what you think your average contribution will be from each backer, as well as how many backers you think you can attract to your campaign. This will give you a very accurate projection about how much you can realistically raise from a reward-based crowd funding campaign.

"I always recommend setting your funding goal as low as possible, which makes it easier to achieve. Potential backers like to see success and realistic goals. If they see a campaign is failing or that it's trying to raise an unrealistic amount of money, they'll be much more hesitant to support it.

"Depending on the project, it might make sense for you to promote a lower funding goal than what you actually need, be able to reach that goal very early in the campaign, and then use the rest of the time in your campaign to reach or exceed your actual goal. This becomes much easier, because backers are excited to be part of a campaign's success."

What do you believe is the best strategy for reaching backers and supporters?

Brad Wyman: "I believe the secret is to effectively use email. I don't care how many friends you have on Facebook or how many followers you have on Twitter. What will bring the most money to a campaign is a well-written and personalized email that's sent to qualified recipients who are part of your target audience. As a result, I recommend building a large and relevant email database before you launch your crowd funding campaign.

"When it comes to crowd funding, email is your most powerful tool. It's the easiest way to convert potential backers into paying and active supporters. If you have a strong email base, you know that people will read your emails. I believe that when it comes to calculating a funding goal for a project, you should anticipate that 15 to 20 percent of your established email base will ultimately help fund your project, if you use email correctly.

"Knowing this, figure out your average contribution from each backer, and you should be able to calculate an achievable funding goal. Don't rely on strangers for your funding. You might be able to attract strangers to your campaign, but the majority of your funding will come from your established network.

"Another strategy for successful campaigns is to try to reach your funding goal as quickly as possible, but then keep up your promotional activities throughout the duration of the campaign. Why stop? Based on your success and the excitement you generate, you should be able to dramatically exceed your initial funding goal.

"One other benefit to using FundAnything is that even once your campaign comes to an end, we do not turn off your store. Thus, you can continue raising funds through presales."

In terms of the promotional video aspect of a reward-based crowd funding campaign, what makes the perfect video?

Brad Wyman: "It's important that you demonstrate your product or project in an earnest way. Keep the video under three minutes in length. It's important that people can clearly see and hear the video, but the overall production value is far less essential than the content of the video. Even an iPhone can shoot 1080p HD video, so there's no excuse to have poor image quality within your video.

"In the video, talk about what you're asking for and why you're asking for it. Talk directly to the audience by looking into the camera, and be sure to offer a demonstration of what you're making or doing. If you're creating and selling a product, have a working prototype you can show off and demonstrate within the video. That's really important.

"I think the focus of the video should be on why someone should contribute to the project. If there's an emotional story involved, tell it. There are no rules for getting someone to financially support a project. A lot will depend on what your project is all about and who you're targeting the video to.

"If you have great video production skills, use them and show them off to create an awesome video. Otherwise, create the best video you can. Within the video, I recommend you avoid using the word 'donate.' Everyone who supports a reward-based crowd funding campaign gets some type of reward back, so it's not a donation or handout. You are not panhandling."

What are some of the biggest mistakes you see people make when using crowd funding for the first time?

Brad Wyman: "People publish a project on a platform and then forget about it. What you should be doing is mounting a multifaceted campaign to drive traffic to your campaign's page. On day one, when your campaign launches, you need to demonstrate you have a lot of supporters already in place. If you don't have that initial support in place, don't bother launching the campaign.

"I like to see a 30-day-long campaign reach at least 30 percent of its funding goal within the first week. That is usually a good indicator it will be successful."

In your opinion, what are the core skills someone needs to create and manage a successful reward-based crowd funding campaign?

Brad Wyman: "To raise any amount of money for any project, you'll need to kiss a lot of ass. However, you need to decide carefully whose asses you want to kiss. You have to understand that your goal when using crowd funding is to get as many backers and supporters as possible to contribute the most amount of money possible to your project. To achieve this, you need to like the people you're approaching, be able to relate to them, and communicate well with them. If you don't like interacting with people, crowd funding is not a good option for you. Crowd funders who have a good crowd and good engagement going into their campaign are always going to do better.

"If going into the project you don't have a good enough network to help support what you're doing, before launching the campaign invest whatever time is necessary to first build up that network. You need to be able to take your social currency and turn it into transactions.

"One exception to this is if you have a really cool gadget you're trying to launch, and you somehow capture the attention of the media, you can run a successful crowd funding campaign. In this case, I strongly recommend seeking publicity from high-profile blogs that cover the types of product you're planning to create. If you manage to get the media to support a crowd funding campaign, it might go viral. This is much easier said than done, however."

Do you have any advice for hiring experts to help create and manage a crowd funding campaign?

Brad Wyman: "First, a platform like FundAnything prides itself on offering the tools and services needed to create and manage a campaign on your own. That being said, keep in mind that crowd funding is still a relatively new concept. Not a lot of so-called experts really have the experience and expertise that they boast. As a result, be very careful about hiring these people. There are some people who have the right skills and experience, who could be very helpful. However, there are plenty who don't."

How do you think crowd funding is going to evolve in the near future?

Brad Wyman: "Our research shows that only about 13 percent of the American public even knows what the term 'crowd funding' means. I think that's going to increase dramatically. I also think that the Jumpstart Our Business Startups Act, once it's fully implemented, is going to change the way equity-based crowd funding works. I think once people can take equity in projects, crowd funding in general will become more popular and become a viable investment opportunity."

CHAPTER 14

Crowd Funding Experts Share Their Secrets

- Hear from lawyers who specialize in crowd funding.
- Discover strategies from independent crowd funding consultants.
- Learn to avoid common crowd funding problems described by experts.

People who have become experts on crowd funding have gathered their knowledge by approaching this topic from various angles. In the previous chapter, you read strategies and advice from executives who represent popular crowd funding platforms.

In this chapter, you'll meet several crowd funding experts who help their clients achieve success using crowd funding, and then in Chapter 15, you'll read about the varied experiences of inventors, small business operators, and creative professionals who have successfully used crowd funding.

You already know that crowd funding is still a relatively new practice that is evolving quickly as it continues to gain popularity. As you'll soon discover, reward-based crowd funding has few legal restrictions and tax implications, but some legal experts who specialize in crowd funding believe this will eventually change, and, as someone hoping to use crowd funding to raise money for some type of business or project, these potential future legal and tax implications are worth considering, and perhaps preparing for.

As you read these interviews, keep in mind you're not being given individualized legal advice. You're simply learning from the personal opinions of lawyers and consultants who specialize in crowd funding. If you have specific legal questions or concerns related to crowd funding issues, consult with an attorney, consultant, and/or accountant directly.

ATTORNEY JOEL FISHMAN DISCUSSES THE POTENTIAL LEGAL AND TAX IMPLICATIONS RELATED TO CROWD FUNDING

Joel Fishman, an attorney with Marina del Rey, California-based Gladstone Michel Weisberg Willner & Sloane (http://gladstonemichel.com), has specialized in corporate securities for almost four decades. Much of his background involves working with clients within the entertainment, new media, technology, and communications fields. For many years, Joel Fishman worked with clients needing to raise money through traditional methods to launch new products, fund motion pictures, or somehow expand their businesses.

In the past, he explained, the main sources for raising capital were friends and family, as well as traditional investors. This meant following strict corporate securities laws and having to give up some equity in the business. Not only do companies need to adhere to federal laws, but state laws also apply. To comply with these legal regulations, lawyers, accountants, and other experts are needed.

In 1997, Joel Fishman first learned about crowd funding from a British band that sought funding in order to be able to record an album. The band turned to its fans and followers using the social media outlets available at the time. Since then, several different forms of crowd funding have become available.

One current crowd funding option involves companies or individuals offering equity in their company or project to investors. This continues to require adherence to strict laws and regulations, but thanks to the Jumpstart Our Business Startups (JOBS) Act, which was introduced in 2012 by President Obama, this type of crowd funding has become more viable to small start-up businesses and other types of organizations. It allows up to one million dollars to be raised without having to use accredited investors.

An accredited investor has an annual gross income of at least $200,000 or a net worth of at least $1 million, exclusive of home value. Additional opportunities, with fewer legal and tax implications, are being put into place (probably by late 2014) that allow companies interested in raising more than $1 million to work with accredited investors through online crowd funding portals that are affiliated with securities brokerage firms.

The second approach to crowd funding, referred to as reward-based crowd funding, is more popular and currently available using many different crowd funding platforms, including Kickstarter and Indiegogo. It allows people, organizations, and companies to fund projects, products, or businesses using a prepurchase, reward-based system that is not yet heavily regulated by any state or federal authorities.

What are some of the potential pitfalls related to the reward-based crowd funding platforms or systems currently in place?

Joel Fishman: "The backers of these projects are not investors, since they do not receive equity or any ownership of the company or project. These backers are basically prepurchasing a product or receiving some type of reward for their support. The backers are not supporting a project with the goal of earning a profit from an investment.

"As a result of the popularity of this form of crowd funding, there is now a huge stream of what might be called 'donations' flowing from backers to project creators. This has caused some lawmakers to begin questioning whether there should be federal or state taxes collected when a backer supports a project.

"Right now, a backer might give \$100 to their favorite up-and-coming rock band, which is using crowd funding. The band might collect \$1 million in total to fund a specific music-related project. Currently, there are no disclosure laws in place that say the rock band needs to explain exactly what it's going to be doing with the funds. If this were purely a fund-raising campaign for a recognized, not-for-profit, tax-exempt organization, it would need to disclose exactly how it utilizes the funds it receives.

"Thus, while a charity needs to adhere to strict fund-raising guidelines, the rules associated with an organization using a crowd funding platform are currently far less strict. Another potential pitfall is what could become tax implications related to reward-based crowd funding.

"From a tax standpoint, the Internal Revenue Service is looking into what the funds given by the backers to a project creator should be classified as, and whether or not those funds should be taxed as income of the project creator or treated as a financial gift, even though some type of presale of a product or reward was made.

"If a backer ultimately receives a product or reward in exchange for their support, theoretically, whatever the reward the backer receives should be subject to sales tax. As of early 2014, these are issues that have come up, but nothing has been addressed on the state or federal level.

"I believe these potential tax implications related to crowd funding will soon be taken up by the courts, and the outcome could dramatically impact the future of crowd funding as we know it today."

What should someone who wants to use crowd funding understand about these potential obligations that as of early 2014 don't yet exist?

Joel Fishman: "Reward-based crowd funding is still in its infancy, and it's unclear what obligations the recipients of the funds have or will have in regard to disclosure, income tax, and/or sales tax obligations. I believe anyone who uses crowd funding today should develop an understanding of what these potential obligations might mean to them financially and legally and prepare to address these issues if and when they become a reality in the not-so-distant future.

"Even with potential legal and tax implications, I am a big fan of crowd funding. It allows for people who are not already multimillionaires to get a project, business, or product funded, plus it allows nonaccredited investors to support start-up businesses that they are excited about. I think both types of crowd funding are really great for our economy, but I am also realistic in believing that more rules will eventually be put into place by federal and state regulators. These will make it a little more difficult to use crowd funding in the future, because project creators will be subject to greater scrutiny than they are now plus they will potentially need to pay taxes to their state and the IRS."

In what time frame do you think some of these new rules and tax laws related to reward-based crowd funding may be introduced?

Joel Fishman: "That's hard to determine. I think a court case will be filed in the near future by either a crowd funding platform or a company using crowd funding, in order to determine if funds need to be withheld for taxes. Plus, a backer could get involved with a case in order to question whether or not there is sales tax liability associated with supporting a project. Once this happens, the process of crowd funding will immediately become more complicated from a legal and tax standpoint.

"When this happens, tax lawyers, corporate lawyers, and accountants will need to get involved to make sure any new laws, as well as state and federal tax rules, are adhered to by the crowd funding platforms, the project creators, and the backers."

In your opinion, should steps be taken by project creators using crowd funding today to prepare for possible new laws or tax obligations in the future?

Joel Fishman: "As a project creator, you might want to sit down with an accountant to determine if it makes sense for your organization to set aside some of the money raised through crowd funding in case a tax obligation related to these funds arises in the future.

"After all, it's unknown if any new tax laws would apply to all present and past crowd funding projects or just to new crowd funding projects moving forward once any new tax laws and/or disclosure laws are put in place. I suspect there will be some grandfathering for transactions that took place before any new laws take effect, but I don't know this for sure.

"If, as a project creator, you plan to put funds aside to potentially pay state and/or federal income taxes, then your funding goal will need to be adjusted, based on the amount of money that's actually needed to fund your project.

"The point is, money raised through reward-based crowd funding is like free money. In the future, this probably won't be free money. However, even if new disclosure laws and tax obligations are put into place, crowd funding is still a sweet opportunity for project creators."

What is a common misconception people have about crowd funding?

Joel Fishman: "Crowd funding is not about raising free money that you can do whatever you want with. Ultimately, I believe a business plan should be put into place, and project creators should adhere to general business practices when operating their business or when bringing their project to fruition.

"If I were planning to use crowd funding to launch a new high-tech product, for example, even though it's not required right now, I would follow the same rules of disclosure as an established business would follow when raising capital using traditional methods. This means creating a carefully put together document, not just a sales piece. I would want to make sure that I inform everyone about the project, who's involved with it, and what the real possible outcomes of the project are. I'd also outline and disclose risks, and create a line-item budget for the project.

"If you use crowd funding now or in the future, you will have greater access to capital, much more easily and inexpensively than you do otherwise using other funding methods."

What is the best way to find a lawyer who specializes in crowd funding?

Joel Fishman: "There are many lawyers out there who have developed a good knowledge of crowd funding. Many of these lawyers really understand the corporate securities side of crowd funding, but not the reward-based crowd funding opportunities. I always recommend someone find an attorney through positive word-of-mouth, and then the client should ask specific questions about the attorney's areas of expertise and experience as it relates to their specific needs."

ATTORNEY MARKLEY RODERICK SHARES HIS ADVICE AND KNOWLEDGE ABOUT CROWD FUNDING

After spending many years working as a tax lawyer, Markley Roderick opted to specialize in business law, handling mergers and acquisitions as well as assisting businesses raise money through private transactions. He has since spent several decades working with companies on what he refers to as "capital formation." Thus, as crowd funding became a viable way for businesses to raise capital, this quickly caught his attention.

When Markley Roderick, an attorney with Flaster Greenberg (www .flastergreenberg.com), first learned of the JOBS Act, he immediately knew that crowd funding would become an enormous event that would fundamentally change the capital formation industry. He then began focusing a tremendous amount of time and effort into learning everything he could about crowd funding and has since become an expert in this area.

Markley Roderick also maintains a blog that covers various aspects of equity-based crowd funding (http://crowdfundattny.com).

How would you say that the JOBS Act has impacted crowd funding?

Markley Roderick: "The JOBS Act, for all intents and purposes, created crowd funding. This term is used generically to refer to any fund-raising that occurs on the Internet. However, the JOBS Act is what made crowd funding legal when you are selling stock or borrowing money on the Internet. Services like Kickstarter, that allow for reward-based crowd funding or that allow for the presale of something, have always been legal.

"It was the JOBS Act that made equity-based crowd funding legal, however. This is where a business is selling or giving up equity or some ownership of the company, for example, in exchange for capital. I believe that in the not-very-distant future, every type of business, large or small, whether it's a start-up or a well-established company, will begin using crowd funding in some way.

"In the short term, it is the coolest, sexiest, and most socially responsible businesses that are currently having the most success using crowd funding. Businesses and projects that in the past would not get easily funded, including socially responsible business ventures and projects, are now able to turn to crowd funding for capital. At the same time, any interesting business venture or project being created by people who know how to fully utilize online social networking, is also experiencing success with crowd funding."

What are some of the ways traditional businesses will soon be using crowd funding?

Markley Roderick: "They're going to use crowd funding in exactly the same way that they've used other money-raising techniques. It's just that now they will be able to do it by appealing to the general public, which has trillions of dollars at its disposal. From a legal point of view, there are two types of crowd funding under the JOBS Act. Equity-based crowd funding allows businesses to seek out funding just as they always have, but they can now advertise to the public to find investors and backers. This represents the most dramatic change to the United States' securities laws since the Great Depression, and it's what makes crowd funding so powerful."

What impact will this have on the traditional methods that companies once used to raise capital?

Markley Roderick: "Eventually, the traditional methods for raising capital will become antiquated in favor of crowd funding. Past methods of raising capital involved relying on and having to pay a lot of different middlemen, such as brokers, investment bankers, finders, and lawyers. These methods relied on developing personal relationships with people who have access to money to invest but included the necessity to go through several different middlemen, each of whom received compensation for the effort.

"Equity-based crowd funding is able to weed out many of the middlemen, which makes the capital raising industry more efficient. Not only will this make it easier for some businesses and inventors, for example, to raise money, it will also make it less costly to seek out and acquire capital. Investors will also get better deals. It will be the middlemen, however, who lose out as crowd funding becomes a more mainstream replacement for raising private capital."

How quickly do you see the popularity of equity-based crowd funding becoming mainstream?

Markley Roderick: "Within 10 years I think a crowd funding portal will have grown large enough and powerful enough to buy Morgan Stanley, for example."

What types of businesses have you seen successfully use equity-based crowd funding thus far?

Markley Roderick: "Many types of business from many industries have already discovered ways to utilize this type of crowd funding. I have seen real estate companies, for example, use crowd funding very effectively. I have also seen exciting, high-tech companies having success using crowd funding, because everyday people want to invest in the next big thing. It's very early to see what types of businesses and industries will benefit the most from the JOBS Act and equity-based crowd funding."

One misconception people have about equity-based crowd funding is that it can only be used by start-ups. However, more and more well-established companies are using crowd funding to fund new products. Is this a trend you see expanding?

Markley Roderick: "It is. Companies are using crowd funding not just to raise money but to test the viability of a new project or product without having to invest their own money in developing the idea before it proves viable.

"For example, if a new product will cost $50,000 to develop, a well-established company might not need the $50,000 to move forward right away on that project. By using crowd funding, it can predetermine if there's a demand for the product and use its backers to fine-tune an idea before spending anything. This dramatically increases the possibility of a new product's success, while reducing the financial risk a company faces when it comes to developing, manufacturing, launching, and marketing new products.

"If enough consumers are willing to prepurchase a product or back a project that's being funded using crowd funding, this is a good indication that the company should pursue it further. Thus, crowd funding is becoming a powerful testing ground that's more reliable than focus groups, for example."

What do you think is a common misconception people have about crowd funding?

Markley Roderick: "From my perspective, it's that people don't understand the difference between an equity-based crowding funding site and a reward-based platform, like Kickstarter. There is a fundamental distinction that many people still don't understand. On the equity-based side, people remain totally confused about the two types of equity-based crowd funding and the rules associated with them.

"When it comes to equity-based crowd funding, there are Title II and Title III crowd funding types. These refer to the sections of the JOBS Act in which they are found. Title II crowd funding allows a company to raise an unlimited amount of money from an unlimited number of investors, as long as all of the investors are accredited, as defined by the U.S. Securities and Exchange Commission. An accredited investor is basically someone who is wealthy.

"Title III crowd funding on the other hand allows a company to raise money from an unlimited number of nonwealthy people, but the most a company can raise is $1 million within a year, and there is a limit as to how much each investor can actually invest. So, you can raise small amounts of money from many individual investors in an effort to raise up to $1 million per year. You can see how, in the public's mind, all of these rules get a bit confusing. Title III crowd funding doesn't become legal until the summer of 2014 at the earliest."

How should a company determine which crowd funding approach to take?

Markley Roderick: "Until Title III crowd funding actually becomes legal and all of the rules related to it are disclosed by the government, it's hard to say whether or not this crowd funding method will be viable at all to any type of business. For most companies, using Title II crowd funding is a no-brainer."

With equity-based and reward/donation-based crowd funding both growing in popularity quickly, which method do you recommend?

Markley Roderick: "It all depends on the company, the project, and what you're trying to accomplish. There is a very limited amount of money that you can realistically raise in a reward/donation-based environment. Yes, there have been some companies that have raised millions of dollars using Kickstarter, for example, but these are few and far between compared to the number of projects published on Kickstarter and similar platforms.

"This limit is because backers are not getting a lot for their money. They're not actually making an investment. They're simply prepurchasing a product or receiving some type of reward for their support. Thus, a company that wants to raise hundreds of thousands of dollars or more will probably need to use the equity-based crowd funding model.

"Every few months, the world of crowd funding portals changes dramatically. So, regardless of which type of crowd funding you want to pursue for your business or project, you'll need to research which platforms are currently the most viable, based on what you're trying to accomplish. Even the most established crowd funding portals and platforms are still in their infancy. It's impossible to say which will ultimately become the most popular."

Is there specific functionality someone should look for when choosing a crowd funding platform or portal?

Markley Roderick: "The easy answer is yes, there is. However, what we're seeing is that all of the new platforms are offering this functionality at their launch. The equity-based crowd funding portals that exist today, like Funders Club [https://fundersclub.com], Realty Mogul [www.realtymogul.com], and Speed Invest [http://speedinvest.com], all have outstanding functionality, which will no doubt improve as time goes on. They will all eventually have the same or very similar functionality.

"What will be the differentiating factor in terms of the platforms/portals is going to be the ones that sign up the best investors and that attract the best companies looking for funding. Right now, it's a chicken-and-egg exercise, which is why the most successful portals will also be very strong marketing companies. They'll all have similar technology, but the successful portals [crowd funding platforms] will be the ones able to market themselves the most successfully to both companies looking for capital and investors.

"It will be the portal's ability to establish and build a thriving online community that will determine its success. Let's look at eBay, for example. It brings about one billion buyers and sellers together on one platform. Someone could launch a competitor to eBay tomorrow that offers better technology and more cutting-edge buying and selling features, but it won't have that established community that makes eBay so successful."

What is the one task or responsibility that's changed about raising capital in terms of what a company needs to do when it comes to crowd funding?

Markley Roderick: "Raising capital with crowd funding is all about producing a really great video. While you can do crowd funding without a video, you'd be foolish to try it. Videos are powerful. Traditionally, when companies wanted to raise money, a thick book was created by lawyers. It talked about the company, the risks, and the benefits. When you compare those documents with the short promotional videos companies are making today, the difference is night and day.

"A company that wants to use crowd funding really needs to make a really good video. I think there are a few things that the video needs to explain, such as the size of the market or demand for the product or project, as well as why the company or investor is uniquely suited to fill that need. I believe a good crowd funding video also needs to reflect some type of social benefit.

"One mistake you want to avoid is using equity-based crowd funding in such an incorrect way that you prohibit your company from using crowd funding in the future. There are several ways this could happen if you don't structure the crowd funding deal correctly. I have put together a sample well-structured deal, which is available on my blog [http://crowdfundattny .com], however, this is where an attorney can be extremely helpful.

"Once you have a well-structured crowd funding deal in place, it can be used repeatedly. There's no need to reinvent the wheel for every deal. This is one way that crowd funding is so efficient. All equity-based crowd funded deals will look the same. This is useful, because investors who want to invest in crowd funded projects or businesses will not want to compare apples to oranges, as far as deal structure is concerned, each time they look at a potential investment opportunity."

For small businesses or inventors that want to use equity-based crowd funding, at what point should they consult with an attorney?

Markley Roderick: "I would suggest that they consult with a lawyer who understands crowd funding very early on. What they should expect from the lawyer is that he or she will have an understanding of the crowd funding alternatives available, so that the advantages and disadvantages are made clear to the company, and that the appropriate disclosures are made.

"The best way to find a lawyer that specializes in crowd funding is through word of mouth. Of course, you can also do a Google search for a lawyer who specializes in crowd funding. There are currently a handful of lawyers who have real expertise in crowd funding. However, within a year or two, most securities lawyers will know at least the basics about crowd funding."

DISCOVER MORE CROWD FUNDING STRATEGIES FROM CONSULTANT PATTY LENNON

After spending 15 years working in commercial finance, Patty Lennon launched her own business coaching company. Her specialty was helping mothers become excellent parents and work as successful business operators. At one point, Patty Lennon wanted to host a conference for entrepreneurial mothers but needed to raise $45,000 to fund the conference.

Instead of using her own money, she opted to use crowd funding to raise the money needed to host the conference. After doing a ton of research about crowd funding and then utilizing her skills in project management and marketing, she launched her crowd funding campaign using Indiegogo.

Based on her research, she knew in order to achieve success she would need to invest 12 to 15 hours per day on the campaign. However, as a mother, that type of time commitment was impossible. So, she invested much more time before the campaign's launch on her preparation efforts. This allowed her to spend less time managing the campaign once it went active.

Ultimately, her campaign was fully funded in 14 days. As part of this process, she developed five strategies for managing a successful reward-based crowd funding campaign. She also determined that crowd funding was a viable business strategy that many of her clients could benefit from.

As a result of her own crowd funding success, she began teaching others, both in groups and privately, about reward-based crowd funding. Ultimately, Patty Lennon (www.momgetsabiz.com/www.crowdfundwithease.com/tag/patty-lennon) became one of the country's leading reward-based crowd funding consultants.

Why did you originally go with Indiegogo as opposed to one of the other crowd funding platforms?

Patty Lennon: "I wanted to use a service that the press would recognize when I issued press releases. At the time, Kickstarter and Indiegogo were the leading crowd funding platforms. When I looked closely at the types of campaigns each service hosted, I didn't feel like Kickstarter would be the best match for my particular project."

Once you decided to use Indiegogo, what was the process for getting started?

Patty Lennon: "Unlike with Kickstarter, there is no preapproval process. On Indiegogo, you simply need to set up a free account and then create your campaign using an online-based step-by-step process. As part of this campaign creation process, you definitely want to link your Indiegogo campaign to all of the social media platforms you're active on."

What was the biggest misconception you had about crowd funding initially?

Patty Lennon: "Before I started doing my research, my biggest misconception was how much time creating and managing a successful crowd funding campaign would actually take. What people don't realize is that doing this correctly takes an enormous effort and a lot of planning. That being said, every ounce of energy you put into it, you get back tenfold in terms of the ultimate benefits, which go well beyond just raising the money you need to fund your project.

"When I first started with crowd funding, I had no experience producing videos. I believe a successful crowd funding campaign must have a well-written and well-produced video. This is where I see a lot of first-time crowd funders fail. When many people or organizations launch a crowd funding campaign, they throw a video online without understanding the importance of that video."

What are the most important components of a good promotional video?

Patty Lennon: "First, the video needs to grab the full attention of its audience within the first 15 seconds. The video also needs to be entertaining, while telling a compelling story about the crowd funding project. There are thousands of projects on these different crowd funding platforms at any given time, and the promotional video is a powerful tool that should be used to differentiate your project.

"During the first 15 seconds of your video, you want to share a compelling image and an important statement, plus have a call to action that's clear. It should ask people to support your project financially and to help spread the word about it. I also recommend using appropriate background music within the video.

"Also, within the video, the person who spearheads the project should be the star, whether it's the company's founder or the product's inventor. However, don't dedicate too much of the video to allowing that person to drone on about themselves. That person simply needs to tell a key part of the story that relates to why they're pursuing the project.

"The person hosting the video or starring in it needs to use the right tone of voice and the appropriate body language to engage the audience and capture their attention. The video should also focus on what the benefits of the project are. People become backers of projects because they want to feel like they're somehow changing the world.

"Funders will hand over larger amounts of money if your video includes a strong 'TLC' message. Within the video, you make someone think. You make them laugh, and you make them care. If you can make them cry, if your project is cause-driven, that helps, too.

"Spend at least 30 seconds of your two- to three-minute video explaining why you're doing what you're doing, and the difference you hope it will make in the world. Spend 30 seconds showcasing people who have been or will be affected by the change you're creating. If you're putting an invention out into the world, talk about how your product will impact the lives of its users.

"Don't spend too much time on how you're doing something within your video. More time should be spent on explaining why you're doing it. Use the text-based campaign summary, not the video, to focus on the how."

Since background music is an important component in a promotional video, what advice can you share about choosing the best music to use?

Patty Lennon: "The music should be appropriate to the underlying message you're trying to communicate and to your target audience. The music should complement your message not distract video viewers from it. The music should also match the feeling you want the video's viewers to have.

"The least expensive option is to use precomposed, royalty-free music that can be licensed. I personally use a music service called Audio Jungle [http://audiojungle.net]."

You mentioned that you did a lot of the groundwork in preparation for your initial crowd funding campaign beforehand, so you could spend more time with your kids while the campaign was underway. What were some of the steps you took to prepare?

Patty Lennon: "One of the first things I did was I went out and found people who were successful using crowd funding and I interviewed them. Based on what I was told, it became apparent that ongoing communication with backers and potential backers is essential.

"One of the first things I did as I was preparing my own crowd funding campaign was to write out all of the different communications I would have with my backers. I prewrote pages and pages of social media updates and messages that would later be posted at various times throughout the campaign. I also prewrote most of my email messages and press releases, and each of these communications was structured differently, based on when in the campaign it'd be used and who it would be targeted to.

"Another thing I did was plan out in advance how my energy would be at each point within the campaign. For example, my messaging when the campaign hit the 50 percent funding mark was prewritten in several ways, using several different tones. The version I ultimately published would be based on whether my campaign hit that 50 percent mark within a few days or after three weeks, for example, once the campaign was active.

"Another strategy I put into place in advance of the campaign's launch was creating a team of advocates who had very specific jobs during the campaign.

"Knowing that direct email is a powerful and important tool for attracting potential backers, not only did I prewrite the key email messages to be used throughout the campaign, I also invested time carefully compiling and organizing my email lists. My email lists were organized based on the type of relationship each person had to my campaign. For example, friends and family members were in one list, while current and past clients were in another list. All of the campaign's top supporters were also included in their own list."

What would you say are the most important skills someone needs in order to create and manage a successful reward-based crowd funding campaign?

Patty Lennon: "One important skill is being able to ask for help and knowing how and when to delegate responsibilities to the appropriate people. If you try to do everything yourself, you'll quickly get overwhelmed.

"Another essential skill is project management. You need to keep all of the details related to the campaign organized and on track. If you don't have solid project management skills, find someone who does, or work on developing those skills before you launch your campaign.

"A third important skill is the ability to communicate effectively in order to market yourself and your project."

Should someone line up outside services to help them preplan and then manage their crowd funding campaign?

Patty Lennon: "This depends on two factors: the skill set and experience you have yourself and your budget. If you are trying to raise $2,500, you are not going to invest $3,000 in a videographer or video production team, for example. Based on your budget, however, hiring a professional video production team is something I strongly recommend. If you can't invest in a full production team, at least rent or borrow a good quality camera and sound equipment.

"If you are not a prolific writer, then you probably want to enlist the help of a copywriter. This would be someone who can help to tell your story using text as you create your crowd funding campaign, write the script for your video, write promotional emails, and compose the status updates and blog entries that will be used as part of your social media marketing campaign. You also want to have press releases and other marketing materials written in a concise and easily understandable way.

"Also, if you or your organization isn't already active on the various social media sites, long before you launch your crowd funding campaign, you need to get onto the various sites and develop a following. For this, you may need to bring on a social media team.

"Finally, I recommend hiring a consultant who is an expert in crowd funding and who can help you efficiently preplan your entire campaign, oversee its management, and help ensure its success. If you can't afford to hire someone to manage your entire campaign, find an expert who will at least review your campaign plan before it goes live."

Once a reward-based crowd funding campaign goes online, what types of communications with backers are important to build and maintain excitement in the project?

Patty Lennon: "Once someone backs your project, they're already excited about it, so you need to post updates on a regular basis. One strategy is to get your existing backers to reach out to their own social networks and promote your campaign on your behalf in order to attract more backers. Every time you hit some type of milestone within the campaign or that relates to your project that is worthy of an update it should be shared publically.

"As soon as someone becomes a backer of your project, it's important to immediately thank them for their support. This should happen within the same day. Depending on the level at which they've supported you, this can be as simple as using an auto-responder email. However, for your more generous backers, a more personalized and direct form of thank-you is appropriate."

Based on your experience, which social media services are the most useful when it comes to promoting a crowd funding campaign?

Patty Lennon: "In my experience, if your project is purpose driven and has a really good story that pulls at people's heartstrings, for example, Facebook can be a powerful tool for sharing that story and converting followers into backers. If you're funding a product that has strong visual appeal, using a service like Pinterest can be useful. If you're doing something that's technology related, Twitter is very useful for communicating with backers and potential backers."

What is one of the biggest mistakes you see people or organizations make once their reward-based crowd funding campaign launches?

Patty Lennon: "I think a lot of people believe that the crowd funding platform is going to attract a lot of potential backers to their project. This is not the case at all. The platform you choose will showcase your project and help you manage your backers, but it's ultimately your responsibility to attract your own backers for a reward-based crowd funding campaign.

"Also understand that very few crowd funding campaigns go viral. Instead of trying to differentiate yourself from all of the other campaigns running on the various platforms, focus more of your efforts on retaining potential backers once you get them to your page and converting them into backers. The easiest way to do this is to start off with a very strong and compelling message.

"Throughout your campaign, make it clear that there is a beginning and an end, and that if your project gets fully funded, it is really going to happen."

Outside of the problems associated with producing a poor video, what are some of the other pitfalls to avoid when planning a reward-based crowd funding campaign?

Patty Lennon: "Avoid offering too many perks or rewards. Brainstorming compelling perks or rewards for a campaign is a skill unto itself. If you offer too many choices, it will confuse your backers. I recommend that at any given time, a campaign should have no more than five to seven available rewards, each with a different level of required financial support.

"The best perks are tangible items or experiences that tie closely to whatever it is you're funding. The core perk should be the product or experience itself that the project relates to. However, for the higher-end perks, include some type of intimate experience with the project creator. Backers want experiences that offer a behind-the-scenes look at the project and/or direct access to the creators. These rewards should appeal to the backer's sense of exclusivity.

"If at the $1,000 or $5,000 support level, for example, you're offering a reward that someone could readily purchase, that probably won't work. You want to make it so that the only way that person can obtain the reward or perk is if they support your project with a higher dollar amount. These backers should also receive significant public recognition for their support.

"For the smaller dollar amount rewards, focus on offering some type of personal gratitude for a backer's support. Depending on your crowd funding campaign, having a $1 reward level may be beneficial or it may be a total waste. I believe that if someone will give you $1, they'll give you $5 or $10. I think the minimum perk offered comes down to what your goal amount is.

"When someone supports your campaign with $10 or less, they should receive an auto-responder email with a thank-you message. For a low amount, don't invest your time and effort creating a reward that will require your time or resources to fulfill. Your distribution costs should be very low. Avoid having to mail these backers something. Make your reward something you can send via email or something the backer can download."

How important is creating a business plan when using crowd funding to launch a business or create a product?

Patty Lennon: "If you're using equity-based crowd finding, creating a traditional business plan is important. However, for a reward-based crowd funding campaign, having a business plan is important only to the extent that it can help you, as the business operator, stay focused and on track. I recommend developing a simple business plan that outlines who you are, who you sell to, what you're selling, and how many you need to sell in order to make the financials work. This condensed business plan should also outline how you plan to achieve your objectives.

"When using reward-based crowd funding, you will not need to share your business plan with others, but this document will help you be an organized businessperson."

Do you have any tips for how someone should set realistic goals for their crowd funding campaign?

Patty Lennon: "Make sure the amount of money you set out to raise is really enough to make your project a reality, and make sure that based on your available resources, you'll be able to reach the right number of people with your campaign. For example, if you determine you'll need to attract 10,000 backers during your campaign, but your existing social media network is composed of a few hundred people, and you have limited financial resources, your ability to attract enough backers is inadequate.

"Begin by analyzing your existing social network. Figure out how many people you can realistically attract as backers, and on average, how much each of those people will be able or willing to offer as their funding amount. On average, expect to receive between $25 and $35 per backer.

"So, if you have 1,000 potential backers in your social media network and each offers $25, theoretically you should be able to raise $25,000 from those people. This figure should represent 40 percent of your overall goal amount.

"From my experience, I have found that 40 percent of your goal amount will come from your core social network, which includes friends and family. The next 40 percent will come from their social networks reached through word-of-mouth, as well as your promotional activities. The last 20 percent will come from a combination of other sources.

"The trick to getting your core backers to help you promote your campaign and spread the word about it is to make it as easy and quick as possible for them to do this. For example, offer them a prewritten email they can forward to their own friends and family, or make it easy for them to share a link to your campaign with their Facebook, Twitter, and/or LinkedIn friends."

One common mistake crowd funders sometimes make is that they set a funding goal that isn't high enough to make their project a reality. What tips do you have for avoiding this pitfall?

Patty Lennon: "I recommend enlisting the help of someone with a financial background who can help you create realistic budgets and projections. I then recommend you add 20 to 30 percent to that amount as a cushion. You may discover that based on how much you need to raise, you don't have enough people in your current social network to realistically fund that campaign. In this situation, I recommend breaking the campaign into smaller parts, and then running two or three separate campaigns. Or, seek out some of the seed money you need from other sources and use crowd funding to make up the difference.

"If you use crowd funding effectively to fund a portion or phase of your project, you may be able to solicit investors or sponsors to help fund the subsequent phases, now that you've demonstrated there's a strong interest in what you're trying to accomplish. People often use crowd funding because they can't prove the viability of their project to traditional investors. Once you're able to prove that viability, investors may look at your project more favorably."

What should someone do if his crowd funding campaign fails?

Patty Lennon: "First, evaluate what you did. Make sure that you did everything correctly, and what you did everything you could have done to promote the campaign. Next, look closely your video and make sure it offered the right message in a compelling way. Determine what aspect of your campaign failed and why.

"Next, based on your analysis, determine if there was no interest in your actual project from potential backers or if your messaging was off. You can do this by asking around and doing traditional market research.

"Third, you might want to sit down with a crowd funding expert and have that person offer suggestions about whether or not you should fine-tune your campaign and try again, perhaps launch the campaign using another crowd funding platform, rework your project idea, make adjustments to your promotional efforts, or scrap the project altogether."

How do you see crowd funding and the crowd funding platforms evolving over the next few years?

Patty Lennon: "The reward-based crowd funding platforms will continue to evolve. We may see a merging between equity-based and reward-based crowd funding. I think that reward-based crowd funding will become more of a marketing vehicle, as opposed to a money-generation vehicle. I think backers are going to begin expecting a more professional approach from the crowd funding project creators and will expect higher production value in promotional videos.

"I also anticipate that a subindustry will be created by video production companies that will provide a turnkey solution for producing promotional videos to be used as part of crowd funding campaigns. This will include the scripting, shooting, and editing of the video. Thus, I think individuals or companies that opt to use crowd funding will need to make a financial investment in their video production.

"I also believe that the crowd funding platforms will become more niche oriented. For example, there will be platforms that specialize in campaigns looking to raise less than $5,000, and others that cater to specific areas of interest or industries.

"We'll also see more do-it-yourself, reward-based crowd funding services that allow you to host your own campaign on your existing website without needing to use a separate crowd funding platform. This will allow companies to presell product ideas, for example, and in the process obtain valuable market research, allowing them to determine if there is a large enough demand for a product idea before investing a lot of money developing that idea."

Do you have any advice for hiring a crowd funding consultant?

Patty Lennon: "Look for someone who has proven experience doing the type of crowd funding campaign you have in mind. If you are looking to raise more than $25,000, make sure you team up with a consultant who can help you with public relations and marketing, as well as planning and managing the campaign itself."

ONLINE MARKETING SPECIALIST ROY MOREJON EXPLAINS HOW A DIGITAL MARKETING AGENCY CAN HELP WITH YOUR CROWD FUNDING CAMPAIGN

Throughout this book, a lot of emphasis has been put on the importance of using the Internet and social media to properly market and promote your crowd funding campaign. If you don't possess the skill and experience needed to use email, Facebook, Twitter, and other social media services as effective marketing tools, perhaps you should hire a digital marketing agency that specializes in this.

Roy Morejon is the founder of Command Partners (http://commandpartners.com), a digital marketing agency with an expertise in promoting crowd fund campaigns that utilize Kickstarter as their crowd funding platform.

Who is a typical client of Command Partners?

Roy Morejon: "We work with clients who have a great idea for a business, product, or project that needs to be funded, and then create a customized marketing plan to promote their crowd funding campaign. In the past three years, we have focused primarily on working with clients who are utilizing Kickstarter as their crowd funding platform, and we've helped more than 75 projects get successfully funded. In total, we've helped our clients raise more than $5.5 million as of early 2014."

At what point should a company that wants to use reward-based crowd funding hire Command Partners or another digital marketing agency?

Roy Morejon: "Ideally, a firm like ours should be hired three months or more in advance of a campaign's launch. However, we have worked with a number of clients who thought they could handle everything on their own, discovered it was a bigger undertaking than they anticipated, and then hired us three days before a campaign's launch or after a campaign is already underway.

"The more time we have to work with our clients and prepare an appropriate marketing and promotional campaign, the greater the chances of success for that campaign. If the campaign will utilize a public relations effort in order to reach out to the media, this takes time to plan and execute.

"We have also been helpful when a campaign gets fully funded quickly, but still has time left before it ends and the project creator wants to raise as much additional funding as possible during that time using stretch goals."

What services does a digital marketing firm handle?

Roy Morejon: "Command Partners handles our clients' online social networking, search engine optimization, PR efforts, and email marketing. We specialize in engagement and driving targeted traffic to crowd funding campaigns. These days, the majority of our clients find us through search engines, our online ads, and through word of mouth referrals. We're one of the top marketing agencies that specializes in crowd funding."

How much does it cost to hire a digital marketing agency to assist with a crowd funding campaign?

Roy Morejon: "We have a flat fee to set up a campaign that includes basic PR efforts and someone managing the social media aspect of the campaign. We also charge a small percentage based on the overall success of the campaign. Thus, we get paid our success bonus only if a campaign reaches or exceeds its funding goal. This motivates us to drive a campaign to raise as much money as possible, because our compensation depends on a campaign exceeding its goal, since our start-up fee just covers our costs.

"We work with a wide range of clients but have seen a growing trend of campaign creators for technology-related products coming to us. We have developed a great rapport with the journalists who write about emerging consumer technologies, so we're able to help generate a lot of positive media coverage for our clients in this field. However, we've also worked with other types of clients, including clothing companies, shoe companies, and movie producers."

What would you say is the biggest misconception people have who want to pursue crowd funding?

Roy Morejon: "Recently, the biggest misconceptions we've encountered among prospective clients is that Kickstarter will do their campaign marketing for them and that all they need to do is create and publish a project on the Kickstarter platform, and then sit back and wait for the funding to come in. These people believe that Kickstarter generates enough traffic from backers that people will automatically find and want to support their campaign once it's underway. This simply is not the case."

Once a client comes to you for assistance, how do you help them determine which crowd funding platform to utilize?

Roy Morejon: "For most projects, our preference is Kickstarter, and it's the platform we have the most experience working with. Right now, Kickstarter has the best reputation, and is the most well-known platform in the reward-based crowd funding arena. We have found that the media is more apt to support Kickstarter campaigns with coverage, plus potential backers trust Kickstarter more than some other lesser-known platforms.

"Also, if you look at the success statistics, 43 percent of all Kickstarter campaigns get fully funded. Beyond Kickstarter, we've also begun seeing a lot of interest in and success with clients using self-hosted crowd funding applications through their own websites."

What have you found that crowd funding campaign creators need the most help with when it comes to creating and managing a successful campaign?

Roy Morejon: "This varies a lot. Sometimes, we encounter clients that have an idea that they're not sure is good enough to pursue, even with crowd funding. We tend to be very helpful when it comes to assisting our clients brainstorm reward ideas for their campaigns and then associating those rewards with funding amounts that are fair. We can also be of assistance helping a client calculate a realistic funding goal, and making sure that based on that goal, they'll still be able to deliver their product or project on time and on budget.

"Command Partners has been successful in helping our clients define and then achieve realistic crowd funding goals. A lot of times, we will help clients calculate their true development and manufacturing costs. We have found that if a campaign's funding goal is very high, potential backers are very hesitant to support it because they don't believe that funding goal will be achieved.

"To calculate a funding goal, the formula to use will vary based on the type of project and its target audience. When it comes to crowd funding for a product's development, a lot has to do with how far along you are in the research and development cycle. Products that are further along and that have working prototypes are much easier to get funded. This gives the company more credibility in the eyes of the backers, plus it gives us something tangible to share with journalists when it comes to generating publicity for a product and its crowd funding campaign."

When using Kickstarter, what is a good campaign length for most projects?

Roy Morejon: "This depends a lot on your ultimate funding goal. The more you're trying to raise, the longer you want the campaign to last. A longer campaign is also useful when you are trying to get media coverage. We have found that the 30- to 40-day campaign length tends to work well and that launching a campaign on a Tuesday is beneficial when it comes to getting media attention about the campaign's kickoff."

If a campaign goes longer, say 30 to 90 days, is it harder to keep up the excitement and momentum?

Roy Morejon: "This is always a challenge. After the first week to 10 days of a campaign, there is often a lull. Steps need to be taken to keep the excitement going for the remainder of the campaign, and to broaden the reach of the campaign so it reaches more potential backers beyond friends and family.

"We have seen a lot of success by introducing new rewards partway through a campaign. Introducing stretch goals for campaigns that are close to or that are fully funded, but that have time remaining in the campaign, is also very useful."

In your experience, what is the best way to attract new backers to a reward-based crowd funded campaign?

Roy Morejon: "We always fully utilize email marketing. It has the best conversion rate, compared to relying on Facebook or Twitter, for example. We have, however, had tremendous success using paid Facebook advertising to promote a campaign to a very targeted group of potential backers.

"It's always easier to attract backers who already understand what crowd funding is and how it works. Using paid Facebook advertising, it's possible to easily and quickly reach these people with a targeted message in a very cost-effective way.

"Backers need to understand that if they're supporting a product, they won't receive that product for several months or even for a year or longer. It is not like purchasing an item on Amazon.com and having it arrive at your door in two business days.

"Crowd funding is still in its infancy and part of managing a successful crowd funding campaign is having to educate some of your potential backers about what crowd funding is and how it works. In the future, this educational component will become less and less important as reward-based crowd funding becomes more commonplace.

"Typically, our first level of engagement as part of our marketing, promotional, and PR campaigns is with people who are already familiar with crowd funding. Once we see some success among that audience, we broaden our scope to people who would be interested in the product or project but who might not be as familiar with the crowd funding process and with Kickstarter."

What advice can you share about what it takes to produce a successful video for a reward-based crowd funding campaign?

Roy Morejon: "We keep all of the videos we produce to between two and three minutes. It's important to discuss the project itself and to have someone on-camera that the audience will relate to. The video needs to tell the story behind the project and discuss why the project is important. Every video also needs to include a very clear call to action. This is where you ask people to support your project financially and also to share it with their online friends.

"After watching the promotional video, the viewer needs to believe in you and the project, and be excited to help fund it. We have done campaigns where the promotional video was shot using the camera built into an Apple iPhone and others where the video was shot by a professional production crew. We have found that production quality is less important than the video's content, as long as the video is in focus and the audio quality is good.

"I believe that promotional videos for start-ups should have a rawness to them. At the same time, they should have some level of professionalism in order to solidify your credibility. Keep in mind that most people who start to watch your promotional video will never watch the entire thing, even if it's less than three minutes long. Thus, within the first 15 to 30 seconds, you need to ensure all of your key messaging is in place and presented in a compelling way.

"If you're editing the video yourself using video editing software on your computer, remember that just because you can include a lot of flashy animations, titles, and graphics, this doesn't mean you should. These elements can be very distracting to the viewer. That being said, using appropriate background music within the video can be a powerful tool. As a general rule, keep your video simple, straightforward, and concise.

"Two things we tend to purposely leave out of the videos we produce are pricing and a description of the rewards being offered as part of the campaign. We want the video to spread across other video platforms such as YouTube, and describing pricing and rewards doesn't fit well on these other platforms. If you also put your video on YouTube, for example, you can still drive traffic to your Kickstarter page.

"Another reason to avoid focusing on pricing is because partway through the campaign, pricing may change, or you may run out of the early backer rewards, and you don't want to confuse or disappoint people."

What would you say are the biggest reasons why reward-based crowd funding campaigns fail?

Roy Morejon: "First, campaigns seek out too much money. Second, the product or campaign didn't nicely fit with Kickstarter. Not every good idea will work well on Kickstarter. In some cases, using another crowd funding platform will be more beneficial. Kickstarter also tends to attract more of a male demographic, so if your project is targeted to women, it may not do as well on Kickstarter as it could on another platform.

"Don't rely just on social media to share your story, but using social media should be a component of your overall marketing and promotional efforts that are put to use every single day that your campaign is underway."

If a company's reward-based crowd funding campaign fails, what should it do next?

Roy Morejon: "A lot of that comes back to marketing and soliciting feedback from the public. Ask the backers why they chose to support your project and learn as much as you can from those people. Not every campaign on Kickstarter will get funded. In some cases, even if a project idea is viable, Kickstarter may not be the place to raise money for it. In some cases, breaking up one campaign into multiple campaigns, each with a lower funding level, can be beneficial, especially when it comes to building momentum."

What tips can you share about creating rewards or perks for backers who support a reward-based crowd funding campaign?

Roy Morejon: "The rewards need to be as simple and concise as possible. Spell out exactly what a backer will be receiving at each level of financial support. Typically, we start a campaign with about seven different rewards. As we progress deeper into the campaign, we introduce a few additional rewards, especially if the early adopters cause some of the rewards to sell out early.

"We always go with a thank-you reward that someone will receive for their support of just $5 or $10. We also offer a reward that is equivalent to the value of the product or experience the campaign is raising money for, which is what the backer receives for their support at that level.

"The average backer will pledge between $45 and $75, based on our own research and experience. Thus, all of the campaigns we oversee have at least one or two pledge rewards within that realm. Then, depending on the project, we'll have rewards with much higher pledge amounts associated with them.

"I believe a project creator should create a few innovative rewards or perks that they hold back until partway through the campaign. These additional perks or rewards can help regenerate excitement for a campaign that experiences a lull partway through."

Many campaigns have a $1 or $5 reward option for backers. Does this low-end reward make sense?

Roy Morejon: "I believe that having a low reward level is beneficial for a few reasons. It allows virtually anyone to show their support for the campaign, plus it allows the campaign to benefit when that backer shares details about it with their own network. There's always the opportunity to upsell those people as the campaign continues, but we have seen a conversion rate of only around 10 percent. The primary benefit of those backers is so the campaign can potentially benefit from the social media aspect when those backers promote the campaign to their online friends."

What would you say are the most important first steps someone needs to take when launching a crowd funding campaign?

Roy Morejon: "The friends and family in someone's social network are critical to a campaign's initial success. As a result, people should have a good size online social network already in place that they can turn to for that initial wave of funding once the campaign kicks off. This initial swell of support goes a long way toward building momentum for the overall campaign."

How do you see the crowd funding process evolving over the next few years?

Roy Morejon: "I believe we will see huge corporations getting involved with crowd funding and the entrepreneurial spirit. I recently took a call from an executive at a major soft drink company that wanted to use crowd funding to help develop new flavor ideas for their soda. At the same time, the company wanted to develop innovative ways to help entrepreneurs fund their projects using crowd funding that was somehow branded to their website. This approach leverages a big brand, but also supports individuals with great ideas for a business, product, or project."

CHAPTER 15

Experienced Crowd Funders Share Their Secrets

In This Chapter

- Learn crowd funding secrets from entrepreneurs, small business operators, inventors, writers, and others who have successfully funded their projects.
- Discover pitfalls to avoid when managing your own crowd funding campaign.

There are two important pieces of advice you should follow as you begin planning your own reward-based crowd funding campaign. First, become active on several crowd funding platforms as a backer. This will allow you to experience firsthand how these services work and get a feel for the types of interactions project creators can have with their backers.

By exploring the various platforms, you can also see for yourself what types of campaigns are currently working, watch dozens of promotional videos for other campaigns to help you develop an approach and strategy for your own campaign's video, and see the types of creative rewards and benefits other project creators are offering to their backers. All of this research will prove to be extremely valuable as you develop your own campaign in hopes of getting your project funded.

Second, seek out project creators who have already successfully used crowd funding, and try to learn from their experiences. This final chapter will help you get started with this aspect of your research.

Here, you'll read in-depth interviews with a handful of people from various backgrounds, each of whom has been directly involved with crowd funding using one of the popular crowd funding platforms.

Learn as much as you can from the experiences and mistakes these people have shared, and then, on your own, seek out a few other people you can talk to who have crowd funding experience.

The people interviewed in this chapter all successfully funded their projects. Even if their project was very different from what you're planning, you can still learn from their experiences and hopefully avoid any mistakes these people made along the way.

NICK EVANS TALKS ABOUT MAKING HIS COMPANY'S HIGH-TECH TILE A BEST-SELLING GADGET

There are more and more crowd funding success stories in which a campaign for a project goes viral and a product becomes a best seller long before it's ever manufactured. The Tile, from Reveal Labs (www.thetileapp .com), is one of those success stories. This small, high-tech gadget can help you locate any item it's attached to.

Nick Evans is a computer engineer who has worked on a wide range of consumer electronics projects that originated in Silicon Valley, including the Pebble smart watch, which is one of the most publicized crowd funding success stories to date, as well as Lockitron, which provides keyless entry for a door and was funded using a successful, self-hosted crowd funding campaign.

Within days after the crowd funding campaign for Tile was launched, it went viral and wound up raising more than $2.6 million, mainly because of the well thought out marketing campaign and expertly produced promotional video that were used to support the campaign on the Selfstarter crowd funding platform (http://selfstarter.us). Selfstarter is an open source crowd funding platform created by Lockitron.

One of the main reasons for the success of Tile's crowd funding campaign was its promotional video. Every second of the two-minute presentation was carefully scripted and shot to ensure that it quickly and effectively explained the idea behind the product, demonstrated how the product worked, showcased uses for the product, and convinced viewers to support the product by preordering it.

This video was supported by a well thought out promotional, advertising, marketing, and public relations campaign, as well as a website that was extremely easy to navigate, well designed, and highly informative.

Why did you opt to use Selfstarter as your crowd funding platform?

Nick Evans: "Lockitron was a high-tech, consumer product that was funded using a crowd funding campaign, but the project was not approved by

Kickstarter. As a result, Lockitron went out and created Selfstarter, which functions very much like Kickstarter, but each project creator hosts the crowd funding campaign themselves. This gives the project creator full control over their project and the funding of it.

"A lot of product developers are turning to Selfstarter because the platform supports preorders. We believed this was where the trend for using crowd funding to launch a consumer-oriented high-tech product was going.

"While Kickstarter and Indiegogo, for example, are great platforms, the project creators need to work in their sandboxes when managing their crowd funding campaigns. We didn't want to have to play by their rules. Using a platform like Selfstarter requires a bit more work, but the end result is much more flexible."

When you came up with the idea for Tile, why did you opt to use crowd funding to fund the project?

Nick Evans: "I was seeing the success of crowd funded projects, like Pebble and Lockitron, and I believed my item locator concept would also be a great project to pursue. The concept of using a small, wireless device that communicated with some other device to help you find your missing stuff had been around for a while. While several companies have released products along these lines, most of them have failed. They were products you'd see in The Sharper Image or Sky Mall, that looked great on paper, but in reality they weren't too useful.

"Tile takes this concept a step further. It works with a smartphone, utilizes low-energy Bluetooth, and takes advantage of online social networking to function if the item it is attached to is lost outside of your home or immediate area.

"The idea for Tile has been in the brainstorming phase and on the back burner for a long time. As the concept for it started to solidify, we always had crowd funding in mind as the way we'd fund the project. However, after seeing the success of campaigns for products like the Pebble, we spent a lot of time researching crowd funding to discover the secrets for creating a successful campaign."

As part of your crowd funding research, what are some of the things you discovered?

Nick Evans: "We discovered there is no predefined plan to follow that guarantees the success of a crowd funding campaign. There are, however, a handful of elements that virtually all successful campaigns share.

"First, for a crowd funding campaign to work, you need to be selling something that people want and that you can create a demand for. This may seem obvious, but if you look at the many campaigns that go online and ultimately fail, it may not be as obvious as you might think. An idea for a product may seem amazing, but it has to also be something that people will want.

"One of the biggest advantages of crowd funding is that you can determine if there's a market for an idea before investing a fortune into the development and production of that idea. The more research you do before starting a crowd funding campaign, the more you'll be able to target that campaign to a specific audience of people who will want it. This will dramatically improve your chances for success.

"We invested a lot of time thinking about how the Tile could be used, why people would want to use it, and what functionality made sense for the product. Once we knew this, we addressed many of these same questions again when producing our video to ensure that every second of the video conveyed the right message to the right audience. Our goal was to make the Tile product itself, and the marketing campaign for it, as simple and pure as possible.

"Second, once you figure out what people want, figure out a simple way to communicate that when developing your crowd funding campaign and your marketing plans for it. The trick is to be able to communicate your message very fast, as in within a few seconds. People will not invest 30 seconds, one minute, or more of their time trying to figure out what you're doing. It is essential that you be able to communicate your message very concisely in a visually interesting and easy to comprehend way."

What crowd funding strategies did you implement that helped to ensure your success?

Nick Evans: "On Kickstarter, there are a lot of art and music-related projects, for example. The message that's being conveyed to potential backers of those projects is, 'Hey, we're trying to do this, and we could really use your support.' There are also a lot of campaigns on Kickstarter that are designed to launch a product and focus on generating preorders. For these, the message is, 'If you want the product, preorder it today so we can make it a reality.'

"Our goal with the Tile was to merge these two types of crowd funding campaign messages using a campaign that lasted for 34 days. We also planned to continue preselling the product after the initial campaign ended."

The promotional video for the Tile crowd funding campaign was brilliantly done. Could you explain some of the creative thinking that went into this video?

Nick Evans: "The two-minute video begins with a simple statement that says, 'This is Tile. Tile helps you find things. Anything.' The video goes on to quickly demonstrate some of the ways the product can be used to solve a common problem while stressing the tiny size of the device and its affordability. The video also features my partner and me inviting people to become backers of the project.

"Within the first 5 to 10 seconds of your video, you need to show and explain what you're selling in an attention-getting way, or you're going to lose your viewer and you won't sell anything. If someone can watch your video for five seconds and knows what you're selling, and then opts to watch more, then you're doing it right. Otherwise, you're not.

"Most of the work for the video was done long before we started filming the first shot or even planning the video. We spent a lot of time determining who would want to use the product and all of the different ways it could be used. Once we knew that information, a lot of the elements for the video fell into place pretty easily, because we knew exactly what our goals for the video were.

"When it came time to put the video together, we worked with an extremely talented videographer. He had experience producing really nice videos that could showcase our product and also tell a really compelling story.

"Keep in mind, aside from the video, if there's any text within your website or your campaign's web page that needs to be read twice in order for someone to understand what you're saying, you're doing something wrong."

What are some elements other people put in their videos that you avoided?

Nick Evans: "Basically, anything that might cause someone to click on the Back button within their web browser as they're watching the video needs to be avoided. For example, I would not invest too much time explaining a backstory behind a project that isn't too interesting or relevant. Also, don't explain things about your product that won't apply to or appeal to the general public. Also, avoid bad acting and poor script writing.

"The first time we watched the final cut of our video for Tile, we knew in our hearts that we were on the right track. We knew that we either had a wild success on our hands, or it would be a beautiful disaster. We knew we could not predict people's behavior, but we believed our video did a good job guiding people in a certain way. I also knew that our video would be setting a new standard for promotional videos tied to crowd funding campaigns."

How important is it to show an actual product in a promotional video that's trying to raise money for a new product or invention?

Nick Evans: "I believe that in the video, if your crowd funding campaign is for a product, you need to have a working prototype. This demonstrates that you know how to build whatever it is you've come up with. You need to be 100 percent positive that you can build the project within the time frame you promise it in. In terms of the video, the prototype allows you to show people exactly what the product will look like. When it comes to describing the look and feel of the product, don't rely on people's imaginations.

"We discovered that it's possible to easily spend any amount of money to create and launch a crowd funding campaign. We have not disclosed how much we spent to produce our video or on our marketing to promote the campaign."

What were some of the misconceptions you had about crowd funding as you got started?

Nick Evans: "Through research and preparation, we tried to iron out all of the potential problems and misconceptions before we got started. However, I don't think we fully anticipated the time commitment and work that is needed to achieve success, before, during, and after the actual campaign. No matter what you hear or what you read, chances are you'll underestimate the amount of work that needs to go into it.

"We also studied many other crowd funding campaigns to see what worked and what didn't and then tried to apply those concepts to what we were going to be doing. This meant studying a lot of successful Kickstarter and Indiegogo campaigns. After a while, you can pretty much tell by looking at a newly launched campaign which ones will be successful and which ones will likely fail.

"I believe once you're able to make these predictions with a good level of accuracy, you have developed a good understanding of how crowd funding works and can apply that knowledge to your own campaign."

What additional preplanning went into your crowd funding campaign before its launch?

Nick Evans: "Behind the scenes, you need to know exactly how much it's going to cost to produce your product, so you can create an accurate funding goal. This means having a good understanding of the manufacturing process and working with a manufacturing company ahead of time. The manufacturer was able to give us price quotes for certain volumes, and then we calculated how many units we'd need to sell at particular price points to be able to complete all of the design and engineering work and ultimately to create the product.

"One of our goals was to ensure that Tile would be highly affordable. This meant we'd need to commit to manufacturing them in a large quantity right from the start. But, we also needed to ensure we could presell those units during the crowd funding campaign. Our initial goal was to presell between 10,000 and 20,000 units. We ended up preselling more than 10 times the number of units we initially projected and ultimately raised in excess of $2.6 million.

"Our initial funding goal was $20,000, which in hindsight was nowhere near enough to get the project off the ground, even if we got fully funded. During the crowd funding campaign, our presale price for Tile was very low. Due to the success of the campaign, we were able to keep that price very low. Even after the crowd funding campaign ended, we continued our presale efforts.

"Using the extra money raised, we hired the additional people we needed, and we were able to go with a really solid manufacturing company that charged us a premium but greatly reduced our risk. Ultimately, due to the extra volume we needed to manufacture, we had to push our production schedule back by several months.

"The problem we now faced was that we needed to make sure the product would work flawlessly from day one once it shipped. We no longer had the chance to ship just 5,000 or 10,000 units to our early adopters and then fine-tune the product. We needed to ship hundreds of thousands of units and make sure the whole concept worked."

Once the campaign was underway, what activities did you pursue to build up excitement for Tile?

Nick Evans: "We utilized a lot of social media, implemented a strong public relations campaign, and simultaneously used paid Facebook advertising. Our goal was to use any tool at our disposal to drive traffic to the website. We had a team of people working on the various components of our marketing and promotion, but my partner and I worked 70 to 80 hours per week during the actual campaign.

"We reached out to everyone we could. I invited hundreds of people to come to our website and 'Like' Tile. Everyone who did that received a personalized message from me thanking them. I used a lot of private messaging. I believe that people hate receiving spam emails, even if it's from a friend.

"Our goal was to generate as much hype about Tile as possible, so that we would generate a lot of funding during the first few hours once the campaign went live. To create and manage a successful crowd funding campaign, I believe someone must have the ability to communicate well. You can't be shy. You also need to recognize when someone is better than you at something, and when necessary, tap the knowledge, skills, or experience of those people.

"There are always people out there who know more than you about marketing, producing a video, or writing promotional copy, for example. Don't be shy. Go and seek out advice. I think you'll discover that people are often willing to share their advice, for free. Think of crowd funding as one big, multifaceted marketing campaign.

"Ultimately, we hired experts to help with our social media campaign, video production, and paid online advertising campaign. We also worked with marketing experts who helped us fine-tune our messaging. Even though we hired people with specific areas of expertise, we worked hand-in-hand with them. Our goal was to hire people who would help us do a better job, not necessarily free up our time and resources. We sought out people who were better at handling specific tasks than we were.

"For example, we hired someone who specialized in creating our targeted Facebook ad campaigns, and then worked closely with that individual. We always made sure we were communicating our brand properly using standard e-commerce marketing techniques."

What went into creating the rewards for your campaign's backers?

Nick Evans: "For us, we focused on preselling the product at an attractive price. We used an introductory price of $19.95 per unit as our presale price. This allowed us to sell the item cheaply, but make enough profit to ensure we would not lose money on each presale. We didn't offer any other rewards, aside from the ability to preorder between one and nine units at a time at a prelaunch discount.

"If someone preordered three units at the discounted price, we gave them one unit for free. If they ordered six units, they received two units for free, and if they preordered nine units, they received three for free."

How do you think crowd funding will evolve throughout 2014, 2015, and beyond?

Nick Evans: "One year from now, I know crowd funding will be very different than it is today. More people will know about it, and more companies, inventors, and entrepreneurs will be utilizing it to fund their projects. But, how it will evolve is difficult to predict. This is why performing your research and due diligence prior to launching your campaign is so important."

MUSICIAN SIMON TAM DISCUSSES HOW HE USED CROWD FUNDING TO PAY FOR HIS BAND'S TOUR BUS

Services like Kickstarter boast thousands of success stories that involve creative people being able to fund their projects. Simon Tam falls into this category. He is part of a band called The Slants, that often tours throughout the country performing 80s-style, new wave dance rock. When his band needed a new tour bus, the group turned to crowd funding and its fans to pay for it.

Professionally, Simon Tam comes from a nonprofit fund-raising background and has single-handedly raised more than $1 million for charities that he's passionate about. When his band needed funds for a tour bus, he saw an opportunity to get the group's fans directly involved.

How did you use crowd funding to build your relationship with the band's fans?

Simon Tam: "Once we launched the crowd funding campaign, we reached out to our fan base and offered unique rewards to our backers. For example, one reward that was offered was the opportunity to have their name, or a message of up to 50 characters, painted on the tour bus. We also offered exclusive, one-of-a-kind merchandise from the band, an exclusive band T-shirt created specifically for the campaign, copies of unreleased songs recorded by the band, and the chance to spend time with band members. Our top-level reward was a personalized guitar and a private concert, along with a handful of other personalized merchandise. These rewards, and the fact we reached out to our fans for their support, helped solidify our relationship with these people.

"Thanks to the enthusiasm of our fans during our crowd funding campaign, we wound up attracting many new supporters for our band and its music, which translated to a larger fan base. I believe the success of any crowd funding campaign depends on having a group of people who are already really excited about the project and who are willing to share details about your campaign with their own online networks."

Why did you use Kickstarter for your crowd funding campaign?

Simon Tam: "For that campaign, we used Kickstarter because it had a strong reputation among musicians and artists. It was also a known name in the crowd funding arena, and the payment system was easy for people to navigate. One feature I liked was that people can back projects by paying using their Amazon account, so for those with an Amazon account, the payment process is streamlined."

What were the steps you went through when launching and managing the crowd funding campaign for your tour bus?

Simon Tam: "When we launched this campaign, we had a very short time line to work with, because our previous bus broke down and we needed a new one fast. This didn't allow us a lot of time to preplan many aspects of the campaign or do a lot of research. Everything was condensed into a very short time period.

"We started the planning process by analyzing our goals for the campaign. Part of this involved creating a budget and considering things like taxes and administrative fees we'd have to pay.

"Once we knew our funding goal, we brainstormed a selection of rewards to be offered at different funding levels. We knew that for our rewards to be attractive to potential backers, they needed to offer something that was personal and special for our fans. We discovered that many people who back projects on Kickstarter do so specifically to gain access to the unique rewards that are offered nowhere else. People like getting something that's very exclusive or limited, and/or that allows them to put their own name on something and get some recognition.

"We built our campaign specifically around offering rewards we knew would be appealing to our band's fans. Then, we set out to shoot a compelling video and send out press releases. We also planned our outreach through social media to promote the campaign, and we created a special hashtag for the campaign.

"Once the plans were in place, we made a point to directly contact a handful of people who we knew would support this crowd funding campaign. As a result, as soon as we launched the campaign on Kickstarter, we had a lot of momentum right from the start.

"As a result of these efforts before and immediately after the start of the campaign, we were able to reach the halfway point for our funding goal within the first 24 hours. Our funding goal was $10,000, and we wound up raising about $14,000 during the 20-day campaign.

"Thanks to the dedication of our fan base, the average level of support from our backers was between $140 and $160, which is significantly higher than the average for most crowd funding campaigns that use platforms like Kickstarter."

What was the biggest misconception you initially had about crowd funding?

Simon Tam: "One misconception I had was that the people who support a reward-based crowd funding campaign are donors. In reality, they're not donors. They are participating in the project itself. In exchange for their financial support, they receive something of value in the form of a reward. For example, our backers received exclusive music, merchandise, and other memorabilia. For other types of campaigns the backers actually prepurchase a product or experience. In other words, backers get something back for their support."

What steps did you take to promote your crowd funding campaign to people outside of your core fan base?

Simon Tam: "We used Facebook, Twitter, and many other online social networks to help get the word out. For us, the single most effective thing that drove backers to our campaign were the direct emails we sent out. This had the highest conversion rate and ultimately brought in the most money. We used email management tools to send out personalized emails to our core fan base.

"When it came to promoting our campaign on Facebook and Twitter, some of our more dedicated followers reached out to high profile and active celebrities and journalists with huge followings on these services, and those fans asked the celebrities to retweet or share a message with their followers about our campaign. Having our fans send out messages to their friends and family asking for support on our behalf became an organic way to spread the world about the campaign."

Do you think raising money for a tour bus helped make your story and crowd funding campaign stand out and get attention?

Simon Tam: "A lot of musicians use crowd funding to raise money in order to record an album or go on tour, for example. We needed a tour bus, which allowed us to position our campaign in a unique way, which resulted in it standing out a bit. That certainly helped. Not only could someone get their name or message painted on the bus, but we made a point to showcase the bus in video blogs and other merchandising and promotions later. As a result, the backers are still able to see what they contributed to when they come to our shows or see our videos, for example."

During the time your campaign was running, how much time did you dedicate per day to manage it?

Simon Tam: "In the beginning, we invested at least 8 to 10 hours per day promoting the campaign and interacting with backers as well as perspective backers. During the middle of the campaign, the time required was maybe two or three hours per day, but toward the final days of the campaign, we wound up putting in 8 to 10 hours of work per day again.

"There was also a lot of time invested a few days before the campaign to get everything ready. This included drafting and sending out the personalized emails to our core fan base, friends, and family."

What tips can you share in terms of producing a powerful promotional video?

Simon Tam: "The biggest piece of advice I can offer about producing a promotional video for a crowd funding campaign is to make the video personal. Know exactly who your target audience is, and cater the messaging within the video to those people. Speak to the people who you know will be the most excited about your project. Don't try to position your video to appeal to everyone. Focus on your target audience.

"Next, keep the video short. In terms of the video's production quality, the picture and sound should be clear. However, you need to keep the production quality in line with the image you're trying to convey, so it meets the expectations of your audience. If you're a well-established business using crowd funding to reach an upscale audience, those people will expect much higher production value in your video.

"For my band's video, we used the web camera built into my MacBook laptop computer, and the video focused on me speaking into the camera. I edited the video using the iMovie software. It was really simple, and it worked for us. The video successfully leveraged our personal relationship with our friends, family, and fans.

"I believe a promotional video should include a specific call to action that speaks directly to your audience. The video should focus on what aspects of your project will be the most appealing to your audience. I would avoid producing a video that's cheesy or over the top."

What advice can you share about setting realistic crowd funding campaign goals?

Simon Tam: "I would recommend sketching out some type of business plan on paper. Develop your strategy and define your goals in advance. Determine who your audience is, and then figure out how much support you can expect to receive from that audience when it comes to funding your project.

"We had an established fan base for our band, which gave us an advantage when we launched the crowd funding campaign. If you don't have a core group of supporters already in place, it's even more important to understand your target audience and develop a plan for effectively reaching that audience quickly and inexpensively, but in a way that will make a positive impression.

"If you can't pinpoint a target audience for your project and the crowd funding campaign you're planning, don't launch the campaign, because it will fail regardless of which crowd funding platform you use. Kickstarter, for example, is just a tool you can use to help you reach your existing core audience. It will not generate that audience for you.

"Another tip I can offer is to create a realistic budget—one that will allow you to raise enough money to achieve your goal and launch your project, but that's also attainable based on the size of your core support group and the size of the audience of backers you believe you'll attract to the campaign."

Are there any major pitfalls someone should avoid when planning or managing their own crowd funding campaign?

Simon Tam: "Don't have the mentality that if you build it they will come. If you want to attract backers to your reward-based crowd funding campaign, it will take a lot of effort on your part. It is much harder to capture someone's attention and get them to become a backer for your project than you might think. Plan on spending time throughout the campaign putting in continuous work if you want it to be successful. You can't just set up the campaign and return in 30 days to collect your money.

"Part of your preplanning process should be to determine ways you'll build up continuous momentum throughout the campaign, not just during the first few days. Know what steps you plan to take beyond just reaching out to your core network. Backers get excited by projects that have a lot of positive movement and support surrounding them. This is something you need to generate right from the start of your campaign, but the challenge is to keep that excitement going throughout the campaign."

What are the most useful skills someone should have in order to create and manage a successful reward-based crowd funding campaign?

Simon Tam: "Crowd funding is all about developing personal relationships. I would say having communication skills and the ability to interact with people is essential. Most of these campaigns rely heavily on using social media effectively. If this isn't your forte, you should reach out to a digital marketing agency or someone who is an expert when it comes to using Facebook, Twitter, and other similar services as a marketing and promotional tool.

"Before launching your campaign, figure out what tasks you'll need to accomplish and what skills will be required to handle each of those tasks effectively. Then, if you don't have the right skill set, find people who do. It's important to have everything handled correctly leading up to and during your crowd funding campaign."

What other tips can you offer that will help someone's crowd funding campaign be successful?

Simon Tam: "As you're getting close to your funding goal, or if you manage to surpass that goal, I recommend setting up stretch goals. For example, if you hit 20 percent above your funding goal, the backers would receive something extra. This is also a great incentive to get backers to offer added financial support or encourage backers to help you promote your campaign.

"Also, as the campaign is underway, slowly release more information about the project in the form of updates. These teasers will help to keep your backers excited, plus help recruit new backers. For example, during our campaign for funding the tour bus, we started posting photos of different potential buses, as well as options we could get and invited our backers to help us make decisions. We also reached out to our backers with artwork depicting what the bus could look like and invited them to vote for their favorite designs.

"Give your backers behind-the-scenes access to what you're doing in the form of an exclusive blog. Let them see what you're up to during the crowd funding campaign and afterward, as you're actually making your project happen. Keeping people well informed and giving them exclusive information will make them feel like they've gotten a good return for their support."

Now that you have a successful Kickstarter campaign under your belt, what would you do differently for your next one?

Simon Tam: "I would definitely start the preparation and planning process earlier. If we had more time to plan and we had incorporated more stretch goals, we could easily have raised more money. As I mentioned, we were under a time crunch when we launched the campaign because our bus had broken down and we needed reliable transportation. I would also have studied other campaigns more closely to see what worked well, and I would have extended the length of our campaign to 30 days."

What should project creators do if their funding campaigns fail?

Simon Tam: "First analyze what went wrong and why. Then figure out what needs to change. When a campaign fails, your backers are going to be disappointed. If you opt to try a new campaign, you'll need to show what you're doing differently and persuade the potential backers to support you based on your revised plan or project. Don't simply try to relaunch the campaign and do the same thing again.

"Crowd funding is becoming more and more popular and gaining more credibility with the public with each passing month. As a result, more people, companies, and organizations are discovering this is a viable way to raise money. In the near future, I believe that project creators will be held more accountable for their actions and the results of their actions, and they'll be held more accountable about how they spend the money that's raised.

"As a result of this added accountability, the project creators will have more responsibility to their backers, and they'll need to ensure that they adhere to and deliver on whatever promises they make."

LEARN FROM AUTHOR TOM STARLING HOW HE SUCCESSFULLY FUNDED HIS CHILDREN'S BOOK USING KICKSTARTER

As an aspiring author, food broker in the restaurant industry, and equal rights activist from South Carolina, Tom Starling quickly learned that being discovered and having a book published by a traditional publisher is a huge challenge. So, when he developed the idea for his children's book, called *Bob the Ladybug: Bob's New Pants* (www.bobtheladybug.com), he decided to self-publish it using money he raised through a Kickstarter campaign.

Why did you decide you wanted to write a children's book?

Tom Starling: "The main reason why I wanted to write a children's book was to educate young people about diversity and to help prevent bullying. The book is written for children between the ages of three and seven. After I wrote this book, I didn't know how to reach out to the major publishing houses, so I felt that the best way for me to get my first book out there was to self-publish it. I decided to use Kickstarter for my crowd funding campaign."

When you decided to self-publish your book, did you realize you'd be taking on many responsibilities, in addition to writing the book, that a publisher would otherwise handle?

Tom Starling: "I did realize that. I wound up teaming up with an artist who did the book's illustrations. My illustrator, Jacquie Gonzalez, also runs an online marketing business, so I felt like that partnership would help to provide leverage for getting details about the book out there."

Why did you decide to go with Kickstarter for your crowd funding campaign?

Tom Starling: "Several friends of mine who are musicians had successfully used Kickstarter in the past to fund their music-related projects, so I knew what Kickstarter was all about and what it could be used to do. Prior to launching the campaign, I did some of my own research, then I sent in my information to Kickstarter in order to get the project approved. The project was quickly approved, and I realized that this was the best crowd funding service to use for my project. At the time, I did not know too much about other crowd funding platforms."

How did you do to learn about Kickstarter and how it works before starting your campaign?

Tom Starling: "I spent time exploring the Kickstarter platform and took advantage of the online tutorials the service offered. I also visited many different campaigns. I talked to my friends who had already used Kickstarter and followed their advice as well. If you can reach out to people with experience using Kickstarter, this will help a lot when it comes to understanding the nuances of how the service works."

How much were you looking to raise from your Kickstarter campaign, and how did you get the word out about your campaign?

Tom Starling: "My funding goal was $6,000, and the campaign length I selected was 30 days. Before I got started with the campaign, I did research to figure out my costs to self-publish the book and then launch a marketing campaign for it. I also calculated into the budget the Kickstarter fees.

"Once I went onto the Kickstarter website and wrote the description for my project, I also shot a short video that described what my book was going to be about. Within the video, we included some sample illustrations that would appear in the book. This information was submitted to Kickstarter for approval. Two weeks later, the project was approved.

"The next step was reaching out to my online network in order to get the word out about the Kickstarter campaign. During the 30 days of the campaign, I constantly promoted details about the project on Facebook and Twitter. I also used direct email to send my contacts a personal message asking for their support.

"I found that Facebook was the most useful for reaching potential backers for my project. Before I started the campaign, however, I invested time using Facebook and sought out individuals to follow and friends who had similar interests as me and what I was trying to accomplish. For example, I reached out via Facebook to celebrities who are also equal rights activists and have large online followings of their own.

"Over an extended period, not only did I reach out to these people on Facebook, I also established contact with them via messages. So, when I introduced them to my Kickstarter campaign, these high-profile individuals already knew who I was, and they were willing to support my project. Through those people, I reached out to their online friends as well, which broadened my own network substantially.

"While this process was time consuming and needed to be done well in advance of launching my Kickstarter campaign, the work paid off. Once the campaign was underway, I spent at least one hour per day managing it."

Prior to launching the Kickstarter campaign, did you put together a business plan for your project?

Tom Starling: "My illustrator and I did sit down and create a business plan for the project. It was not extremely detailed. Our goal was not to make a lot of money from the book. It was more to get the book published and use it as a tool for conveying an important message to its young readers. Our hope was that based on the initial success of the self-published edition of the book, a major publisher would ultimately pick up the project and publish it.

"One of my goals was to donate many copies of the book to schools and libraries, just to get the book out there and to promote the antibullying message conveyed within it."

What was the biggest misconception you had about crowd funding and Kickstarter before you actually used the platform for your campaign?

Tom Starling: "I thought that the Kickstarter platform would drive people to my campaign who were interested in supporting a project like mine. Ultimately, I found that it was entirely my responsibility to find and solicit backers, and it was challenging to convince potential backers to support the project.

"As a result, I had to reach out to many more people than I initially anticipated, and I had to spend time prequalifying those people to make sure they'd be interested in my project. I had to make sure that my emails, Facebook, and Twitter postings were written in such a way that they would touch the recipient's heart and not simply be deleted or overlooked.

"Another misconception I had was that millions and millions of people spend countless hours on Kickstarter reviewing all of the different projects on there looking for interesting things to support. What I discovered was that unless someone had some type of personal connection to you, or a personalized invitation from you, driving traffic to the Kickstarter campaign page was a challenge."

In terms of your campaign's promotion video, what did you do to make it interesting for potential backers?

Tom Starling: "I purposely made the video very colorful so it would be of interest to anyone who wanted to support a children's book. I produced the video myself using a high-definition camera. I wrote up a script and then sat in front of my camera and shot it.

"I had watched a lot of Kickstarter videos that looked more professional than mine, but I am not sure that having higher production quality than what my video offered would have done a better job than my video. I think you need to establish a personal connection with the viewer. It can be a turnoff for potential backers if it looks like you spent a lot of money producing a flashy video that looks like a television commercial.

"Within the video, I talked about how I was bullied as a child and provided a brief biography. I also talked about how I wanted to make the world a better place for our children. I showcased several sample pages from the book and discussed how it was going to read. Most of the video involved me looking into the camera and talking. My goal was to establish a strong eye connection with the viewers. Then, when the pages from the book and illustrations were shown, I used voice-overs to explain what people were looking at. I purposely did not use any flashy graphics within the 90-second video.

"Ultimately, I think the 90-second length was perfect for my project. I don't think people would have spent any more time watching a longer video. The video allowed people to see the main bullet points related to my project and learn about me and my goals."

Do you have any tips for producing an attention-getting promotional video?

Tom Starling: "I believe it's important to showcase who you are as the project creator and be able to show off samples of what your work will look like. Also, when producing the video, make sure there's no background noise or anything else that will be distracting to viewers. Take your time shooting the video. Make sure you speak slowly and clearly, so everyone can understand you and your message."

What tips can you offer when it comes to setting realistic goals for a crowd funding campaign?

Tom Starling: "Start off by taking a close look at your existing network and figure out who will be willing to support you financially and how much support you believe you can count on from each of those people. If you figure out that the maximum support you'll receive from a friend or family member is $100, don't expect those people to offer $500 once your campaign begins. If you don't have connections who are very wealthy, your crowd funding campaign will be that much more challenging, since a huge percentage of your overall funding goal will most likely come from your core network."

Based on your experience, what is the biggest pitfall to avoid when using Kickstarter or a similar reward-based crowd funding platform?

Tom Starling: "Don't just assume that by publishing a project online that your campaign will attract backers and you'll automatically raise the money in a short period of time. Make sure you have the right connections in place before you launch your campaign, and make sure you have a plan for effectively reaching those people.

"When you are reaching out to potential backers, try to quickly establish a personal connection. If your project or idea will somehow touch their hearts and capture their emotions that will be to your advantage. People give with their hearts.

"Also, while the campaign is underway, it's important to publish regular updates. Within these updates, share details about how the funding of the project is going, but also disclose new information about the project itself, as well as your time line for getting it underway and completed. I tried to do an update every week to keep all of the backers and potential backers in the loop."

What skills do you think are essential for creating and managing a successful crowd funding campaign?

Tom Starling: "I think it's important to be able to write well and speak well. It's essential that you are able to quickly and effectively communicate your ideas and tell your story. It's also important to understand how online social networking works and to have a network already in place. You need to be proficient using Facebook, Twitter, and other online social networking services and understand how to use these services to reach people in your target audience.

"Once you successfully attract backers or supporters to your project, it's essential that you communicate with them on a regular basis in order to keep them up-to-date on your project. I tried to do this at least once per week. I also made a point to send each backer a personalized thank-you for their support.

"After the book was printed, I sent out another thank-you to everyone and asked that they stay in touch. I wanted to make sure we'd be able to keep our network excited about the project, since our plan was to publish a second book in the future."

As part of your Kickstarter campaign, how did you handle the rewards for your backers?

Tom Starling: "I created a number of different rewards at different price points. The majority of the incentives included autographed copies of the book from its first printing. Obviously, if people were going to support the publication of a book, they'd want a published copy of it.

"I also created a series of autographed prints and limited edition posters that were illustrations from the book and offered those as our rewards. For higher levels of support, we offered to name characters in the book after people's children. The highest priced reward involved me traveling anywhere within the country and bringing 25 copies of the book to a private party and autographing them for the attendees after a book reading.

"When creating your rewards, make sure that you don't overextend yourself or overpromise things that you won't be able to fulfill in a timely and cost-effective manner.

"Ultimately, my campaign attracted just over 100 backers, and the average level of financial support was between $25 and $50. This turned out to be along the lines of what I projected."

Once the Kickstarter campaign ended, what happened next?

Tom Starling: "We collected the funds we raised from Kickstarter, minus their fees. We then spent the next three months creating the book and having it published. This was the timeline we planned on. By the end of the third month, our backers received their published copies of the book. The book also has its own website [www.bobtheladybug.com], and it was available for sale on Amazon.com.

"Between the time the crowd funding campaign ends and when the project is actually completed, it's important to keep your backers up to date on your progress, and to give them realistic projections as to the project's completion date. As long as you keep your backers informed, they'll be patient. I made a point to say the books would be shipped out to backers in November, but I actually got them shipped out in October, so people were really pleased with that.

"If you think your project is going to take three months to complete, build four months into your time line. This gives you wiggle room if you run into problems.

"What I noticed was that after the book was made available for sale to the general public, many of our backers made a point to share the website's link, and we received orders from their friends and family members, as well. I have also received emails from backers saying how they've taken the book to their child's classroom and read it to the class."

Do you have any additional pieces of advice that will lead to the success of a crowd funding campaign?

Tom Starling: "Once you launch the campaign, stick with it. Make sure you're open and honest about what you're trying to do, you have a plan in place to keep people motivated throughout the length of your campaign, and that you communicate regularly with your backers and potential backers. The more you can get other people excited about your project, the more willing they'll be to offer you help when it comes to promoting it."

PIET MORGAN'S COMPANY, HAMMERHEAD, USED CROWD FUNDING TO CREATE A PRODUCT FOR BICYCLE ENTHUSIASTS

Back in 2006, Piet Morgan rode his bicycle from New Haven, Connecticut, to San Francisco in order to raise money for Habitat for Humanity. It was on that trip that he discovered how difficult it is to navigate while riding a bicycle. Later, in 2013, even with the navigation capabilities of the latest smartphones, nobody had yet developed an elegant GPS navigation solution for bicycles.

As a result, Piet Morgan launched a company, called Hammerhead (www.hammerhead.io), with the goal of leveraging the technology people already had within their smartphones, using the navigation information they are able to generate and displaying it in an easy-to-view way on their bicycles' handlebars.

The technology is combined with a specialized app that runs on the smartphone. Ultimately, he developed a simple and elegant $85 device that attaches to a bicycle's handlebars and wirelessly syncs with a smartphone. Using multicolored light pads and a set-it-and-forget-it approach, the Hammerhead device displays all of the navigation information a bike rider needs to know.

At the time he created this invention, Piet Morgan lacked the capital needed to develop and manufacture the product. For him, crowd funding was a perfect solution. His goal was to use crowd funding to demonstrate the existence of a market for his idea and simultaneously to raise the capital needed to develop and build the product.

Using Dragon Innovation's crowd funding platform, Hammerhead raised more than $190,000 and exceeded the campaign's funding goal (www.dragoninnovation.com/projects/23-hammerhead).

At what point did you decide to pursue crowd funding after coming up with the idea for Hammerhead?

Piet Morgan: "Initially, my partners and I created a prototype on our own. We needed to see if it could be done. We determined what the solution would look like, and put my idea into a tangible form. Next, we created a three-dimensional printed model of the device. Once we had that, we were able to start putting some electronics into it.

"Ultimately, we were able to build a prototype that actually worked. A big part of our objective was to determine if the concept for Hammerhead was viable. A lot of ideas for products look good as a concept, but once you go about trying to create it, you run into hiccups and discover the idea isn't viable. By creating a working prototype, we proved the product idea was viable. We were then confident that if we raised the funding we needed, we could create and manufacture the actual Hammerhead product and launch a real company.

"I don't think that everything that could be made should necessarily be made. One of the beautiful things about crowd funding is that it helps determine if there's an actual demand for a new product or invention very early on, before a lot of resources are invested into its development. For me, using crowd funding allowed me to validate the idea and prove there was a demand for it among bicycle enthusiasts.

"From a business standpoint, I thought that if we could fund the project initially using crowd funding, this would make us more attractive to traditional investors and bankers in the future."

Once you decided that crowd funding was the way to go for your invention, how did you choose which crowd funding platform to use?

Piet Morgan: "I chose to use the Dragon Innovation platform after meeting with one of the company's executives. This occurred while we were seeking advice related to the feasibility of manufacturing the Hammerhead after our prototype was completed. The folks at Dragon Innovation sat down with us and explained exactly what it would take to actually manufacture the Hammerhead, and we were very impressed by their knowledge and level of engagement with us.

"About two months later, we received a call from Dragon Innovation. They told us they were launching their own crowd funding platform designed specifically for companies developing consumer technology. I was so impressed with the new platform and Dragon Innovation, we wound up launching our crowd funding campaign on the Dragon platform on the same day the platform actually launched."

What was your funding goal, and what steps did you take to ensure it was adequate?

Piet Morgan: "We came up with a funding goal of $145,000 after the experts at Dragon Innovation vetted the Hammerhead for manufacturability, so we had a very accurate idea of how much money we needed to move forward. Before the campaign began, we had also sourced product suppliers and looked carefully at manufacturing facilities.

"Based on our funding goal, we projected that we needed to presell just under 2,000 units through our crowd funding campaign to make the project a reality. Unlike Kickstarter and other crowd funding platforms, the Dragon platform allowed us to focus on presales without using a reward system for backers. We didn't have any special rewards for our backers. We simply offered a preorder opportunity."

When you got started in crowd funding, what were the biggest misconceptions you had, and what mistakes did you make early on as a result of those misconceptions?

Piet Morgan: "Crowd funding relies heavily on the Internet. However, the Internet is an extremely busy place. I had this romantic view that as soon as we launched the campaign it would go viral and within a few hours, the project would be fully funded. I figured the campaign would organically grow and drive its own traffic. I was quickly made aware that this was not the case.

"Under the hood of most successful crowd funding campaigns is a lot of hard work. On day one of our campaign, we received support from our close friends and family, but very little happened. That was disconcerting.

"The duration of our campaign was 35 days. At the time, my business partner and I were living in a one-bedroom apartment in New Jersey, and we had little additional money to spend. During the first few days of the campaign, we quickly learned that we needed to drive our own traffic to it.

"We also discovered that many of the most successful campaigns had invested in marketing and public relations experts to assist with the creation and management of their campaigns. Dragon stepped in and was helpful in teaming us up with press agents and online marketing experts who helped us quickly implement a marketing plan that kicked in about a week after the campaign had launched.

"Because our product was unique, the press picked up the story and started to run with it. From that point on, we spent our entire day, every day, promoting the campaign. We woke up at 8:00 A.M. and went to bed at 1:00 A.M., and spent our time seeking out reporters and bloggers who would write about the Hammerhead. We also spent time being active online within biking communities trying to bring people to our campaign's web page.

"We used Facebook and Twitter to help drive traffic to our campaign. Initially, I was skeptical about how useful social media could be, but Facebook become a powerful tool for us. More than one-third of our traffic came from Facebook. We tried to create content on our Facebook page that people would be interested in, and we shared it online.

"Ultimately, we wound up using paid Facebook advertising to target people who would be interested in our product. That paid ad campaign proved to be very effective. We were seeking out bicyclists who were also technology enthusiasts."

What went into the production of the promotional video for Hammerhead?

Piet Morgan: "We did research prior to the campaign and found a very strong correlation between well-produced videos and successful crowd funding campaigns. We also found that the most successful videos were around two minutes in length to ensure maximum engagement.

"We then had to figure out how to demonstrate the product and convey our message in those two minutes. To accomplish this, we set out to learn how to do small-scale filmmaking, because we didn't have the budget to have the video professionally produced for us. I recruited a friend who knew a lot about cameras and who is passionate about cinematography. He was able to explain what we needed in terms of equipment to get started.

"We found an equipment rental company in New York and rented lighting and sound equipment and used a Canon 7D camera that we borrowed from a friend. We edited the video ourselves using Final Cut Pro, and learned how to edit by watching YouTube video tutorials.

"The whole video production took longer than we anticipated. The most challenging thing was shooting the action scenes on the bicycle. In order to do that, we needed to mount the camera on the bike and come up with our own rig for doing this. There were a lot of stability issues we had to overcome in order to capture smooth footage—from the angles we wanted—of the bike in motion with the Hammerhead in use.

"During the course of the crowd funding campaign, we went through six different versions of the video. For example, in the first version of the video that we presented, people were very upset that the rider was not wearing a helmet. We made the decision to skip using a helmet because we didn't own one that looked modern. The helmets we owned were all older and brightly colored. They didn't fit in the video visually.

"Once we started getting negative emails about the lack of helmet, we went back and had to reshoot some of the scenes with the rider wearing a helmet. Another video-related challenge we encountered was having consistently good sound quality. We wound up needing to use a separate microphone from the one built into the camera to capture acceptable sound quality. Improving our sound quality dramatically improved the perception people had when viewing our video.

"We shot a lot of footage that we really loved. However, we gave ourselves a strict two-minute limit for the video, so a lot of it had to go. We knew what we were trying to say in the video, and then we kept going back and making sure that every second in the video communicated something important. Nothing could be redundant. We kept looking for ways to shorten our message without losing impact."

What tips can you offer about populating the crowd funding campaign's web page with useful content?

Piet Morgan: "Regardless of which platform you use, a crowd funding campaign's page has several distinct elements, and each can be used to convey relevant information. The campaign page is composed of video, text, and photos. You need to use each of these three mediums to their utmost advantage to articulate your information in the most efficient and best way possible.

"The video has the unique ability to showcase a product actually working. For us, that was crucial. We wanted to show as much footage as possible of Hammerhead in action.

"I saw a lot of campaigns where the same information was conveyed three times, using the same message with the video, descriptive text, and product photos. I don't think that's very effective. Each medium should be used to convey a different aspect of your message in the clearest, most concise way possible."

Looking back, did the crowd funding campaign for Hammerhead achieve its goals?

Piet Morgan: "Yes. It allowed us to presell units, receive a capital influx, prove that our product idea was viable, and demonstrate that there is a demand for it. We also got a lot of exposure among potential investors, plus we received inquiries from a lot of really talented people looking for jobs. Part of launching a successful business is hiring the right people. Our crowd funding campaign wound up helping us find and hire some key people who are now on our team.

"The exposure we received from our crowd funding campaign also opened the doors for us to participate in other activities that were extremely beneficial to our company's future growth that would not otherwise have been possible. This has allowed us to build our business a lot more aggressively than if we were to do it on our own.

"Once the campaign ended, we continued to remain in contact with our backers, who have provided us valuable feedback during the final design phase of the Hammerhead."

Do you have any advice about setting realistic goals for a crowd funding campaign?

Piet Morgan: "From the time we started creating a prototype of the Hammerhead to our anticipated shipping date of the product to our backers, it will be almost a two-year, full-time commitment. A lot has to happen behind the scenes to bring a product idea to market, and people need to be prepared for that. Also, people need to realize that building and running a crowd funding campaign becomes almost a full-time job if you want to do it correctly. It requires a hell of a lot of work. Make sure you understand what will be involved before you move forward.

"To succeed on a crowd funding platform, first and foremost, you need to be offering something that people want. In some cases, there may be a demand for a product, for example, but it may not be feasible to use crowd funding to reach the right audience. If your target audience is not Internet savvy, for example, reaching those people and getting them online to help fund your project is not going to be easy.

"At this point, crowd funding is still supported primarily among males within a certain age group. If you're not targeting that demographic, crowd funding might not be the way to go. In addition to determining if there is a demand for your product, you need to establish that your product is a good fit for the crowd funding audience and the crowd funding platform you opt to use.

"It's also important to understand that if you'll be creating and managing the crowd funding campaign primarily by yourself, you'll need to develop a very broad skill set that focuses on strong written and verbal communication skills. If you don't have the right skills, you need to bring the appropriate people on board, and figure out how you'll pay for their talents."

What tips can you share about interacting with backers during and after a crowd funding campaign?

Piet Morgan: "One of the things we did was engage people through personalized email. We thanked people for backing us, for example, using a personalized email. We also have taken steps to keep our backers engaged now that the campaign has ended.

"It is common for a project to experience delays once it's been funded. However, to avoid losing the support of your backers, it's essential that you continue to communicate openly with them. Explain what's happening every step of the way. I recommend using email and producing short video updates.

"If your project does experience extensive delays, always give people the option to leave. If they get frustrated, offer them their money back. You do not want backers to get agitated and then voice their negative thoughts publically. Be proactive, and be very responsive to incoming emails from backers and supporters.

"At one point during the campaign, we were receiving more than 100 emails per day, and we made sure that each one received a personalized response that same day. I believe this responsiveness was very important to our success."

How do you think crowd funding will evolve over the next year or two?

Piet Morgan: "I think backers and supporters will become more selective and more demanding. They'll have higher expectations. Thus, project creators will need to be more prepared. I believe the production quality of promotional videos will need to be higher and more consistent. I also think it will become increasingly more difficult for projects to stand out on these various crowd funding platforms.

"On a positive note, I think more and more people will become acquainted with crowd funding, and the pool of potential supporters and backers will increase dramatically. I also predict that crowd funding will be used more and more by existing companies as a marketing and market research strategy as well as to generate presales for products."

Index

A&E network, RocketHub and, 38, 164, 167
Acquaintances:
  as part of network, 80
  personalized emails for, 108–109
Adobe's Premier Pro video editing software, 102
Adorama, 96
Advertising:
  budget considerations and, 73–74
  scheduling of, 58
  target audience and, 81, 83–84, 86
Aleph Objects, Inc., 23
Apple's Final Cut Pro video editing software, 102
Athletes, Prizeo and, 44
ATS Rentals, 96
Attorney. *See* Legal considerations
Audio, in promotional video, 90–91, 97, 98–101
Avid editing and production software, 102

B&H Photo-Video, 96
Backers:
  attracting with blog, 80
  For Backers Only updates to campaign web page, 127–128
  defined, 4, 5
  distinguished from investors, 5, 199
  gaining experience as, before creating project, 24–27, 225

Girouard on, 176
importance of regular communication with, 123–124, 131–132
Kickstarter and reward levels for, 153–155
Lennon on, 212
meeting in person, 121–122
Miller on, 183, 184
Morejon on, 220–221
personalized emails to, 123–124
promotional video and emotions of, 91
repeat backers on Kickstarter.com, 151
rewards and, 56
shipping rewards to, after campaign, 141, 142–144
suggestions for information to share with, 128–130
targeting of, 79–87
tax liabilities and, 200
updating on stretch goals, 130–131
using blog to stay in touch with, 124–127
using YouTube to communicate with, 125, 127
Wyman on, 193
Background location, of promotional video, 91
Background music, in promotional video, 100–101
Lennon on, 210